MORE PRAISE FO

"I commend Father Benedict C ....rew noter, O.P. on the publication of *A Living Sacrifice: Guidance for Men Discerning Religious Life.* Here young men as well as Vocation Directors will find solid material to help in discerning a vocation to religious life. The information is at once practical, giving details on the various forms of religious life which a candidate might seek to explore, and rooted in the tradition of the Church. The example of many saints provides concrete testimony to the charisms of the various religious orders which go to make up the rich mosaic of religious life in the Catholic Church. This book will undoubtedly prove invaluable in helping young men respond in a confident and trusting way to the promptings of the Holy Spirit as they discern God's call."

Robert Cardinal Sarah, Prefect, Congregation for Divine Worship and the Discipline of the Sacraments

"This book is a 'must read' for any man considering the religious life. Practical, accessible, and packed with information, it is also a work of profound wisdom, a theologically rich and spiritually challenging book that presents and explains the religious life in the ultimate context of Trinitarian life and love. Highly recommended!"

Carl E. Olson, Editor of *Catholic World Report*

"This book offers to young men the opportunity to explore the Trinitarian mystery by listening to Jesus Christ, the poor, chaste, and obedient One."

Archbishop J. Augustine Di Noia, O.P., Vatican City

"I'm delighted to see this book made available. It offers practical guidance with valuable pastoral/theological principles for young men discerning religious life. I pray that many will benefit from the wisdom contained within its pages."

Most Rev. Paul S. Coakley, Archbishop of Oklahoma City

"When the desire to commit one's whole life arises in the heart as the most appropriate response to the call of the One who comes to reveal God's friendship with the world, the path that then opens up before us is both exhilarating and intimidating. It is then that we are glad to find companions on our journey who extend their friendship to us by sharing their experience, by making our steps sure, giving them both realism and daring, and by placing trust in our ability to find our path as we allow ourselves to be guided by the Spirit. This little book comes from such invaluable companions."

fr. Bruno Cadoré, O.P., Master of the Order of Preachers, Santa Sabina, Rome

"*A Living Sacrifice* proclaims the reality of the vowed consecration in ways so practical, spiritual and inspirational that one experiences sitting at the foot of the masters and drinking from the springs which have nourished saints through the ages. Above all, this treasure trove gives a precious glimpse into the joy of such a vocation to religious life.... a particular joy that radiates throughout the entire world from age to age!"

Sister Joseph Andrew Bogdanowicz, O.P., Dominican Sisters of Mary, Mother of the Eucharist

"Balancing practical information, personal narrative, and Catholic tradition, Fr. Benedict and Fr. Andrew have compiled an excellent resource for men at all stages of discernment."

John Garvey, President, The Catholic University of America

"*A Living Sacrifice* is specifically written for young men who are discerning a vocation, but it would also benefit those who promote vocations among the men in their parish community. Everyone should consider themselves a promoter of religious vocations, so everyone should read this book!"

Most Rev. Shawn McKnight, S.T.D., Bishop of Jefferson City

"Spiritually sound and eminently practical, *A Living Sacrifice* is a rare find that will inspire men who desire to give the totality of their lives to God with generosity and courage through the profession of the evangelical counsels. The world today needs zealous, faithful religious, and this book offers us hope that God is indeed still calling!"

Mother Anna Grace Neenan, O.P., Prioress General of the Dominican Sisters of St. Cecilia, Nashville

"In every generation, the Lord calls some men to follow him in radical ways, even to share intimately in His own way of life, poor, chaste and obedient. If the Lord is calling you to this privileged life of belonging totally to him, then this book will give you the foundational principles and real-life examples to help you respond with generosity and trust."

The Most Reverend Andrew H. Cozzens, S.T.D., D.D., Auxiliary Bishop of Saint Paul and Minneapolis

"This book asks the fundamental question of the discerner who is genuinely seeking holiness, 'Am I called to live for Jesus alone as a living sacrifice?' Every man discerning the priesthood should read this book. It will give clarity to the vocation God has created him to live in this world, whether that is religious life or diocesan priesthood."

Fr. Jeff Eirvin, Vice President, National Conference of Diocesan Vocation Directors

"These pages are filled with indispensable advice on realizing one's vocation in Christ that is at once sensible and sanctifying. Religious life must always be discerned in community and this book brings its readers into contact with not only the figures and theologies of religious life's earliest beginnings, but also with all the lived realities of the 21st century."

Fr. David Meconi, S.J., Director, Catholic Studies Centre, Saint Louis University

"Like the authors of *A Living Sacrifice*, I was helped by Benedictine monks in my priestly vocation. The world needs more monks, canons, friars, and other religious. This book will be of great service to a young man discerning a calling to religious life."

Very Rev. Joseph C. Taphorn, Rector, Saint Paul Seminary

"Sensitively written, its deep theological insights wrapped in accessible prose, *A Living Sacrifice* offers solid practical guidance for Catholic men discerning religious life. The authors draw wisdom from Fathers and Doctors of the Church, especially St. Thomas Aquinas, as well as recent Magisterial teachings. Expertly avoiding the twin pitfalls of overpsychologizing and overspiritualizing, they provide a candid account of the joys and challenges of living out the vows of poverty, chastity, and obedience."

Prof. Dawn Eden Goldstein, Holy Apostles College and Seminary, author of *The Thrill of the Chaste*

"As parents who pray that our children will be docile to the prompting of the Holy Spirit, wherever it leads them, we could not be more grateful to Fr. Hofer and Fr. Croell for *A Living Sacrifice*. At points deeply theoretical and tremendously practical, this book is a tour de force on men's religious life. The reader will find tips for discernment, counsel for thinking about and conducting oneself during a visit, as well as the trials and temptations which await one after entering a community. In addition, the Church's teaching on religious life—as an eschatological sign of the Kingdom—comes across with beautiful clarity, as well as a treatment of essential Christian virtues, with a particular emphasis on their application to an aspiring religious (e.g., faith, hope, charity, and prudence). In this work, the Church explains herself and speaks with the wisdom of the ages, both past and present. Any young man (or anybody helping young men discern and commit to a vocation) will find this book indispensable. What a gift to the Church!"

Dr. Andrew Swafford, editor and contributor, *Great Adventure Catholic Bible* & Sarah Swafford, author of *Emotional Virtue*

A LIVING
SACRIFICE

A LIVING SACRIFICE

GUIDANCE FOR MEN
DISCERNING RELIGIOUS LIFE

Fr. Benedict Croell, O.P.
&
Fr. Andrew Hofer, O.P.

VIANNEY VOCATIONS

Vianney Vocations, Valdosta, Georgia
© Fr. Benedict Croell, O.P. & Fr. Andrew Hofer, O.P.
All rights reserved. Published 2019
Printed in the United States of America

ISBN: 978-0-9896212-8-1

LCCN: 2019937865

Nihil Obstat:
Rev. Basil Cole, O.P.
Censor Deputatus

Imprimatur:
Rev. Msgr. Charles V. Antonicelli, V.G.
Moderator of the Curia
Archdiocese of Washington
February 14, 2019

The *nihil obstat* and *imprimatur* are official declarations that a book or pamphlet is free of doctrinal or moral error. There is no implication that those who have granted the *nihil obstat* and the *imprimatur* agree with the content, opinions, or statements expressed therein.

Cover photo by Ricardo Moraes, Reuters

To the Immaculate Heart of Mary

TABLE OF CONTENTS

PART FIVE: Hearing from Other Religious

FOREWORD

Each man's story of his journey to priesthood or religious life is unique. God meets each of us where we are on life's pathways and invites us to proceed forward. This journey to religious life marks a sacred passage into the loving and mysterious call of God to each of us. Too often we can be tempted to think that the voice of God in our life is something that knocks us over to make the point. Sometimes that can be true, but most often, God's Spirit speaks to us, even whispers to us in the quiet of our human heart. The important posture remains one of attentive listening. What is God saying in this passage of Sacred Scripture? What is the meaning of this event in my life? Could God be speaking to me through this person? Why is there so strong a feeling of belonging when I am with this community of dedicated men? God's ways of communication with us can be subtle or direct, quiet or clashing, peaceful or even frightening. But to listen attentively, this we must do.

The very title of this book gives us an initial insight into the call to religious life. A "living sacrifice" demands our response to God's invitation to follow Christ within the context of a community. The word "sacrifice" means "to make holy." Holiness calls for a willingness to take hold of God's initiative and invitation, from which flows our readiness to follow the will of God. Thus we are made holy by our human will in cooperation with God's grace, God's initiative. If we read the *Confessions of Saint Augustine*, this holy man came, in hindsight, to see how God was constantly in communication with him. The grace was present there, but it also took his willingness to cooperate with that invitation; and sometimes that process can take a long time. (I heartily recommend Saint Augustine's *Confessions* to anyone in a process of discernment.) Being the good Father that He is, God keeps inviting us instead of forcing us to draw close to the divine life offered in religious life. We must take the step forward in answering God's invitation and call.

From the very beginning of the Scriptures we see how God calls individuals to be His servants, instruments of divine goodness. Our father in faith, Abraham, was called to leave his homeland and family, and go to an unknown place. Faith enabled him to follow the holy bidding which gave birth to a nation of people who became the people of the promise. Moses, who did not think himself as having a cultured tongue, was called to go before pharaoh and persuade him to free his fellow Hebrew slaves; with his brother Aaron, he did this, and this gave rise to the covenant which transformed Hebrew slaves into the people of God. When we read through the prophets, we hear their stories of how they were given a call to make a U-turn in their life, so as to be ambassadors of God's word, peace and reconciliation among the people they served. And we all know the story told three times in the Acts of the Apostles of Saint Paul's call (cf. Acts 9:1-19; 22:4-16; 26:12-18; see also, Gal 1:13-24), a life-altering invitation which has communicated to people through the centuries the great mystery of Christ.

We also see how Mary, the mother of Jesus Christ, was called in a way so mysterious, so profound, and so holy. The account of her calling in the Gospel according to Luke shows her struggle with the message of the angel: "How can this come about since I have no knowledge of man?" (Lk 1:34). The young maiden of Nazareth took so great a leap of faith that God used her faith to bring forth the Savior of the world. It is not an exaggeration to say that we are also called to be instruments of God's goodness in our world. For the great majority of us, our impact will not be likened to that of the Virgin Mother, but God can employ our goodness to be channels of divine goodness, whereby people experience God's mercy through us. And significantly, the author of the Epistle to the Hebrews places on the lips of Jesus these words, quoting Psalm 40(39), "Here I am; in the scroll of the book it is written, I come to do your will,

O God" (Heb 10:7). God's word in the Psalms became an avenue to knowing God and discerning His will for Jesus, His Son.

In all the stories of great men and women who are called by God, they followed the path which was laid out to them. They came to live for God alone, and for Saint Paul, for Christ alone. They found "the pearl of great price," and they sold everything to obtain it. Christ became their all. And that is an important thing to keep in mind. We don't join a religious community because of a friend, or even an inspiring leader, because persons and things change. We come to a community to follow Christ with a group of men who share a common vision with us, who support us in our love of Christ, who encourage us to grow in the ways of God. How important it is to also say we come to community because we know our own weakness, our need for continual help in the journey toward God through Christ. That is one of the great gifts of community life—seeking God together, striving to do the divine will together. "Whatever you do, do it from your heart for the Lord, not to impress others. And know that you will receive from the Lord a divine inheritance; be servant of the Lord Christ" (Col 3:23-24).

On a personal note, I remain so grateful to God for my call to be a member of the Benedictine monks of Conception Abbey in northwest Missouri. Though I was first a seminarian for the Archdiocese of Chicago, I knew that community life was something I truly needed and wanted. I really wanted to search for God through a common life of prayer and service. I sought a community where the liturgy stood at the center of the community's life, where there was a common apostolate to work at together, and where the sense of fraternity among the monks was very strong. I thank God each day for my call to be a monk of Conception Abbey. Now God's will has called me to a unique position in the Benedictine Order, after serving as the Abbot of Conception Abbey for twenty years; now I am in Rome serving the worldwide Benedictine Confederation at Sant'Anselmo to the best of my ability. Challenging as the work can be, I thank God every day for the call to monastic life and to the community to which God initially called me, and now calls me.

The authors of this book have provided for you a very wise guide in your consideration of a vocation to religious life. They write from their own experiences and those of others; their experiences are rich with examples that are practical and real. You will find examples from the lives of men very much like yourself, searching for a way, stumbling and then getting up, and then stumbling again and rising from the experience. May God grant you the insight to know His will for you, for in knowing and following it, you will find the peace, joy, and hope for which God created you for an eternal destiny.

Abbot Gregory J. Polan, O.S.B.
Abbot Primate of the Benedictine Confederation

Acknowledgments

With all thanks and praise to the Blessed Trinity, we acknowledge our many debts to those who have helped us in writing this book.

We want to thank Sam Alzheimer of Vianney Vocations, who commissioned us to write this book, and the entire Vianney Vocations team who worked on the book's production. We also thank Elly A. Brown for her proofreading.

We owe a debt of gratitude to the Abbot Primate of the worldwide Benedictine Confederation. Elected in 2016 by the Congress of Abbots, a gathering in Rome of Benedictine major superiors from throughout the world, Abbot Primate Gregory Polan, O.S.B., serves at Rome's Sant'Anselmo Abbey as the Benedictine Confederation's unifying representative and administrative head. He accepted our request to contribute this book's foreword.

For an earlier version of Chapter 2, no. 5, see Andrew Hofer, O.P., "How to talk to your family about your vocation" in VISION Vocation Guide, vocationnetwork.org, published by the National Religious Vocation Conference. We are grateful for the permission to re-use that material.

We are grateful to our Dominican brethren who have contributed in various ways to this work. We want to thank especially our Prior Provincial, the Very Reverend Kenneth R. Letoile, O.P., who granted the *imprimi potest*, and Father Basil Cole, O.P., the deputed censor and one of the world's preeminent theologians on religious life. We also thank Father James Brent, O.P., Father John Corbett,

O.P., Father Michael Mary Dosch, O.P., Father Joseph Fox, O.P., Father Jacob Bertrand Janczyk, O.P., Father John Chrysostom Kozlowski, O.P., Father John Baptist Ku, O.P., Father Gregory Maria Pine, O.P., Father James Sullivan, O.P., Father Sebastian White, O.P., and the brothers in initial formation of the Dominican Province of St. Joseph, especially Brothers Jude Grieshaber, Linus Martz, Titus Sanchez, and Nicodemus Thomas in the 2018-19 novitiate class, who have given their assistance.

We are very appreciative of the men from many other religious communities who contributed to this book: Brother Angelus Atkinson, N.O.S.B., Brother Stephen Balletta, S.M., Father Michael Berry of the Heart of Jesus, O.C.D., Father Donald Calloway, M.I.C., Brother Isidore Colm, O.S.B., Father Ambrose Criste, O. Praem., Father Thomas Esposito, O. Cist., Brother Joseph Michael Fino, C.F.R., Brother Leven Harton, O.S.B., Father Richard Goodin, O.F.M., Frater Urban Hannon, O. Praem., Brother Tim Jones, O.F.M. Cap., Father Benedict Jurchak, T.O.R., Father Emmanuel Mary Mansford, C.F.R., Father Charles McCoy, C.S.C., Abbot Austin G. Murphy, O.S.B., Father Bill Murphy, S.J., Brother Christopher Patiño, F.S.C., Brother Jerome Simpson, O.S.B., Father Neil Wack, C.S.C., Brother M. Anthony Weber, O.C.S.O., and Father Benjamin Maria Wilkinson, S.E.M.V.

We express gratitude to those many others who have offered their strong support through endorsement, encouragement, suggestions, and prayers that this book might be helpful to souls.

We realize that some may disagree with our interpretations of religious life. (We two authors have disagreements among ourselves at times, too.) Grateful for the help of so many in producing this book, we take responsibility for its errors. We hope that the book will serve the broad spectrum of men's religious vocations.

Authors' Preface

This book is written for Catholic men who are thinking about the possibility of religious life. We want what is best for you as you discern your vocation!

One of the most distinctive features of religious life is its fraternity. Many men want brothers who can inspire them to live for Jesus Christ. You really can't join a community of one. We are two Dominican friars of the U.S. Eastern Province of St. Joseph, and this book comes as a product of our own religious brotherhood. It began when we were both at the Dominican House of Studies in Washington, DC. Now one of us remains in Washington, but the other is assigned to Rome. A true brotherhood can stand the test of time and separation.

Throughout the book, when we refer to ourselves, we use the first-person plural. On the following pages we introduce ourselves separately so that you can hear a bit of our own vocation stories and see how our experience in living religious life can be helpful to you. But we don't talk about ourselves too much. We want to keep the focus on your relationship with God and your possible vocation to religious life.

Father Benedict Croell, O.P.

When I was a sophomore in college, my mother passed away after a battle with cancer, and to help grieve her loss my father took my brother and me on a pilgrimage to Europe. In my vulnerable state, the Lord opened me up to his grace, and after days of quiet prayer, he worked a miracle of conversion in my life. I returned home with a renewed devotion to the Blessed Virgin Mary and a hunger to learn everything I could about my Catholic faith.

Not long after returning, while living in a fraternity house at Colorado State University, I was praying the rosary in my room. As I prayed, I was overcome with a profound longing to be near Jesus in the Eucharist. At that moment, I somehow knew I was being called to live a radical life for Christ. I knew I had to do something big—and that I had to change in a big way. As this desire welled up in me, I thought the obvious decision was to become a priest. (Like many young men, I mistakenly thought that priesthood was the only radical choice in life after a conversion, though of course this is not the case.)

Thankfully, the Lord directed my zeal, and I did become a diocesan seminarian, though I was not to remain one for long. I was sent to seminary at Conception Abbey in Missouri and while there, became deeply impressed with the Benedictine monks who taught me. I was attracted to their lifestyle—and frankly, to the significance of their religious habit. I remember thinking, "Now *that* is what I want to do with my life." Religious life is all encompassing, and the habit—while "it does not make the monk" as the traditional saying goes—it surely helps. Even more than that, though, their fraternity and spirituality drew me in. I had discovered a way of life that had eternal significance. I began to wonder, "Could I become a religious?" I asked for this grace, and in his love, the Lord gave me the desire to offer myself to him. To this day, I know the desire for religious life clearly came from God, not from me. If, like me, you discover that desire within yourself, know that it is a holy, wonderful thing.

In time, I found my way to the Dominicans and have now served as a religious priest for more than twenty years. Through my priesthood, the Lord has helped thousands of people on their way to heaven—and he can do the same for you. If the Lord is calling and if you are generous in responding to his call, you will affect thousands of people for eternity. Being a religious priest is truly a radical vocation.

Religious life is an adventure, too. Since becoming a Dominican priest, I have been blessed to help with other people's vocations as a parochial vicar, foreign missionary, novice master, graduate student/university chaplain, parish mission preacher, vocation director, and now mission advancement director for the Pontifical University of St. Thomas Aquinas—the Angelicum in Rome. One of the greatest joys and challenges of my life was my time as a missionary in the East African missions, where I served as novice master in western Kenya.

It just so happened that my co-author, Fr. Andrew, was also in Kenya teaching for two of the years I was there. His friendship and support both in Africa and more recently at the Dominican House of Studies in Washington, DC, enabled me to work vigorously to help young men find their vocations. During the last eight years, while I served as vocation director and Father Andrew was involved in formation, some one hundred men entered our formation program.

Looking back, if I had tried to thoroughly explore all the various forms of religious life before making a decision, I never would have entered. There are so many options that I would still be doing research and visiting communities. That's the danger of trying to explore everything: you may never pull the trigger for fear of making a bad choice. While my generation suffered from over-analysis, the current generation sometimes seems to be paralyzed by it. Our hope is that this book will help you overcome hesitation and second-guessing and forge ahead to find your true vocation.

You'll see from this book that our advice to you has some central themes. Pray hard. Depend on Divine Providence. Explore what is in front of you. You don't have to turn over every rock to see what's underneath, but you do have to trust in the Lord Jesus and the powerful prayers of his mother, Mary. When the time comes, you must act! Do not delay. As a student master in our Dominican province used to say, "Do not deprive God of the best years of your life."

Father Andrew Hofer, O.P.

"Nerd Herd member." That was one way I was known when I attended Benedictine College in Atchison, Kansas. My friends and I relished being nerds. I grew up on a Kansas farm, and I've always enjoyed rhyming, so Nerd Herd sounded to me like an apt description. We even had a Benedictine monk as our own honorary chaplain.

Religious vocations are practically planted in the soil of southeast Kansas where I grew up. In 1847, the Jesuits founded my hometown, located five miles from my family farm. The town was originally called Osage Indian Mission, which became the Jesuit center of mission activity throughout southern Kansas. After the Osage Indians were forced to move to Oklahoma and the Jesuits left later in the nineteenth century, then came the Passionists, who staffed the parish in St. Paul, Kansas until 1987. According to the 2010 census, the town had 629 people—but it has produced about 200 men and women religious since its founding. That's a bumper crop.

Because I'm the tenth of ten children in my family, I sometimes joke that I'm the family tithe for religious life. I was confirmed "Thomas Aquinas" at the age of sixteen. During my undergraduate years at Benedictine College, all four philosophy professors were Thomists, and they introduced me to St. Thomas's writings. I kept my vocation a secret from my family and friends, but one Benedictine priest was especially helpful to me in answering God's call to be a religious priest. Many other Benedictine monks and sisters, as well as my Nerd Herd friends, supported me in the faith.

During the month that I graduated, May 1994, my Grandma Smith was dying, and it was also the right time to announce that I thought God was calling me to be a Dominican priest (like St. Thomas Aquinas, who had been first educated by Benedictines). Little did I know until that month that my Grandma—my only grandparent alive during my lifetime—had prayed for me to be a religious priest since my birth. My final time with her on earth, before she passed on May 26, 1994, was to pray a rosary together. I offered my Mass of Priestly Ordination on May 24, 2002 for the repose of the souls of my grandparents, in gratitude especially for my Grandma Smith's love.

Since my ordination God has filled my life with blessings. I finished a License of Sacred Theology at the Dominican House of Studies in Washington, DC, ministered as a parochial vicar in Rhode Island, was sent to Kenya to be a missionary and seminary teacher of men from many religious and apostolic communities (Salesians, Consolata missionaries, Comboni missionaries, Missionaries of Africa, men from the Society of African Missions, Discalced Carmelites, Camillians, et al.), worked as a Ph.D. student in theology at the University of Notre Dame (where I lived for five very happy years at Moreau Seminary of the Congregation of Holy Cross), and received the great joy of being a formator for eight years at the Dominican House of Studies, with the last six years as student master. So now you know something of how this Kansas farm boy and Nerd Herd member has been doing for over twenty years living religious life. God's providence has been abundantly evident in my life.

When I wrote my request for solemn vows to my Prior Provincial, after over four years of formation, I said that I did so in part because of my Dominican brethren. I come from a big family, but God gave me a much bigger family in religious life. I love them. To give you just one example, my co-author, Father Benedict, was a student brother who helped me when I was applying to the Order of Preachers. Little did I know that we would serve together in Kenya and at the Dominican House of Studies years later. It's an honor now to collaborate with him on this book for you.

Father Benedict and I both want to help you commit your life to be formed in Christ. We pray, through the intercession of the Blessed Virgin Mary, that the Holy Spirit comes to you while you read this book and ponder the possibility of religious life. Read with great expectation of God's grace. Come, Holy Spirit!

THE LORD'S INVITATION TO YOU

"Brothers, I beg you through the mercy of God to offer your bodies as a living sacrifice, holy and acceptable to God your spiritual worship. Do not conform yourselves to this age but be transformed by the renewal of your mind, so that you may judge what is God's will, what is good, pleasing and perfect."
~Rom 12:1-2, taken from the Morning Prayer reading for the Common of Holy Men

D

o you see problems in the Church today? We do. So do many young men we've worked with over the years. Their complaints may be familiar to you. Priests who don't teach what the Church teaches. Catholic schools that are Catholic in name only. Scandals in their home diocese. Declining Mass attendance. Poor catechesis. Woefully inadequate youth ministry. The impoverished neglected. And the list goes on.

It's plain to see that the Church today suffers from a crisis of faith and morality, which has profound effects on regular Catholics. Think about your own experience of the Church. You've probably been inspired by some excellent witnesses of the faith, but we imagine that you have also seen (or heard about) corruption, ignorance, abuse, apathy, hypocrisy, dishonesty, and lust damaging the Church.

But is that the end of the story? No! When a man awakens to

these problems, something stirs in his heart. It's like suddenly seeing people you love in danger. You have an instinct to leap into action, to come to their aid as quickly as possible. Most Catholic men we've encountered—those serious about their faith, that is—yearn for a transformed Church. They want to be personally involved in making the Church stronger. And more than that, they themselves want to be transformed. Most are already active in the Church, but they sense that wholesale transformation will take more than volunteering a few times a week (as laudable as that may be). Deep inside, they know it will require their lives.

Throughout the centuries, many men just like yourself have reached this point. They felt the Lord tapping their shoulder, whispering an invitation, but they couldn't quite make out the words. They needed help to hear.

If you're having a hard time interpreting the Lord's call, you're in good company. Saint Francis of Assisi had the same problem. When he was twenty-four years old, Francis received a profound call from the Lord. Some decades later, St. Bonaventure wrote this account of it:

> One day when he went out to meditate in the fields, he walked near the church of San Damiano, which was threatening to collapse because of age. Impelled by the Spirit, he went inside to pray. Prostrate before an image of the Crucified, he was filled with no little consolation as he prayed. When his tear-filled eyes were gazing at the Lord's cross, he heard in a marvelous way with his bodily ears a voice coming from that cross, telling him three times: "Francis, go, rebuild my house which, as you see, is all being destroyed!"[1]

As the famous story goes, Francis originally thought that the

---

1. St. Bonaventure, *Life of St. Francis*. These words are found both in Bonaventure's long account, chap. 2, and short account, chap. 1, fifth lesson. See *Francis of Assisi: Early Documents*, vol. 2: *The Founder*, eds. Regis J. Armstrong, O.F.M. Cap., J. A. Wayne Hellmann, O.F.M. Conv., and William J. Short, O.F.M. (New York: New City Press, 2000), p. 536 and p. 686.

Lord wanted him to do physical church repair. But he then came to realize that he was to rebuild the living Church, the people that Christ purchased with his own blood. That Church is composed, as St. Peter tells us, of "living stones" built "into a spiritual house to be a holy priesthood to offer spiritual sacrifices acceptable to God through Jesus Christ" (1 Pet 2:5).[2] That Church, like an abandoned church building, seemed to be falling into ruin.

If you are familiar at all with St. Francis, you know that like our Lord, he gave his life for the sake of the Church. In his desire to imitate Jesus Christ, he was even granted the stigmata, the very wounds of Christ imprinted on his own body, which he bore for the last two years of his life. In a most amazing way, Francis became "a living sacrifice." In all this, even in the midst of terrible suffering in his own body and in the world around him, he radiated joy.[3]

"Yes, but I'm no St. Francis," you may be thinking. But you may not be as different as you suppose. In the thirteenth century, St. Francis knew of the sins in the Church and the sins within himself. Though young, his life already had its ups and downs. He came from a family that had some money, and he liked women and parties. He wanted to be a knight to fight for the honor of his hometown of Assisi—only to find himself in prison after Assisi lost a battle against another town. He suffered heartache, illness, and misunderstanding.

In the end, Francis repented of his sins and received the grace

---

2. Most biblical quotations are taken from the *New American Bible, Revised Edition*. At times, other translations are used.

3. On joy, Pope Francis, the first Jesuit Pope in Church history and the first religious since 1846 to be Pope, writes: "[T]he old saying will always be true: 'Where there are religious, there is joy.' We are called to know and show that God is able to fill our hearts to the brim with happiness; that we need not seek our happiness elsewhere; that the authentic fraternity found in our communities increases our joy; and that our total self-giving in service to the Church, to families and young people, to the elderly and the poor, brings us life-long personal fulfilment." See Pope Francis, *Apostolic Letter to all Consecrated People on the Occasion of the Year of Consecrated Life*, November 21, 2014; no. II.1. All English translations of the magisterial documents of the Catholic Church cited in this book are available online.

to live the Gospel radically. Francis said yes to God's call in an unreserved manner. It was answering that call that made him a great saint—one of the greatest in Church history. It is certainly possible that you, too, may be called to religious life—to be a holy religious. The Lord continues to give his invitation to follow him *closely*.

There is one very important point that we must make before continuing. You may already know that holiness is everyone's first vocation. Thus, in every Christian state of life, God gives the grace to become holy. For example, there are many very holy married people. However, *the Church teaches that religious life has advantages over any other kind of life for holiness.* St. John Paul II affirms that religious life has "an objective superiority" compared to the clerical and lay states in showing forth the Church's holiness.[4] You certainly don't have to be a religious to be a saint, but it definitely helps.

Why is religious life such a privileged path to holiness? Stated simply, it is a consecration that mirrors Christ's own life of being poor, chaste, and obedient. These three qualities of Christ's life are called the "evangelical counsels," by which he invites his followers to draw closer to him by giving up material goods, the possibility of marriage, and self-determination. Thousands of religious saints can attest that renouncing these very good things makes way for even better things. For the glory of the Lord and for the salvation of souls, we in religious life are called to love like Christ without counting the cost. And that love takes a toll on our bodies. Each of us is meant to be *a living sacrifice*.

Questions and Concerns about Religious Life

This book is written to help you hear if God is calling you to religious life, to live for Jesus alone as a living sacrifice. Religious life is a profound way to reject conformity to this world and instead be transformed by the renewal of your mind. It is not for everyone, but if you are reading this book, and you take its advice to heart, you may discover that religious life is your vocation.

---

4. St. John Paul, *Vita Consecrata*, nos. 18 and 32.

If you are like the young men we have worked with for the past several years, you probably have many questions and concerns:

How do I know for sure if I'm called to religious life?

What really is religious life, anyway?

I have a beautiful girlfriend. Doesn't that mean I'm not called to be a religious?

I did some stupid and sinful things in my past. That means I shouldn't become a brother or priest, right?

Why should I trust a religious community with my life?

My family isn't supportive of a religious vocation and I don't want to upset them.

What's the difference between becoming a diocesan priest and a religious priest?

What's it like to live day after day, year after year, as a religious priest or brother?

The Church has a lot of problems, so why enter religious life now?

It's not just others in the Church who have serious problems. I have serious problems too.

This book will address all these questions and fears—and more. (That's why it's so long!) We cover a lot of ground and try to offer satisfying answers. We even cover areas that you may not realize are important. Also, we emphasize what is most important in the Christian life and what is most important in religious life: love. A religious knows that he's loved by God in a unique way and wants to love fully in return.

As much as possible, we draw on examples from our experience. We have encountered men from all different backgrounds, with all sorts of weaknesses and strengths. Some were not called to religious life and others are thriving as novices, professed brothers, and young priests. Sometimes we introduce you to characters who are fictional but whose situations are real. We think the experiences we describe will be of great benefit to you.

Throughout the book, we appeal to Scripture, Tradition, the Magisterium of the Church, and the wisdom of many saints. We feature the teaching of one saint in particular, the "Common Doctor," St. Thomas Aquinas. The Second Vatican Council singled him out as the special teacher in the Church for all men studying to be priests, and the *Code of Canon Law* reiterates that privileged status.[5] He's a wise and holy guide for our thinking about God and the things of God.

Overview of the Book

A Living Sacrifice is comprised of five parts, each composed of three chapters. The first part is entitled "Getting Started," and it addresses rather basic matters. The very first chapter is on ten truths to set you free from discernment traps. The next two chapters are top ten lists: things to do and things *not* to do.

In the second part, the book enters the deepest of all mysteries: the Blessed Trinity. God is Father, Son, and Holy Spirit. From all eternity, the Three Divine Persons live in a communion of unspeakable bliss yet chose to create to share their happiness with created persons—with you and me. Chapter 4 helps you think about God the Father and his plan for our happiness. Chapter 5 is about our Lord Jesus Christ, and his call to share in his own life of poverty, chastity, and obedience. We'll look at how religious men become like Jesus Christ in living out these evangelical counsels. In Chapter 6, we consider the Holy Spirit and his gift of holiness in religious life. If you don't want to be holy, why in the world would you want to enter religious life?

------

5. Second Vatican Council, *Optatam Totius, Decree on Priestly Formation*, no. 16, and *Code of Canon Law*, can. 252 §3. The Second Vatican Council also singled out St. Thomas Aquinas among all doctors of the Church as a model for study at Catholic colleges and universities. See its *Gravissimum Educationis, Declaration on Christian Education*, no. 10. St. Thomas is that important for the Church's thinking.

The next part of the book details the distinctiveness of religious life. Chapter 7 looks specifically at discerning the differences among diocesan priesthood, religious brotherhood, and religious priesthood. Sometimes men want to dedicate their lives to God in a radical way, but they really don't know these basic differences. Chapter 8 considers the dizzying array of religious communities as they developed through the course of history and are present today. Chapter 9 looks at some all-stars, if you will, of religious life. Have you ever wondered why so many of the Church's most popular saints are religious? Here we will find some of these great saints and see how they can help you consider living for God in the religious life.

In the fourth part we have a section called "Applying, Entering, Expecting." In Chapter 10, we offer many tips concerning how to apply to enter formation. Then we walk you through religious formation in Chapter 11. Although religious communities vary widely, the Church does have some common rules and guidelines for communities to follow. After that, we have a "reality-check" chapter on what to expect, and not to expect, in religious life. If you want to know what it's really like to enter religious life as a young man, Chapter 12 will be invaluable to you.

The fifth and final part before the Conclusion allows you to explore specific aspects of religious life from the perspective of various religious men. Chapter 13 gives you snippets of writings from holy religious of the past, and Chapter 14 shares "day-in-the-life" accounts by a monk, a canon, a friar, and a priest in a religious congregation. You may be inspired both by the saints and by what these men have to say about religious life. Chapter 15 shares the answers from several of today's religious men to the question: "What is the most important piece of advice you want to give to men discerning religious life today?" We think you will be struck by the simple counsel that these religious offer regarding your future.

Our Conclusion is focused on Our Lady, and how you can turn everything over to her in your vocation. We're dedicating this book to her Immaculate Heart. She has never been known to fail anyone who seeks her protection. By the time you reach the end of the book, you're going to have a lot more clarity about religious life and be equipped to make a much more informed decision about your vocation. It is our prayer that you experience a deep sense of joy in answering the Lord's invitation, just as St. Francis did.

Blessed Virgin Mary, cause of our joy, help me to see the possibility of becoming a living sacrifice as a religious.

—PART ONE—

GETTING STARTED

CHAPTER 1

TEN TRUTHS TO SET YOU FREE FROM DISCERNMENT TRAPS

"If you remain in my word, you will truly be my disciples,
and you will know the truth, and the truth will set
you free" (John 8:31-32).

In your discernment, do you at times feel trapped? Sometimes men want to do the right thing, but they don't know what to do. They have a jumble of thoughts, feelings, and motivations within them, and they can feel tied up. They also labor under ignorance and misinformation about basic principles regarding a vocation from God, and that can make their future course seem hazy. On one hand, the possibilities seem endless, but on the other hand men feel immobilized to take the next step.

The world loves what philosophers call "potential." You may have heard it said, "He can do anything." Well, the problem is that you certainly can't do *everything*. And if you can do *anything*, then you haven't yet made commitments. Good commitments free us to be excellent in a chosen way of life. Think about it. A married man can't do *anything*—if he wants to stay in good relationship with his wife in the sight of God.

Or take this example from carpentry. A good piece of wood can be made into all sorts of objects, but only when it is actualized by a skilled craftsman can you see that it has been used to form a crucifix. Once it's a crucifix, it is not useful to be a plank in a treehouse. Your life is like that piece of wood. Do you want it to resemble Christ crucified? If so, your life needs to be cut and carved into the service which perfects you for who *you* are meant to be. At the end, you won't be able to do *anything*, but you will have the freedom to be who God intends you to be.

Jesus wants us to experience that true freedom. This is not mere freedom of choice among many options. That's how the world usually understands freedom. The freedom that we propose is freedom for excellence.[6] As St. Paul says, "For freedom Christ set us free" (Gal 5:1). We are freest when we have the unencumbered capacity to become who God wants us to be as disciples of Jesus Christ.

Each section in this chapter begins with a statement of truth, followed by a scenario in which a man has fallen into a discernment trap. We follow with a brief meditation on the truth as applied to that man's life. Keep in mind that none of the examples we give will perfectly fit everyone's situation, because every person's life is unique and extraordinarily complex. Each person is influenced by his culture, family, time, and place. For example, Luis lives in California, and is preparing to graduate from high school. He is the seventeen-year old son of faithful Catholic parents who have a strong marriage. His story is quite different from Ian, a twenty-seven-year old lawyer from New York who is a recent convert and who was raised mostly by his fallen-away Catholic mother and agnostic stepfather, each of whom had a messy divorce. Despite these differences, we have observed that there are common patterns of sin, patterns of ignorance, patterns of how God works, and patterns of achieving true freedom. We now propose some basic truths that you can apply to the unique complexities of your life.

---

6. For more on freedom for excellence vs. freedom of indifference, see Servais Pinckaers, O.P., *The Sources of Christian Ethics*, 3rd ed., trans. Sister Mary Thomas Noble, O.P. (Washington, DC: Catholic University of America Press, 1995), especially pp. 327-456.

1. God provides for your life

Jacob is at his wit's end worrying about his vocation. He is a junior at a large Midwestern state university and is concerned about the massive amount of student loans he will have after graduation. His family doesn't have the resources to pay off his debt. Jacob has such high anxiety that he's thinking maybe he should just give up the idea of religious life because it seems so impractical. He's also worried about his grades, worried about his sins, and worried about his younger brother who has started getting into drugs. Perhaps he should take the advice of his uncle. Uncle Pat has been a father figure in his life after Jacob's dad had an affair and abandoned the family. Uncle Pat tells him to get the idea of religious life out of his head. He told Jacob to be more practical about providing for himself by getting the right jobs and looking for a woman who will be a good wife. As Uncle Pat says, "You gotta grow up and be productive."

Uncle Pat is right, in part. Jacob does need to grow up, to be a mature man. All young men need to mature and take responsibility for their lives. A huge part of spiritual maturity is recognizing that we are not in complete control of our lives. A mature man does not give in to the incessant worrying that plagues many men today. He can identify the problem, ask God to make it stop, and place his trust in him as Father. The Lord Jesus preaches: "I tell you, do not worry about your life, what you will eat or drink, or about your body, what you are to wear. Is not life more than food and the body more than clothing? . . . Your heavenly Father knows that you need them all. But seek first the kingdom of God and his righteousness, and all these things will be given you besides" (Matt 6:25, 32-33).

If you are a worrier about all sorts of things concerning a vocation, be freed by knowing that *God provides for your life.* He made you. He loves you. He has a plan for you. He is, as theologians like to say, provident. Your Creator directs your life back to himself, just as a prudent man makes a detailed plan of action.[7] You belong to God. He has great love for you and will not fail you.

2. God gives grace to respond freely to his call

Michael went to a public high school in Houston and thought about a religious vocation a couple of times, but never pursued the idea seriously. He used to go to confession about once a year and attend Mass on Sundays and most Holy Days of obligation. He is now a freshman at a university in the Lone Star State. Recently, he attended a Catholic campus ministry retreat which included Eucharistic adoration during which the idea of becoming a priest or religious surfaced much more strongly than ever before. The retreat preacher talked about Jesus' presence in the Eucharist and Michael felt a great longing to be close to Jesus—even to dedicate his life to Christ. Several weeks after that experience, he still feels drawn to Jesus by going to Mass almost every day and Eucharistic adoration once a week. Still, Michael doesn't fully grasp the meaning of his Eucharistic experiences. Because of the academic demands of college, he is tempted to set aside his longing for the Eucharist and concentrate on his studies until he graduates from college. After all, he's young, and has his whole life ahead of him.

Michael doesn't need a refined sacramental theology to apply the grace of the sacraments in his life. It is precisely through the sacraments that we have the surest and most wonderful contact with God's grace. He can go to confession and Mass far more regularly than every Sunday and Holy Day of obligation. That is where we most especially find grace. The sacraments communicate the grace of God to free us from all sorts of traps. By having a frequent sacramental discipline, he may also find that he can become more disciplined in his studies and get more work done. After all, sacramental study breaks are much more conducive to a life of study than typical college partying.

7. See St. Thomas Aquinas, *Summa Theologiae* I, q. 22, a. 1. The *Summa*'s translation by "Fathers of the English Dominican Province" is available online.

When you don't know what to think about your vocation, continue to frequent the sacraments of grace, especially the Most Holy Eucharist and confession. God gives grace in these sacraments for you to think more clearly about who he is and about your life in him. Be freed in knowing that *God gives grace to respond freely to his call.* Because God is not in competition with his creatures, the more grace you accept from him, the freer you will be to become the person God wants you to be. You may find that more order in your life enables you to say yes to all sorts of commitments appropriate for your growth in human and spiritual maturity.

3. God created you with natural desires

Juan is in the process of applying to be a Benedictine monk at the abbey that founded his college. For about two years he has been set on this path, but before he finished the application process, he heard some news about his former high school classmate, Maria. He secretly had a crush on Maria for as long as he could remember, but thought she was too beautiful and popular for him. Well, not only did a couple of Maria's friends tell him that she was very interested in him, but he was at a dance where he found out that it was most certainly true. He felt happy and excited to be with her—a feeling he'd never felt with any other woman. Now he's thinking that maybe he should forget about trying to become a Benedictine monk.

What Juan is experiencing is the goodness of a natural desire at work within him. It is good for him to be attracted to Maria. Yes, Maria is a lovely Catholic woman, and so his attraction could be spiritual as well as natural. We should expect Juan to be attracted to her. If he becomes a monk, he will most likely be attracted to her for years to come. His attractions will not disappear simply because he becomes a religious.

Religious life is not for those who have had their natural desires pulverized. *God created you with natural desires.* With the Psalmist you can pray to God: "I praise you, because I am wonderfully made; wonderful are your works! My very self you know" (Psalm 139:14).

But do not confuse the natural desire to be with a beautiful woman with the supernatural desire to be exclusively with God in the grace of religious life. Your answer to the vocation God gives you should not depend upon whether a particular woman likes you. Don't think of religious life as your second-best option, or that religious vocations happen only when a man doesn't fall in love with a woman who returns his love. Religious life offers the possibility of a *greater* love.

4. God plants in your heart holy desires through special graces

Tyler and his girlfriend, Madison, go to Eucharistic adoration together on Sundays at five o'clock. He loves taking her to that chapel. He also loves taking her back to her apartment where they would spend the rest of Sunday evening together. Eating Chinese take-out, they talk about their successful jobs at the same bank, their families, recent news, and life's big questions. But one day, Tyler realizes that he would prefer being alone with Jesus in the Eucharist and that Madison is distracting to him. He finds that he is thinking more and more about the possibility of becoming a religious priest who helps the poor, like a Franciscan. He feels guilty for thinking so seriously about the possibility of a religious vocation because Madison would make the perfect wife. He had told her as much months ago, and ever since she has been expecting him to propose. He's thinking maybe he should get this crazy vocation idea out of his head. But perhaps there's something to it?

Tyler has been touched by God with something that surpasses General Tso's chicken, his work as a loan officer, and even the very lovely Madison. The desire to give up his girlfriend and his lifestyle in order to imitate St. Francis surpasses what the world can give. Wanting to be before the tabernacle without his girlfriend is a special grace from heaven. Tyler should take the opportunity to explore his holy desire by telling Madison that they need to separate so that he can concentrate on discerning with the Franciscans.

If you are surprised by certain holy desires at work in your heart, do not ignore them, but feed them. *God plants in your heart holy desires through special graces.* You may find yourself drawn away from a girlfriend, away from a successful job, away from whatever the world can offer you—because all of that is not enough for you.

5. God forgives your sins and redirects you to himself

Aiden is ashamed of the choices he has made regarding chastity. A few years ago, he started watching pornography and masturbating. He felt he couldn't help himself. For a brief time, he experimented with homosexual male pornography, after he became fascinated by lesbian pornography. He loathed his life because he kept imagining beautiful bodies which were different from his and those around him. Fortunately, he attended a weekend retreat where he had a very powerful experience. Late that Saturday night, he imagined the Sacred Heart of Jesus in prayer and sensed deep within himself Christ saying, "You are within my heart."

Aiden is now a junior in college. With the help of regular confession, Mass twice a week, a strict plan about his phone and computer usage, and some counsel from a wise priest, Aiden is able to avoid pornography. He occasionally becomes buzzed with alcohol, maybe once every few months, and he masturbates while recalling images he saw years earlier. In the past few months, he's been thinking about the possibility of becoming a religious brother. But his past is haunting him, even in his prayer.

Aiden knows that he repeatedly made big mistakes with respect to chastity, and he thanks God that he no longer suffers the indignity of looking at porn late into the night. Yet, he wonders if his past has trapped him from even the possibility of becoming a religious brother. How could he be a brother, when he has seen and felt so much against God's call to be holy? By the grace of God, he can realize even more deeply that God is merciful. Jesus did not come to call the righteous, but sinners.

If you are like Aiden, haunted by certain sins from your past, know that *God forgives your sins and redirects you to himself.* It is true that certain actions of our past can be impediments, or obstacles, to what we might want to do later. Do not be naïve. But do not think that just because you sinned against chastity, you can't be a religious. That is a thought from the devil, who wants nothing more than to take you away from God and distract you from the call to be holy. Religious life is meant for sinners who seek mercy in the discipline of being poor, chaste, and obedient with Jesus Christ.

6. God opens your mind to think about religious life

A sensitive artistic type, Caleb makes many decisions based on how he feels. For example, he decided to buy a car not because of factors like affordability and safety, but because he had a really good feeling when looking at its shade of cobalt blue. Caleb is now in a discernment group for young adult men. In that group, individual feelings are very much stressed, as opposed to what is more objective. Caleb feels rather torn, as he has some feelings that point him toward staying at his job at a coffee shop, some feelings that push him toward asking out his fellow barista, Olivia, some feelings that motivate him to try religious life, some feelings that incline him toward becoming a philosopher, and some feelings that tempt him just to binge on Netflix. He finds that he has more and more feelings without any order or prioritization.

Not every discernment group has helpful principles. Caleb is being exposed to a kind of discernment so subjective that it's crippling him. He needs "to get out of himself." Life is more than the feelings he has. This means that Caleb should think more about what is real. He needs to think less about himself and more about the people God has put in his life. When he does that, he will be in a better position to sacrifice lesser loves (such as Netflix and fantasies about being a famous philosopher) to focus on what is truly important.

If you feel knotted up by lots of conflicting feelings, know that *God works beyond your feelings to open your mind to think about religious life.* It's true. You are more than what you feel, and your life can be much more than your feelings. When you contemplate the objective goodness of religious life, it can temper flighty emotions because it focuses your mind on an external truth rather than interior emotions. By subordinating mere feelings to real commitments, you may find that your feelings will be re-ordered and what you truly desire will become clear.

7. God offers many different paths to holiness in the Church

Connor is a senior chemistry major who has a very strong sense that God is calling him to be a priest. His parents think he's crazy because Connor could have a lucrative career in the pharmaceutical industry like his dad. Connor is wondering whether he should apply to be a priest back home in the Archdiocese of Los Angeles or whether he should be a Norbertine or a Dominican. He occasionally thinks about becoming a Cistercian, even though he's never visited a Cistercian abbey. God hasn't given him an unmistakable sign from heaven about where to be a priest. He doesn't know what to do, and he wishes there were some formula he could use to determine his vocation. He wonders whether there is a difference between the degree of holiness possible for a diocesan priest and the degree of holiness possible in religious orders.

Connor should learn to appreciate how God offers many different paths of holiness in his Church. He already appreciates that his parents have a path of holiness; they got married in the Church twenty-five years ago. But he is confused about the other vocations. For example, Connor doesn't yet realize that the diocesan priesthood is not a form of consecrated life. He has a sense that the diocesan priesthood is different from living in a religious community, but he doesn't know much else. If he were to become a religious, it doesn't mean that he himself will be holier than his dad or his hometown parish pastor, who is a diocesan priest of Los Angeles. But he can learn how the Church teaches that the consecrated life has an objective superiority in holiness in comparison to other states of life.

Religious do have some objective advantages in attaining a holy state of life, as will be made clear in this book. But religious do not have an exclusive hold on holiness. Be freed to know that *God offers different kinds of holiness in the Church.* If you desire what has been considered for many centuries to belong to "the state of perfection," and you think you have a vocation to be a priest, then look at the religious communities with priests to which you are most drawn. If you think you are called to be a priest, but don't feel called to community life or to receive religious consecration, then asking a diocesan vocation director about the diocesan priesthood would be a better path for you.

8. God invites all sorts of people to consider religious life

Logan has a knack for repairing things. He has fixed cars, tractors, computers, radios, ovens, kitchen blenders, and clothes dryers. He prefers hands-on learning rather than being stuck in a classroom. After high school, he took classes at a trade school to learn more about electronic and mechanical repairs. His great uncle is a diocesan priest and he has a second cousin who is in the Priestly Fraternity of St. Peter seminary in Nebraska. Logan doesn't feel called to the priesthood, but he wonders if he could put his talents to use elsewhere in the Church. He is happy with his new job at the grain elevator ten miles from his home, but he would like to serve the Church more explicitly. His parish church already has a custodian to take care of the property. He doesn't really know what he can do with his life, though recently he has an urge to do something big. But what?

Logan has been given some great talents and has used them well. He wants to put them to use for the Kingdom of God. He should realize that religious life has many different varieties of people, including those who hate being in a classroom. Many communities have men who seem, on the surface, to be quite average, but have rather surprising talents in cooking, information technology, agriculture, architecture, music, etc. Sometimes their former talents are put to extraordinary use precisely in living out the obedience of their vocation. Ultimately, Logan can also learn that a religious vocation is not given because of our skills, but because of God's generosity made known in our hearts.

If you are like Logan, wondering how God can use the gifts given to you, know that *God invites all sorts of people to consider religious life.* You can find religious who love to learn languages and argue about hard-to-understand philosophical terms, but you can also find men who love to do mechanical work. Many religious communities would welcome someone who can fix things. After all, St. Paul says, "There are different kinds of spiritual gifts but the same Spirit; there are different forms of service but the same Lord; there are different workings but the same God who produces all of them in everyone" (1 Cor 12: 4-6).

9. God gives distinctive charisms, recognized by the Church, to religious communities

Carlos was an award-winning debater all through high school and college. He loves to argue and he loves to win. He has been planning on entering law school but something happened which has him debating himself. During the fall semester of his senior year, he heard a powerful homily about the consecrated life at his college's Newman Center. He unexpectedly felt drawn to give up law and to become a priest instead. He has no idea where to go or what to do because there are so many religious communities in the Church. He doesn't trust the community that staffs his hometown parish because he thinks they oppose the Church's teachings.

If Carlos is especially drawn to debate, he probably shouldn't try to be a Carthusian unless he expects to receive an extraordinary grace to be silent. Instead, Carlos would do well to find a community that emphasizes a charism, or special gift from God, which involves oral communication. It's possible that an order of teachers or a community dedicated to preaching may make Carlos feel they were made for him, and he for them.

God gives distinctive charisms, recognized by the Church, to religious communities. If you do research on religious communities, you will find that there's a tremendous breadth. If you are meant to be a religious, you will find a community that will be your home. What they consider to be most important, you will also consider to be most important. If some community has a great reputation, but their apostolates don't seem like a good fit for you, then consider other communities. Approach a community whose gifts would be an appropriate place for you and your gifts.

10. God works both through you and the religious community in a mutual consideration

Jackson heard from a friend about a religious community which is supposed to be one of the best in the Church today. Unfortunately, Jackson didn't get past the first in-person interview with the vocation director. He was told that he didn't have a vocation to that community because of his ADHD. Jackson is dejected and wonders whether there is hope for him with any community.

It can be devastating to hear "no" from a vocation director. What happened to Jackson happens to quite a few men. It is common to think, "Hey, I'm here. Take me. Thank me for coming to you. I'm God-sent!" Such men need to learn that a religious vocation doesn't work like that. If Jackson, or any man in his shoes, wants to follow Jesus in religious life, he should seek a religious community willing to have a man with a certain level of ADHD.

In fact, just because you apply to a religious community, or even enter and make first profession, it doesn't guarantee that the religious community will accept you and approve you at every stage of initial formation. Realizing that there is a two-way street in a religious vocation can be freeing. *God works both through you and the religious community in a mutual consideration.* Jackson can now be confident that he's not meant to pursue a call with the first religious community, and he can be encouraged to look at one that would be more suitable for his strengths and weaknesses. If you are like Jackson, it is important to see how a religious community reacts to you. They may encourage you to apply to their community, or to look elsewhere. Just because someone thinks a particular community is the "best" (whatever that means), does not mean that it is the best for you. Also, it's much better to listen to a priest or brother who knows about the realities of religious life than to an uninformed friend who is eager to give advice.

Conclusion

Let us give a word of caution. Do not try to compare yourself to others. God has made you unique, and he loves you uniquely. Sometimes men focus on what God seems to be doing for others—and then fall into a sin like envy or pride.

Also, we want to emphasize that in giving us grace, God frees us. Grace transforms us through the virtues, the gifts of the Holy Spirit, the fruits of the Holy Spirit, and the beatitudes. By the gift of grace, we become the persons God intends us to be. When we receive a share of God's own nature, making choices to live only for God becomes more natural for us.

Mother of the Truth, pray that I may be freed by your Son to think rightly about a religious vocation.

CHAPTER 2

TEN THINGS TO DO WHEN CONSIDERING RELIGIOUS LIFE

"Be on your guard, stand firm in the faith, be courageous, be strong. Your every act should be done with love" (1 Cor 16:13).

S t. Paul is not afraid of telling people what to do. Notice in these few simple words from First Corinthians that he not only gives instruction, he also gives a brief pep talk. We all need to be encouraged from time to time to do the right thing. In the encouragement he gives us, St. Paul emphasizes what is most basic to every Christian action: love.

After our discussion of ten truths that free you from discernment traps, it's now time to go over what we recommend you do. This book is not just meant for you to have some good ideas about God's call to religious life, but for you to develop an action plan.

1. Talk with God

The word "vocation" comes from a Latin word that means "call." It is God who calls. Are you able to listen to him? Be in conversation with him, especially in the Church's sacred liturgy.

Are you able to attend Mass each day? You should make every effort to do so. The Mass is the greatest conversation that we can have with God in this world. In the Mass, heaven is joined to earth.

Here is a general question to ask yourself: What would I be doing if I were already in religious life? What are those spiritual practices that I can do before I enter? Daily Mass should always rank high on that list. If you are not able to find time in your day to attend daily Mass, consider re-prioritizing your day.

The Church's sacred liturgy includes not only the sacraments, but also the Liturgy of the Hours. If you don't know how to pray the Divine Office, you could ask someone who does, or seek a group that prays together. The core of this liturgy is praying the Psalms, the book of prayers that God's people have been praying daily for millennia.

If you can't pray the Liturgy of the Hours, see if you can pray over the Sacred Scriptures each day, not necessarily for a long time. A traditional monastic term for this is *lectio divina*. Among this book's appendices you will find a guide for how to pray over the Scriptures, especially in view of your vocation.

Is there a Eucharistic adoration chapel nearby? If so, spend some time there in daily prayer. If there is no adoration chapel, find a Catholic church that is open at a regular time each day. Quiet yourself before the Lord and listen to him. Learn to spend time with him in peace.

In fact, your life should be marked by prayer and conversation with the Lord throughout the day. St. Paul says, "Pray without ceasing" (1 Thess 5:17). Remember, unless you commit mortal sin, the Lord dwells within the tabernacle of your own soul through sanctifying grace. Even if you do commit a mortal sin, God is still with you by mercy, although not by sanctifying grace. He is with you always. Prayer recognizes that divine presence. Turn inward to talk with God throughout the day, beginning with a morning offering to give your day to God. It could go something like this:

> Most merciful Father, I thank you and praise you for the gift
> of this day. I unite all my prayers, works, joys, and sufferings
> of this day to your Son's sacrifice made present in the Holy
> Mass for these intentions (name them), and especially that I

may do your will in responding to my vocation to be holy. I ask this in the name of your Son, our Lord Jesus Christ, who lives and reigns with you in the unity of the Holy Spirit, and I call upon the intercession of the Blessed Virgin Mary and the saints: Immaculate Heart of Mary, pray for us! (Continue with invocations of your favorite saints, with the plea "pray for us!")

2. Talk with the Blessed Virgin Mary each day through the rosary

Talking with God naturally leads to conversing with the holy ones in heaven, who are with God. One of them is above all the others; she is the Star of the Sea, who can guide us as we sail along on the choppy waters of this world. We all experience a certain amount of incertitude as we question ourselves: "Where am I going?"

But when you pray the rosary and are faithful to Our Lady, you will realize more and more that she is always faithful. If you go to the mother of our Savior, you will be helped to answer as she did. She said yes to God, and the Incarnation of the eternal Son came about through her. Your vocation will come about through her prayers and tender love. Our Blessed Mother makes things simple in life, especially in regard to your vocation. You may hear from her about Jesus: "Do whatever he tells you" (John 2:5). When you pray the rosary each day, offer it for the specific intention to know God's will and to have the strength to do it.

3. Talk with a spiritual director

It is important to find a wise priest in whom you can confide. We do not live in this world alone, and a prayerful consideration of a vocation to religious life is best done with the guidance of a trusted spiritual director or mentor (preferably a priest, to whom you can also go for the Sacrament of Confession). With him, you can be honest about yourself, your thoughts, your motivations, your emotions, your desires, your fears, etc. In a word, he is someone with whom you should be comfortable to be appropriately vulnerable in sharing who you truly are.

A good spiritual director sacrifices significant time to meet with you. Don't waste his time. When he asks you to do something you should follow through with it. If what he asks you to do does not make sense, ask him why he is suggesting it to you. A spiritual director can accompany you in the process. Again, he should be someone to whom you can bare your soul. Even though you may not be discussing this within the sacrament of confession, your spiritual director and you are communicating in what is called the "internal forum" during spiritual direction sessions. The "internal forum" means your discussions are confidential, which protects your privacy when you share intimate details of your life. This is distinct from the "external forum," which means that those with authority may discuss your formation with one another. Your meetings with a vocation director, for example, are in the external forum, as he will need to discuss you with his superior.

Meetings with your spiritual director should cover: your prayer life, how to pray better, your motivations to join religious life, concerns of chastity, and questions about the Catholic faith and the practices of the Church. Eventually, with the help of your spiritual director you might put together a reasonable plan for how to answer the Lord's call to be holy. What makes sense, and what does not make sense? Some men, left to their own devices, might imprudently bite off too much and not be able to follow through with their plan.

Ask your spiritual director to be honest with you and be ready for some constructive criticism. Everyone needs to grow. In fact, you don't present yourself for entry into religious life because you are perfect. Rather, you come in order to be perfected. Do you see the difference? All of us are a work in progress until death—and purgatory can continue the purification. Be humble when accepting coaching from your spiritual director. Even if not completely accurate, criticism is information that can be useful to you about how you are being perceived.

If you are not docile or unable to take criticism, what good will it be to go to spiritual direction or to enter formation in a religious community? If the process of spiritual direction is not working for you (or for him, for whatever reason), be honest about that. It can be a good idea to have an agreement from the beginning that, if it is not working either for you or for him, both of you should feel perfectly free to suggest that you part ways without offense; and you should find another spiritual director. Working with a spiritual director can help you grow in humility, docility, and self-knowledge—all very important in the Christian life, and especially religious life.

4. Talk with a vocation director

Most men do quite a bit of research online before talking with anyone about their vocation. However, it is particularly helpful, even after a short period of research, to reach out to a vocation director of a community that interests you. Keep in mind that just because you contact a vocation director or visit a community does not mean you will join them. Many vocation directors want men to understand the different forms of religious life and to have experience with the community before applying to enter formation. A general principle when talking with a vocation director is to be confident and humble about what the Lord is doing in your life in leading you to this point. For example, tell the vocation director something of your prayer life and your desire to be pleasing to God. Remember that your vocation is more about God and less about you.

The vocation director will have questions for you. Be prepared to have questions for him. Ask intelligent questions about the community: its charism, its formation, its prayer, its ministries, etc. Listen to what the vocation director tells you and ask what he recommends for your next steps.

5. Talk with your parents

Once you're ready to do so, if at all possible, talk with your parents. For some, this comes after talking with a vocation director. For others, it's before. It depends on your relationship with your parents. If you and your parents speak easily and they would support your entering a religious community, that is a great blessing not to be taken for granted. You don't need coaching about how to have that conversation. For many, however, it's tough to talk about a religious vocation with parents, because they may not be supportive. If you are in that situation, and your parents are opposed to a religious vocation, here's some step-by-step advice.

Have you respectfully listened to your parents' reasons for objecting to a religious vocation? Before you try to explain the mystery of a vocation to them, allow them to express their concerns. Their reasons could range widely. They may think that you don't really listen to them or honor them. They may want you to have a "normal" life that would include marriage and their expected grandchildren. They may think that you have abandoned them and won't see them. They may think that you need to have several years of experience after college before you can make a decision. They may think that religious communities are full of misfits, or that religion is a scam. They may think that you will be happier and be more productive in doing just about anything other than becoming a religious.

Remind your parents of your unconditional love for them. Allow them to know that you will always be their son. Give them the honor and gratitude that they deserve. St. Thomas Aquinas says, "It is not possible to make to one's parents an equal return of what one owes to them."[8] In the virtue of piety, you are forever in your parents' debt. Let them know that. Let them also know that your love and prayer for them can actually increase in religious life.

Are their objections to a religious vocation conflated with other natural concerns? At times, parents may be reluctant to have

---

8. St. Thomas Aquinas, *Summa Theologiae* II-II, q. 8, a. 1; cf. *Summa Theologiae* II-II, q. 101.

their son grow up. Maturation takes much longer in Western society now than a century ago. This may be due to various reasons, such as an unhealthy dependency of the son on his parents, or the parents on their son. A young man seriously thinking about a religious vocation needs to show independence from parents. If you were to join the military and go overseas, would your parents also be concerned? Do they realize that even in entering a marriage "a man leaves his father and mother" (Gen 2:24)?

Let your parents know that there are safeguards to prevent you from making a hasty decision about religious life. A man cannot make a life-long vow until at least four years have lapsed after entering the novitiate. Entering the novitiate does not mean that everything has been settled.

Let your parents know that you place the Lord above all else. Perhaps you even learned that basic truth through their faith. The Lord says, "Everyone who has given up houses or brothers or sisters or father or mother or children or lands for the sake of my name will receive a hundred times more and will inherit eternal life" (Matt 19:29).

Be ready to give them a witness about why you believe the Lord might be calling you. Let them experience something of your joy and excitement in thinking about a religious vocation. Show them that your response to God's call is precisely for happiness. You know that God wants you to be happy, perfectly happy. St. Thomas Aquinas says, "To those indeed who take this sweet yoke upon themselves God promises the refreshment of divine enjoyment and everlasting rest for their souls."[9] Allow your parents to see how a man who could have had marriage, family, and normal jobs in the world can thrive in a life that is a special gift from God. He has a much bigger and much more wonderful plan than we do. Be patient with your parents if they don't fully understand or accept your desire to become a religious. Also, let your parents know that the brethren within a religious community look with affection on the

---

9. St. Thomas Aquinas, *Summa Theologiae* II-II, q. 189, a. 10, ad 3.

parents of one of their own. If you do enter a religious community, your parents may find that they are not losing a son as much as gaining many more sons.

6. Write a brief spiritual autobiography

Many vocation directors ask an applicant to write what could be called a spiritual autobiography. It could range from ten to thirty pages. Writing down what the Lord has done in your life is a helpful exercise, even before you are ready to apply to a community. We suggest that it cover such aspects as: your family, your growth in faith, your desire for religious life, your ability to work, how you are able to recognize failure, and what you can learn from that failure. There's no need to try to write your own version of St. Augustine's long *Confessions*, but, like him, try to identify singular moments of grace in your life.

If you write a spiritual autobiography (even as a rough draft), we think you will be helped in the following ways. First, it will help you connect the dots in your life, deepening your self-knowledge. Some people are not very perceptive about the patterns of their life, the significant moments, and the workings of God's grace. Writing may help you express truths about yourself that you have never actually articulated. For example, if you like manual labor or enjoy intellectual labor, then that may come across in your writing. If you have had outstanding spiritual friends, you may gain insight into their influence on you. If you write about your family, and you can think only of problems, it may reveal issues that need forgiveness and healing.

Second, writing a spiritual autobiography may tell you more about who God is and what God is doing in your life, as you see that he is the primary author of all our lives. In his providence, he has put certain people in your life. He has given you many good things. God declined to prevent certain hardships and brought some good out of those sufferings. Your own word choice may surprise you as you write out the story of your life in God's presence.

Third, your spiritual autobiography can be written in conjunction with your spiritual director. The writing will help him to know you better. He may guide your writing, such as advising you to omit details that are better left to the internal forum.

7. Love intensely

Some people think that by becoming a religious you put love away. That's ridiculous. Entering religious life is a great act of love. Love is the very end or purpose of religious life, as we will see later. Listen to what is read at Night Prayer of the Liturgy of the Hours on Saturday night:

Hear, O Israel! The Lord is our God, the Lord alone! Therefore, you shall love the Lord, your God, with all your heart, and with all your soul, and with all your strength. Take to heart these words, which I enjoin on you today. Drill them into your children. Speak of them at home and abroad, whether you are busy or at rest. (Deut 6:4-7)

Our Lord Jesus ties this passage with Leviticus 19:18: "You shall love your neighbor as yourself" (see Matt 22:34-40). True love of neighbor is for the sake of God. God doesn't just get some of your heart, while other parts of your heart are divided up among various neighbors—and yourself. How much of your heart does God get? All of it. And God wants you to love your neighbor in him.

To love intensely, do corporal and spiritual works of mercy in preparation for the possibility of entering religious life. Mercy is a particular kind of expression of Christian love for those who are in need. Develop a more generous heart. In mercy, someone's need touches your heart, and you respond out of love. Be merciful, as your heavenly Father has been merciful to you (see Luke 6:36). Because mercy is so basic to the Christian life, you will find it to be foundational in the various forms of religious life.

Let your intense love build up the Church. A man who feels a call to follow the Lord in religious life must recognize that what he has received in love from the Lord can now be passed on to others in order to build up the Church. Be active in your parish church or campus ministry. That can be one of the most significant preparations for entering religious life. "Zeal for your house consumes me!" (Ps. 69:9)

8. Be vigilant in your resolve to be chaste

When the world thinks of love, it often turns to things that counter true charity, such as sexual sin. We live in a world where temptations against chastity abound. You must not play dumb regarding these realities around you, or subject yourself to negative influences that could derail your response to Christ's invitation. Plan a path to navigate through dangers to chastity with the wisdom of your spiritual director. Most men need to cut back significantly on the amount of media to which they subject their senses. Avoid excessive screen time, go outdoors to spend quality time in God's creation, and be mindful to the presence of God in all places and all times. He is always present to you. You also need to be patient and to persevere. God's grace is more powerful than your sins. In your resolve to be chaste, stay close to Jesus in the sacrament of penance. Recall that with God, all things are possible (see Luke 1:37). If you find this extremely difficult, recall these words: "In your struggle against sin you have not yet resisted to the point of shedding your blood" (Heb 12:4).

9. Make a "Come and See" weekend

After some research, it is a good idea to make a "Come and See" weekend at a religious community. The phrase "come and see" appears early in John's Gospel. Andrew and an unnamed disciple hear from John the Baptist that Jesus is the Lamb of God. They start following him. Jesus turns around and asks them what they are seeking. They ask him where he is staying. Jesus then says, "Come and see" (John 1:39).

That invitation is what the Lord continues to offer men who visit a religious house to see how the Lord is present there within the community. Most communities require a man to be at least of college-age to make a vocation weekend. Don't be surprised if the vocation director wants to ask you many questions before you come to visit them for a weekend. The community has a right to know your general history before you come.

Even if you make a vocation weekend but don't enter that community, the visit can help you. Each religious community has its own culture. Getting to know that culture will help you to become more familiar with the basics of religious life. It will also help you to understand the differences among various religious communities.

Remember that attending a "Come and See" does not equal: "I must join." Unfortunately, many young men think this is the case. Then fear stops them from even visiting a community. Going on a "Come and See" should not be an experience of anxiety. Such a visit will likely make you a better Catholic man. So relax! It's a wonderful opportunity that will give you some concrete exposure to religious life, and the chance to meet men already living this way of life.

10. Be a man, grow out of childish dependence, and make sacrifices

St. Paul urges us to grow "to mature manhood, to the extent of the full stature of Christ, so that we may no longer be infants, tossed by waves and swept along by every wind of teaching arising from human trickery" (Eph 4:13-14). What does that mean for your life right now? Be a man and stop childish things. Learn how to make sacrifices in little things so as to be found worthy to make sacrifices in big things. Here are a couple of examples. Naturally, you may need to adapt this advice to your cultural, family, financial, and health conditions.

If you are in college and want to enter a religious community after graduation, think about how you can show greater maturity in the different aspects of your life. Do well in your courses. Volunteer in your campus ministry and in social outreach programs. Get a job during the summers and during the school year to show that you know the meaning of money. Pay off any debts you might have. Be respectful to your family, especially parents and grandparents, and other persons who deserve your respect such as teachers and mentors. Make mature decisions regarding friendships, parties, and other social interactions. Be able to have friendships with both men and women. Know the importance of chastity in your interactions with women. Be responsible in your behavior throughout the week. For example, if you are accustomed to party on Friday nights, think about how Friday each week is traditionally set aside in penance to honor the Passion of our Lord. Yes, a religious community has many celebrations, but religious life itself is a penitential form of life.

If you are finished with college, it would make very good sense to live on your own as you strive to live for God. That is part of what it means to grow up. Religious life can certainly order your life, but it will not automatically solve the personal problems younger men sometimes experience. There are priorities that a man must make to live in the world and not be of the world. A young man must make these choices himself—free from the pressures of parents or other influences for a time. A mature man makes sacrifices all the time. Be the man God is calling you to be by sacrificing various creature comforts. Only a self-possessed man can give himself in love. Look at it this way: if a man who is considering a vocation is able to live on his own, have a full-time job, pay his own bills, cook his own meals, do his own laundry, and make the Lord his priority by doing the things listed in this chapter, then that is a young man who has the foundation to flourish in religious life.

In any case, it is important to be in a position of strength which will enable you to launch. By launching, we mean gaining a measure of freedom and independence to set out on the great adventure of life—which may be religious life. Only a man who has some independence, an understanding of marriage, and the value of material goods, can make the sacrifices involved in obedience, chastity, and poverty. You can't give what you don't have; only a self-possessed man can give himself in love.

Most powerful Virgin, ask your Son to give me the strength to do what I need to do, at this time in my life, to be ready to follow him wherever he goes.

CHAPTER 3

TEN THINGS NOT TO DO
WHEN CONSIDERING
RELIGIOUS LIFE

*"Do not be haughty but associate with the lowly; do not be wise
in your own estimation. Do not repay anyone evil for evil. ...
Do not be conquered by evil but conquer evil with good"
(Rom 12:16-17, 21).*

St. Paul gives this list of don'ts in Romans 12, along with several other commands. We especially need to hear the don'ts when we are tempted to do what is wrong. Sinning is always wrong for us, because it takes us away from God in whom alone is our happiness. Sin can cloud your thinking about the possibility of becoming a religious. Yet there are still other actions, although not sinful, that can also muddy the waters.

Take a college student by the name of Brayden as an example of what you shouldn't do. He contacted ten religious communities at the same time. He thought he was casting his net wide, but instead he was in the process of throwing away a possible religious life. He made the ten contacts during one of the break-ups in his relationship with Emily, a girl he had been seeing on and off for over a year. He was half-hoping that Emily would find him more attractive if he had a reputation as "discerning." Also, Brayden thought his mother would be very pleased by this discernment, and he would score some points with her. He knew his dad, a non-practicing Catholic, would get angry when hearing about his discernment. "That's just fine," thought Brayden, because he really wanted to get back at his dad for being a crummy father. When he visited four of the ten religious communities within a span of two weeks one summer, Brayden kept thinking and praying about Emily and his family dynamics. During a conversation in the Dominican priory he visited, he slipped and called the friars there Benedictines. That did not go over well.

Don't follow Brayden's example. Now we'll look at some specific things for you not to do.

1. Don't date Katie

If you are seriously considering religious life, don't date. Some men thinking about religious life are so deeply involved with a woman that they are looking at engagement rings. If you are in that situation, and you want to consider the possibility of religious life, you must tell your girlfriend that you need to stop the momentum of your relationship and separate on account of your relationship with God. If you don't want to consider religious life, then, of course, put this book away and proceed with your relationship with your girlfriend. It is a holy thing to get married in the Church. What we want is some honesty in your life during this time. You cannot be in a relationship with a woman and seriously consider religious life at the same time. If you are dating Katie while you keep thinking about religious life, it is not fair to her, not fair to yourself, and not fair to God.

Often enough, a man meets some beautiful woman right in the very process of applying to enter a religious community. This might happen to you, and you might become enormously attracted to the Catholic woman of your dreams. Of course, this woman is not from the devil, but she may be distracting you from a greater good than marriage. The Church considers the consecrated life objectively higher than marriage because it affords greater fidelity to imitating the life of Jesus. Do you want to aim higher? If so, realize the nature of making a sacrifice now. Sacrifices usually aren't easy. If you do become a religious, you will not cease being attracted to beautiful women. Your love of beauty and your emotions don't just disappear once you make a religious profession. Face the reality of how you are being called to love and to be loved.

The question comes down to love. What kind of love do you want to receive? If you have the sense of a vocation to religious life, God may be asking you: "Is my love enough for you?" Answer him. How do you want to love and to be pleasing? St. Paul says: "An unmarried man is anxious about the things of the Lord, how he may please the Lord. But a married man is anxious about the things of the world, how he may please his wife, and he is divided" (1 Cor 7:32-33). Say with St. Paul: "forgetting what lies behind but straining forward to what lies ahead, I continue my pursuit toward the goal, the prize of God's upward calling, in Christ Jesus" (Phil 3:13-14).

2. Don't succumb to the FoMO

While you may not be dating, you may still be falling victim to the peer pressure of doing what everybody else is doing for entertainment. If you are serious about considering a religious vocation, you will need to disconnect from some things in your life that you may have considered important. In the name of Jesus and his love for you, cast out the "Fear of Missing Out."

Thinking seriously about a religious vocation will likely change your outlook on life. A young man might reason, "I want to be fresh for my holy hour in the morning, so maybe I should go to bed earlier . . . but that means leaving the party earlier." If your friends discourage the change, try to gently and non-judgmentally bring them along. If they can't be made to understand, that's unfortunate. But unless you hate father and mother (and party friends), you can't be Christ's disciple (see Luke 14:26).

Yes, conversions of heart bring changes to your life. For example, there might be some friends who are a bad influence on you, or there might be bad situations in which you have regularly put yourself in the past. If you know that being with such friends or in such situations has led you down the wrong path before, you must avoid them beginning right now.

Some people's social life consists mostly of using social media. This is, to put it bluntly, pathetic. If your problem is not going out every Friday and Saturday night, but rather spending hours perusing what other people put up on social media, just stop. If you feel compelled to post vaguely interesting things that you just saw or ate or heard, just stop. Unplug yourself from social media and cultivate real relationships independent of screen-time. Does this mean deleting your social media accounts? It might. Or it may mean simply reducing how frequently you check your accounts. Generally speaking, young men are far too connected to screens.

Again, we are not asking you to cut off your friendships. Commenting on Aristotle, St. Thomas Aquinas observes that no one in his right mind would want to live without friends.[10] Develop stronger and more loving relationships with both men and women. But don't worry about missing out. God has his own plans for you—plans for lasting joy, happiness, and friendship.

3. Don't block out your family

All sorts of young people have family problems. Perhaps you are afraid that your family will shun you if you apply to a religious community. In any case, it is important not to block your family out of your life or repress hurt feelings that arise from your family. Here are two reasons why you should exercise special care regarding your family and its problems.

The first reason is that you will always be a member of that family. You can't change that, even if you enter some monastery

---

10. St. Thomas Aquinas, *Commentary on the Nicomachean Ethics*, Book VII, lecture 1, no. 1539.

across the world. Entering religious life should be an action of great maturity, and a mature man is aware of the strengths and weaknesses of his family. We recommend that you spend extra time with your family before you enter a religious community, as that may reassure your family that you aren't running away from them.

The second reason is that your familial relationships affect your community life. If you begin initial formation without trying to resolve a given family issue, your effort to be formed could suffer. Sometimes those with bad relationships with their parents have unnecessarily strained relationships with authorities in the community. Sometimes those who have problems in relating to siblings have problems with their religious brothers.

Coming from a dysfunctional family certainly does not prevent a man from becoming a religious priest or brother. But a man who has repressed a painful childhood in his dysfunctional family and refuses to face those issues may need the help of a good spiritual director and perhaps of a professional Christian therapist to achieve some healing. It is best to do these things before entering religious life both for the sake of your family and for the sake of your future community.

Believe us. It is very important to practice Christian virtues such as love, mercy, piety, and gratitude within your family if you are thinking about entering religious life.

4. Don't develop unhealthy patterns of life

It is so sad to meet young men who are interested in religious life, but who have unhealthy patterns of mind or preventable physical health issues. No matter how much they may want to be religious, they shouldn't enter religious formation. Being of good physical and mental health is one of the few prerequisites to entering a religious community, but today all sorts of men are destroying their opportunities to enter. Almost all religious communities will ask for a psychological and a physical examination of their applicants. We will discuss this in our chapter on applying to enter a community. If you are doing unhealthy things, ask God for the grace to stop and get the help that you need. Here are just a few examples.

Are you obese? It's true that too many religious are very overweight. But if you are very overweight, and you are still young, what do you think you'll be like twenty or thirty years from now? Don't neglect your physical health now. Take care of yourself and be a good steward of what the Lord has given to you.

Do you have addictive behaviors? You need the powerful grace of God and the help of others to stop addictions involving sex, alcohol, drugs, gambling, or electronic entertainment. Yes, to stop is easier said than done. Too often addicts don't even realize that they are addicted to behaviors until they try to stop—and can't.

Do you have recurring thoughts that indicate anxiety or depression? Such conditions are increasingly common among young people today. If you need some counseling before you apply for religious life, get that help. If you are a college student, you may very well find that counseling is provided through your college's psychological health services. In any case, be careful to consider any counselor's advice in view of the Church's teaching on faith and morals.

5. Don't look at pornography

Although this recommendation is quite focused, it merits its own consideration. Pornography and masturbation are perhaps the most common reasons why men hesitate to consider religious life. These vices prepare a man for no vocation at all—least of all a religious vocation. The man who is looking at porn is not in a position to enter initial formation. In fact, a man who views porn would also have problems in entering a Christian marriage. Pornography is a scourge upon the Church and society—and it is so easily accessible. If this is a problem for you, ask God for the grace to get it immediately out of your life entirely. No compromises! Do everything in your power to stay away from pornography. Talk bluntly with your spiritual director and make a concrete plan to leave such things behind. Even with respect to images that are not pornographic, it is highly advisable for you to limit the amount of media you take in through your senses. Screens will not bring you happiness.

6. Don't judge a religious community as if you were the Lord

It may happen that you do not find what you see in a religious community to be very appealing. Remember that you are a guest in that community, and that you are assessing their life in a short visit. You need only to decide whether you should continue thinking about that community or not. Most religious communities today are not bursting with vocations. Could it be that the Lord is calling you to join one of those communities? If not, then still be appreciative of their hospitality and the venerable tradition of their community in the Church. And learn from the experience. It is important that men who enter have some understanding of the breadth of religious life, and that they be grateful to God for the good that many religious communities are doing.

7. If you can't enter religious formation this year, don't delay preparations for a future entrance

Lots of young men consider entering religious life when they are still years away from the possibility. Do not think, "Oh, I'm too young to prepare to become a religious." This book can help you think, pray, and work to prepare—even if your entrance is years away. You may think that something like four years is such a long time. But time flies. Four years will come and go before you know it. Some tell themselves they will sort out the "vocation thing" or the "holiness thing" later. This is not rational thinking. It is better to consider a vocation when the Lord calls you and not delay. Take a close look now at a community and keep in touch with the vocation director as you make progress. You need time, and you can ask for the grace to be consistent in being a disciple of the Lord now.

8. Don't be afraid

Repeatedly in the Bible we hear such encouragement as "Fear not!" "Do not be afraid!" and "Do not fear!" This is extremely important not only in your Christian life, but also in your thinking about the possibility of becoming a religious.

What are the fears that you need to face at this time? For some, it's the fear of the unknown; for others, the fear of being rejected by family and friends; for still others, the fear of making the wrong decision; for yet others, the fear of being told no by the religious community. Some are afraid of applying and being accepted, but then needing to leave at some point during formation. Some men have all these fears.

Let Jesus Christ, your Lord, strengthen you so that you may overcome your fears and have the courage to respond to your vocation. You don't know everything that will happen, but you can cast out your fears by loving the Lord wherever he leads you.

9. Don't despair of God's mercy

Sometimes men have an experience of something so remarkable in religious life that they feel like saying what Simon Peter said after the miraculous catch of fish: "Depart from me, Lord, for I am a sinful man" (Luke 5:8). We want to emphasize what St. Benedict gives as the last item of his long list of instruments of good works: "Never despair of God's mercy."[11] Yes, religious life is a life of great holiness, and it's meant for *sinners* to receive. Do not become discouraged when you encounter the holiness of God at work in a religious community, and you become more conscious of your sinfulness. In his mercy, God brings good even out of what is evil. Think of how terrible it was that our sins put Jesus to death, and recall that the Lord's mercy conquers our sinfulness. Do not despair. We are not worthy of being close to Jesus, but the Lord says, "I have called you friends" (John 15:15).

---

11. *Rule of St. Benedict*, chap. 4.

10. Don't endlessly discern

Some men have been "discerning" for a decade—or even two. They go back and forth between religious communities or between religious communities and girlfriends or between the hot pursuit of religious life and no interest at all. Vacillating constantly between options, they never decide to try religious life. They suffer. We don't want anyone to suffer like that.

Do the research and decide which communities you would like to visit. Some men know where they want to visit. They visit, and they enter. Other men might take more time and visit several communities. Some men, after seriously considering religious life, realize that they're not called to be religious. They can move on with their lives. Every vocation from God is holy, and offers the opportunity for growth toward perfect love!

Do not join the "Order of Perpetual Discernment." If you recognize that you have been discerning too long about what you want to do with your life, then ask God to give you the grace of insight and decisiveness. God wants you to look with his eyes and love with his heart. Also, a spiritual director can often help nudge you in one direction or another.

Most holy mother, please stop me from doing what I should
not be doing at this time in my life.

—PART TWO—

THE TRINITARIAN CALL TO RELIGIOUS LIFE

CHAPTER 4

GOD THE FATHER AND OUR DESIRE FOR HAPPINESS

"Blessed be the God and Father of our Lord Jesus Christ, who has blessed us in Christ with every spiritual blessing in the heavens, as he chose us in him, before the foundation of the world, to be holy and without blemish before him" (Eph 1:3-4).

Jayson is confused about what to do. He wants to do the right thing in life, but he knows quite painfully that he has failed in various ways. His father and mother divorced when he was just ten years old. Each of his parents tried to spoil him, in part to win his affection. He always got what he wanted: special food, the latest electronic upgrades, nice clothes, the best guitars, time to be left alone with his friends without anyone questioning him. His father promised to pay for his college education, and is now preparing to find Jayson a job after he graduates. When he was fifteen, Jayson became caught in a cycle of lust, anger, and self-loathing—becoming addicted to pornography and masturbation. In his second year of college, he was able to break free of that vicious cycle through the help of a religious priest, Father Michael, and the companionship of some very supportive Catholic friends. He began to develop real discipline in prayer and control of appetites—what Father Michael calls "asceticism." But he still struggles in various ways. Jayson admires Father Michael and the other religious he sees at his college. He wonders if he could become like them, but fears that may be unrealistic for him. He's confused. He doesn't know what he wants in life.

What do *you* want in life? There are all sorts of answers to this question. But there is a bottom-line principle, recognized by many philosophies and religions, and it pertains to us all. *Everyone wants to be happy.* People may want all sorts of different things in order to try to find happiness, but all are united in a quest for happiness. It's not selfish to want to be happy. It's being human.

In your own search for happiness, do you feel the desire for something more than you already have? God has put a restlessness in our hearts that cannot be filled except by him. We instinctively yearn for something more. Our yearning is not a sign of the inadequacy of grace, but rather a sign of its efficaciousness. In other words, the gifts that God is giving you now are only a shadow of what will come. Grace helps us see that there is much more to our life than simply the world we see with our eyes. God wants us, chosen in Christ his Son, to experience *every spiritual blessing in the heavens.* He wants us to share in his glory where the Church will be as Our Lady already is, *holy and without blemish before him.*

This is the path of love. The perfection that God wants of us is the perfection of love. God is love, and he calls us to be like him—full of love. Men who have said yes to God's call to enter religious life can find, in loving and being loved, God himself as a fulfillment of their desires.

Some people are suspicious of desires, acting as if all desires should be stifled. To the contrary! We think that our desires for goodness should be fanned into a raging fire! C. S. Lewis famously writes:

> Indeed, if we consider the unblushing promises of reward and
> the staggering nature of the rewards promised in the Gospels,

it would seem that Our Lord finds our desires not too strong, but too weak. We are half-hearted creatures, fooling about with drink and sex and ambition when infinite joy is offered us, like an ignorant child who wants to go on making mud pies in a slum because he cannot imagine what is meant by the offer of a holiday at the sea. We are far too easily pleased.[12]

Are you fooling about with "drink and sex and ambition"? Jayson was. Know that infinite joy is offered to you. C. S. Lewis contrasts mud pies in a slum with a beach vacation. Perhaps we can think of more relevant, contemporary examples. Don't be satisfied by playing video games and looking at other people's self-portrayals in social media when God wants you to have a real life of everlasting happiness with him. Don't be lured into pornographic fantasies. If you spend your life looking at a screen of some unreality, whether that be the gravely sinful viewing of sex for fleeting pleasures or the inane wasting of several hours of your day on the latest video game craze, your life will go nowhere.

Don't give up on truth, goodness, and beauty in your life. Rather than looking at a screen to find your life, look to God. God alone satisfies. He knows how many hairs are on your head. He has made you precious in his eyes. He loves you and made you to love and to be loved.

By desiring to understand better how God alone satisfies, we will understand better who we are. By desiring to understand better who we are, we will understand better who God is. Answering our vocation reveals to us not only who God is, but who we are.

That was Moses's experience at the burning bush. In Exodus 3 we read that God reveals himself to Moses, "I am who am." That little line of divine revelation has sparked millennia of thought and debate about God's own being. But what shouldn't be overlooked is that God also reveals Moses's own identity. Moses asks, "Who am I that I should go to Pharaoh and bring the Israelites out of Egypt?"

---

12. C. S. Lewis, *The Weight of Glory* (New York: Harper Collins, 2001 [reprint]) p. 26.

God answers, "I will be with you." Moses wants to know his own identity as he begins his mission to free the Israelites from slavery. God's answer is quite simple: "I will be with you."

If you were talking to Moses after he heard that from God, you could say, "Hey, Moses, that's who you are! Don't you get it? *God is with you.* That's your identity. That's how you will free God's people from slavery. It's not about you. In finding out who you are, you find God himself. In fact, it's *all* about God!" Something similar is happening to you right now as you think about your vocation.

Because it is all about God, let's begin at the beginning—when there was only God—and reflect on why God created the human race. After that, we'll look at how you were created to be a man. Then we will consider our goal: heaven. In this chapter's conclusion we'll discuss what it means to become a "man of desires," full of desire for the One who reveals our vocation. If you are like our Jayson featured above, experiencing some confusion about what to do in life, turning to God the Father's purpose in creation can be of great help.

Created in the image of God

God is Father, Son, and Holy Spirit. From all eternity, the Father has generated the Son, and the Holy Spirit has proceeded. These three persons are all equally God, and each is God whole and entire. They live in unspeakable joy and are without any need.

There are lots of errors today among Christians about the nature of God. These errors can really derail our lives. If you don't get God right, how can you get your vocation right? For example, if you erroneously think that God needs you for his own happiness, you might conclude that God uses you without regard for your own happiness.

The *Catechism of the Catholic Church*, in its very first sentence of the first paragraph says: "God, infinitely perfect and blessed in himself, in a plan of sheer goodness freely created man to make him share in his own blessed life."[13] Think about that. God has no need to create. Rather, it is a plan of sheer generosity. St. Irenaeus of Lyons in the second century says:

> Service rendered to God does indeed profit God nothing, nor has God need of human obedience; but he grants to those who follow and serve him life and incorruption and eternal glory, bestowing benefit upon those who serve him, because they do serve him, and on his followers, because they do follow him. But he does not receive any benefit from them: for he is rich, perfect, and in need of nothing.[14]

A defective image of God creates a defective image of man and God's plan for him. As you think about your vocation, fix your eyes on the all-powerful God, and renew your faith in his plan for you. He created you for a great purpose.

Created to be a man

Let's face it. Our culture seems to be getting stranger each year regarding what it means to be human. Now people can create their own gender identities. But it was not so in the beginning. Created in the image of God, we express that image as men. What does it mean to be a male, an adult man, in God the Father's plan?[15] How does the religious vocation for men accentuate rather than evacuate our male identity? After all, if you want to be a religious brother or to be a spiritual father in religious life you need to be a man with human and Christian maturity. Religious life isn't for the immature. Jayson, so spoiled in his childhood years, will need to continue to learn what it means to be a man. The lesson is something learned

---

13. *Catechism of the Catholic Church*, no. 1.

14. St. Irenaeus of Lyons, *Against Heresies*, 4.14.1. *Ante-Nicene Fathers* translation by Alexander Roberts and William Rambaut available online and slightly altered here.

15. We highly recommend that you read the apostolic exhortation of the Bishop of Phoenix to the men of his diocese, Bishop Thomas J. Olmsted, *Into the Breach*, September 29, 2015, available online.

over time—with mistakes, heartaches, and God's merciful love. Let's first consider what it means simply to be human, as we must be human before being adult men.

The Second Vatican Council's *Pastoral Constitution on the Church in the Modern World* reads:

> The truth is that only in the mystery of the incarnate Word does the mystery of man take on light. For Adam, the first man, was a figure of Him Who was to come, namely Christ the Lord. Christ, the final Adam, by the revelation of the mystery of the Father and His love, fully reveals man to man himself and makes his supreme calling clear.[16]

The great Pope Saint John Paul II had an ardent love of the truth that Jesus Christ reveals man to himself. In his inaugural encyclical of his pontificate, St. John Paul quotes from this same Pastoral Constitution:

> Human nature, by the very fact that it was assumed, not absorbed, in him, has been raised in us also to a dignity beyond compare. For, by his Incarnation, he, the son of God, in a certain way united himself with each man. He worked with human hands, he thought with a human mind. He acted with a human will, and with a human heart he loved. Born of the Virgin Mary, he has truly been made one of us, like to us in all things except sin.[17]

When we look into the eyes of Jesus, we look into the eyes of God the Father. As Jesus says, "Whoever has seen me has seen the Father" (John 14:9). He reveals to us how to know God our Father as his sons. Jesus reveals how to be both human and male.

Today many men like Jayson find themselves confused about what it means to be a man. Various philosophies and movements

---

16. Second Vatican Council, *Gaudium et Spes*, Pastoral Constitution on the Church in the Modern World, no. 22.

17. St. John Paul II, *Redemptor Hominis*, no. 8, quoting *Gaudium et Spes*, no. 22.

in our society have undermined once widely received standards of true masculinity. For example, it was once widely understood that a man was supposed to protect his wife and his children. But today it is common to see men escorting their pregnant girlfriends into abortion clinics. It was once widely understood that sexual intimacy with a woman was the privilege that comes with making a life-long commitment to her in marriage, but today the widespread use of pornography has dramatically eroded a sense of intimacy in human sexuality.

Furthermore, the shifting demands of feminist ideology have sent mixed messages to men about how they are to act around women. Is the man supposed to pursue the woman in a romantic relationship, or is he to be pursued? Is he supposed to pay for her dinner as a sign of gentlemanly respect? Or is he to let her pay in acknowledgement of her self-sufficiency as a woman? Maybe you have encountered these social paradoxes yourself. These are only a few of the host of everyday confusions confronting men.

There are two extremes at work in our society. At one extreme we find a kind of hypersensitive male: insecure, indecisive, excessively preoccupied with his emotions and how he is perceived by others. At the other extreme, we find a kind of macho male: egotistical, emotionally hard, indifferent to others, and ready to use women for his own pleasure. How are men today to navigate these competing stereotypes and discover the true meaning of masculinity? How is discovering your true masculine identity connected with discerning a religious vocation?

Jesus Christ is the way. Jesus stands as the point of balance between these two extremes. He is gentle but firm, he is full of strength and power, but places that strength and power at the service of all, including women. He speaks with women and interacts with women, always telling the truth and always affirming their dignity and worth. Even though he is filled with the power to cast out demons, to heal and to walk on water, he is meek and humble of heart. He radiates love, joy, peace, patience, kindness, purity, and self-control. He even lays down his life on the cross, crucified in weakness (2

Cor. 13:14). He emptied himself and took the form of a slave (Phil. 2:7). In these ways, Jesus shows us what true masculinity is.

Jayson learned from Father Michael that all men are called to imitate Jesus, but it is not easy. In fact, it is impossible on our own. This perfect masculinity, in its total mastery and balance of the emotions, is too difficult for us to attain by our own natural strength. But the good news is that Jesus—now risen from the dead—offers to men everywhere a share in his own true masculinity. The true masculinity of Jesus is a gift offered to us in grace—for which we should earnestly ask.

Sometimes people get the impression that religious life is emasculating. After all, how can a guy who gives up his independence, a salary-earning job, and a wife be a real man? Religious life seems to take away three things that men often use to show off their masculinity: big money, beautiful wife, and dominant autonomy. But it is precisely here that religious life shows its power to make someone a real man. The vows of poverty, chastity and obedience remove the illusion of finding fulfillment in these things alone, as we will see in the next chapter. A man who is called to religious life is called to identify with Jesus in a profound way, and by identifying with Jesus, he finds the meaning of what it is to be created as a man.

Happiness with God forever

Now that we have considered God's design of creation in the beginning, and our place in that creation as men, let's think about the end. Think about your life as having a purpose or an end.

Consider the example of an archer. In making choices, especially those choices that are lifelong commitments, you move your life in a certain direction—just as an archer moves an arrow by releasing it from an outstretched bow. The question is, where is the target? In what direction do you aim?

Answering a vocation presupposes a maturity through which you take responsibility for your future actions. Your vocation is about the rest of your entire life. Jayson is daunted by the seriousness of this, but he shouldn't abandon the idea simply because it is so demanding, so costly. It's giving up all sorts of possible "lives" in order to be committed to God in a particular way of life until death. You are not merely making a short-term decision about your education, your employment, your health, or your friendships. As important as these decisions are, they are not of the same significance as directing the totality of your life in answering a vocation. This is not like choosing the right college for yourself. Don't you ultimately want heaven as your target, to be with the Father, Son, and Holy Spirit forever in happiness? There we will be able to see God as he is in what is traditionally taught as a beatific vision. Our Lady and the angels and saints behold God face-to-face and praise him forever in bliss, utter joy.

The Christian life is aimed at this goal, and the religious life is, in a certain way, an intensification of pressing on toward that goal. In other words, a man joins a religious community so that he may more intensely order his life toward God as the goal of his life. Religious life is sometimes described as "an eschatological sign." *Eschatological* comes from the Greek term that means last or final things. Our belief in the last things has special relevance to how we respond to the possibility of a religious vocation.

You are going to die. Have you realized what that means for your life now? Some are afraid of death; some don't have an authentic hope in heaven. Religious have traditionally had various ways of putting into practice the Latin adage, *Memento mori,* which means "Remember death." As St. Benedict says in his *Rule,* "Remember to keep death daily before your eyes."[18] One of the reasons that Jayson was able to think about the possibility of becoming a religious is that Father Michael impressed upon him the shortness of his life and how his life is such a precious gift from God.

Religious life sets us more intensely on the path to heaven. One important connection between religious life and heaven is what

18. *Rule of St. Benedict,* chap. 4. Various translations available. One available online is at www/ewtn/library under the section of many resources titled "Priests, Religious, Vocations."

our Lord Jesus says in the Gospel about marriage and heaven. Jesus says in response to the Sadducees who do not believe in the resurrection: "At the resurrection they neither marry nor are given in marriage, but they are like the angels in heaven" (Matt 22:30). Now connect this with Christ's revelation that some "have renounced marriage for the sake of the kingdom of heaven" and that "whoever can accept this ought to accept it" (Matt 19:12). Renouncing marriage for heaven now is already sharing in the way of living that all the saints in heaven have. There are many, many, many saints in heaven who were married on earth, but there is no marriage in heaven—except the wedding feast of Christ and his Church in the heavenly Jerusalem.

This desire to live now something of the heavenly life, a life of praising God freed from certain earthly pleasures, is itself a supernatural gift from God. The very thought of making such an offering of yourself to the Lord is not explainable by human reason alone. It is a work of grace. Looking back on his teenage years, Jayson is amazed at how God has been so good to him. He would never have imagined when he was sixteen that he would one day be seriously thinking about religious life. The fact that you are reading this book is itself a sign that the Lord has planted a holy desire in your heart.

Conclusion: Becoming a "man of desires"

In some translations of the Book of Daniel, we read that Daniel is called a "man of desires" (Dan 10:11). By God's grace, we too can become like Daniel and be men of strongly-ordered, holy desire for God himself. Have your desires be ordered and ardent. In a mystical consideration of how contemplation makes our mind tend toward heaven, the great Franciscan St. Bonaventure writes:

> No one can enter by contemplation into the heavenly Jerusalem unless he enters through the blood of the Lamb as through a door. For no one is in any way disposed for divine contemplations that lead to spiritual transports unless, like Daniel, he is also a man of desires. Now such desires are enkindled in

us in two ways, to wit, through the outcry of prayer, which makes one sigh from anguish of heart, and through the refulgence of speculation by which the mind most directly and intensely turns itself through the rays of light.[19]

If you are considering the possibility of becoming a religious, be a man of great desires. Do not desire the little things. Desire the greatest. Desire God. Have great hunger for great things, especially for God himself. Feed your holy desires. Be faithful to prayer, especially the prayer that arises from the anguish of your heart, and constantly consider the truth of things as God originally intended.

Too often, in our experience, men have the spark of religious life, but it is blown out by worldly compromises, the lust of the flesh, and the lure of the devil. Sometimes, men don't attain the maturity to make a lasting commitment—to anything or anyone. Jayson is resolved by God's grace not to turn back to childish ways. What about you? Ask God for the grace to be faithful to him and to reveal his direction for your life. Then you can be a true man of desires.

O Blessed Virgin Mary, my mother, you are blessed among women. Help me to be an adopted son of God the Father, after the pattern of your own Son. Help me to desire to be blessed among men.

---

19. St. Bonaventure, *Journey of the Mind into God*, trans. Philotheus Boehner, O.F.M., edited with introduction and notes by Stephen F. Brown (Indianapolis: Hackett Publishing, 1956 [1990 reprint]), Prologue, no. 3, p. 2.

CHAPTER 5

CHRIST'S INVITATION TO BE POOR, CHASTE, AND OBEDIENT WITH HIM

"Peter began to say to him, 'We have given up everything and followed you.' Jesus said, 'Amen, I say to you, there is no one who has given up house or brothers or sisters or mother or father or children or lands for my sake and for the sake of the gospel who will not receive a hundred times more now in this present age, houses and brothers and sisters and mothers and children and lands, with persecutions, and eternal life in the age to come'" (Mark 10:28-30).

S ebastian hates making important decisions. Growing up, his parents made decisions for him and he just went along with what he was told. He has always tried to be a good kid. Now he's a junior in college and is continually asked what he will do after graduation. The clock is ticking. Through his campus ministry, he had a conversion when he was a college freshman, which helped him avoid the wrong crowd and cultivate a healthy group of friends. He feels he's on the right track, but he doesn't know where the track is headed. Sebastian simply has not developed the skills to carefully weigh his options. He admits to himself that he is unequipped to navigate life after college.

Do you hate making important decisions like Sebastian? When confronted with big decisions, how do you deliberate? Do you ever consult others? Scripture advises, "Seek counsel from every wise man" (Tobit 4:18). The counsel of friends, family members, or experts can be very helpful, depending on the decision you're facing. If you are wondering about whether to have a medical procedure, it's advisable to ask medical experts. If you're wondering whether you should choose one job opportunity over another, you may want to consult a friend or family member who knows you well, can listen to you, and help you come to the right decision.

In thinking about the possibility of entering religious life, to whom do you turn? At some point, you should obviously talk to a religious brother or priest about your interest. But before that, there is a more fundamental approach. Turn to the words and commands of Christ himself. For example, on the night before he died, Jesus said, "I give you a new commandment: love one another. As I have loved you, so you also should love one another" (John 13:34). That is a universal commandment, and it's not optional.

Jesus also offers advice on how to achieve this love, which the Church calls "evangelical counsels." The Church traditionally enumerates poverty, chastity, and obedience as the three evangelical counsels. A "counsel" is not a commandment or precept, but rather something like advice—though in this case, it is very important advice, as it comes from Christ himself.

The Evangelical Counsels: An Overview

When St. Thomas Aquinas reflects on the evangelical counsels, he makes an obvious but profound observation:

> The counsels of a wise friend are of great use, as it is said in Scripture: "Ointment and perfumes rejoice the heart, and the good counsels of a friend rejoice the soul" (Prov 27:9). But

Christ is our wisest and greatest friend. Therefore, his counsels are supremely useful and fitting.[20]

The evangelical counsels provide a particular way that we may be conformed to Jesus and imitate his life in charity.[21] His love is perfect, and he wants us all to be perfect in love. The commandments, especially those direct commandments from the Lord to love, forbid sin and direct us most clearly to what all are obliged to do. Grace gives us the ability to love as God wants us to love. The counsels of Jesus allow us to love to the point of giving up even good things, such as possessions, marriage, and our own freedom to choose, in view of something even better. St. Thomas Aquinas says:

> The perfection of charity is the end of the religious state. And
> the religious state is a school or exercise for the attainment
> of perfection, which men strive to reach by various practices,
> just as a physician may use various remedies in order to heal.[22]

St. Thomas continues that just because the end is perfection, it does not mean that those who enter it must be perfect. Thank God! The apostles, who practiced the evangelical counsels in their close relationship with Jesus, weren't perfect when they were called by the Lord. It's rather that all those who profess the counsels should have as their goal the perfection of charity. They set aside even some good things in order to attain a higher and better goal.

Moreover, St. Thomas thinks that because Christ himself recommends poverty, chastity, and obedience, one should not be distracted about whether or not religious life is an objectively greater good and originates from God. St. Thomas writes: "It is certain that entrance into religious life is a greater good, and the one who doubts about this, insofar as religious life is considered in itself,

---

20. St. Thomas Aquinas, *Summa Theologiae* I-II, q. 108, a. 4.

21. The *Code of Canon Law*, can. 575 says: "The evangelical counsels, based on the teaching and examples of Christ the Teacher, are a divine gift which the Church has received from the Lord and preserves always through His grace."

22. St. Thomas Aquinas, *Summa Theologiae* II-II, q. 186, a. 2.

detracts from Christ, who gave the counsel."[23] Since Jesus Christ the God-Man does not give bad counsel, we can rest assured that religious life is good and holy. Now a community may doubt that a man is meant to be accepted or to remain in initial formation with them, but the man himself should always know that a desire for the religious life is a holy desire that comes from the Holy Spirit—even if that man is not meant to be in religious life.[24] God's counsel is certain, even if a man in his particular situation should not be in a particular religious community or in religious life in general. Do you see the difference?

Men like Sebastian, who are confused and don't know what decision to make, can be reassured by certainties. Just because the evangelical counsels are certainly higher goods, it doesn't mean that you need to enter religious life. After all, these counsels are forms of advice meant for all to consider—not specific commands for you to perform. This mystery testifies to the objective goodness of the Lord's call to religious life—given in a sort of universal way to all sorts of people: male and female, young and old, rich and poor, educated and uneducated, those patently known to be sinful and those who have a reputation for holiness.[25] Individual communities may have all sorts of restrictions, and a young man may have various impediments like fragile health or prohibitive debt. But for St. Thomas, the religious life offers a tremendous good, objectively recommended to be preferred to others because it is a special acceptance of the sweet yoke of Christ.

As we saw in the Scripture passage at the beginning of this chapter, Simon Peter says to our Lord: "We have given up everything and followed you" (Mark 10:28). Those of us who accept Jesus' good advice of the evangelical counsels want to live like Jesus, who

---

23. St. Thomas Aquinas, *Summa Theologiae* II-II, q. 189, a. 10.

24. See St. Thomas Aquinas, *Summa Theologiae* II-II, q. 189, a. 10, ad 1.

25. Consider the *Code of Canon Law* on entrance into a community. Can. 597 §1 says: "Any Catholic endowed with a right intention who has the qualities required by universal and proper law and who is not prevented by any impediment can be admitted into an institute of consecrated life."

was poor, chaste, and obedient. We want to give up everything: everything of personal control over external goods through poverty, everything of the possibility of delights of marital union, and everything of our own free will through obedience. We want to do these things, because we want to be close to Jesus. It is out of love for him that we voluntarily accept poverty, chastity, and obedience, because he voluntarily accepted poverty, chastity, and obedience out of love for us. Not everyone can accept this invitation. These counsels can and should be practiced to some degree by all Christians, but religious have the public profession of the counsels in an extraordinary degree as defining their existence. It is a grace, a gift given to live this special discipleship with Jesus Christ.

This form of following Christ through poverty, chastity, and obedience opens our minds to God in a deep way. St. Thomas Aquinas says:

> "Now, the perfection to which these three counsels give a disposition consists in detachment of the mind for God. Hence, those who profess the aforesaid vows are called religious, in the sense that they offer themselves and their goods to God, as a special kind of sacrifice: as far as goods are concerned, by poverty; in regard to their body, by continence; and in regard to their will, by obedience."[26]

All religious are called to make that sacrifice, following Christ who gave up his life in sacrifice out of love of us.

But what about how different religious have different practices of these vows? You might say, "I don't see the Dominicans living the poverty of the Missionaries of Charity." Yes, you will find variety in how communities live the evangelical counsels, and the Church encourages a legitimate diversity: "Each institute, attentive to its own

---

26. St. Thomas Aquinas, *Summa contra Gentiles* Book III, chap. 130, no. 6. For a translation of this work, see *Summa contra Gentiles*, trans. Anton C. Pegis (Book 1), James F. Anderson (Book 2), Vernon J. Bourke (Book 3: Parts 1 and 2), and Charles J. O' Neil (Book 4) (Notre Dame, IN: University of Notre Dame Press, 1975 [reprint]).

character and purposes, is to define in its constitutions the manner in which the evangelical counsels of chastity, poverty, and obedience must be observed for its way of living."[27] As the Church must approve an institute's constitutions, such specification is not simply up to the whim of some religious founder or superior. Moreover, the Church continues in her concern for religious: "all members must not only observe the evangelical counsels faithfully and fully but also arrange their life according to the proper law of the institute and thereby strive for the perfection of their state."[28] These counsels are for the entirety of the life of religious so that they may reach perfection in Christ.

So what do these counsels actually mean in real religious life today? How can we be united to Jesus through observing them? Let's look at each in turn, both in the life of Jesus Christ and in the lives of religious today.

Poverty

Our experience is that young men are frequently attracted by the idea of radical poverty. Many men enthusiastically think, "If we're going to do this, let's go all the way!" It's easy to imagine yourself dramatically giving up everything and entering a form of religious life that lives absolute poverty to the point that the religious don't wear shoes or sandals and allow showers only on Sundays and solemnities. Say, for example, you imagine yourself in a new community that lives poverty so radically that they go barefoot even though the community is in Minnesota and has an apostolate to the poor on the streets of the twin cities of St. Paul-Minneapolis. Well, it all might seem very holy and impressive for a while. Then imagine after a few weeks of bitter winter cold... it may not be too attractive; rather, it may simply be stupid. However, the vows are not stupid. They are also not lived simply for practicality. We can even say that they are not lived simply for a witness value—as great

---

27. *Code of Canon Law*, can. 598 §1.
28. *Code of Canon Law*, can. 598 §2.

as that is. No, this counsel of Jesus Christ has great foundation and wisdom because Jesus and his disciples embraced it. The ways the Church traditionally considers this vow to be radical, we believe, will surprise you.

Jesus was poor. But the primary understanding of this poverty in the life of Jesus Christ is something even more profound than Jesus' not having money on his person to pay the Temple tax (Matt 17:24-27) or not having a place to rest his head (Matt 8:20). It is the Incarnation. The Incarnation is the very "emptying" of the all-powerful Son of God in accepting the weakness of our human nature. St. Paul says in his Letter to the Philippians that the Lord Jesus, who was in the form of God, "emptied himself, taking the form of a slave" (Phil 2:7). Our human condition, in comparison to that of God's, is that of a slave. From that perspective, all humans are poor just by being human. St. Paul says elsewhere: "For you know the gracious act of our Lord Jesus Christ, that for your sake he became poor although he was rich, so that by his poverty you might become rich" (2 Cor 8:9). Early Christians understood this to mean that the Lord's Incarnation leads to our deification. The Lord became poor (human) so that we might become rich (divine). Think of this. All of Christ's life of lowliness is meant for our exaltation.

Now that we have the context of how Jesus Christ is nothing less than God made man, we can see the wonder of his acceptance of a life of poverty. His family was unable to find a place for him to be born. St. Luke tells us that the Virgin Mary "wrapped him in swaddling clothes and laid him in a manger, because there was no room for them in the inn" (Luke 2:7). St. Joseph and the Virgin Mary had to utilize a trough where animals feed—a manger. That is Christ's Eucharistic poverty. God chose to make himself like the poor of this world and to live among the poor so that we who recognize our lowliness may be fed by him. The poverty of his birth led to the poverty of his cross and tomb. On Good Friday, everything was stripped from him. He died out of love for us, and was buried, wrapped in a different sort of swaddling clothes, a linen cloth, thanks to the benefaction of Joseph of Arimathea (see Luke 23:50-56).

Is not having control over money actually something good? There are lots of ways to consider how poverty plays out in the world today. This counsel from Jesus places God first and everything else at the service of God. It places before religious priests and brothers, and their communities, the call to a profound reliance on Divine Providence. Poverty is about being with the Lord in a particularly close way. St. Jerome coined the saying *Nudum Christum nudus sequere*—"Naked, follow the naked Christ."[29] This idea proved to be a kind of battle cry for those courageous enough to follow Jesus in absolute poverty to the cross. But St. Jerome didn't go buck naked down the streets of Bethlehem where he lived to be close to the birthplace of our Savior. Rather, he stripped himself of all sorts of possessions in order to dedicate himself completely to the Word whom he so loved.

The tradition of consecrated religious life looks toward the vow of poverty as that counsel from Jesus to moderate, or even completely abandon, personal goods—depending on the proper law of the community, that is, the community's own rule of life.[30] Jesus gives us this counsel so that we might be free of worldly concerns, and think more of God and less of ourselves and our personal needs. In religious life lived today, poverty does not mean that one lives in squalor. Rather, poverty means that each member lives poverty in fact and in spirit as specified in the constitutions of the religious institute, relinquishing his control over goods. The community provides for your basic needs. Usually there's not a lot of extra money to do extra things. But normally, a young man has what he needs.

The reality of poverty was brought home to young students

---

29. St. Jerome, Letter 125.20, to Rusticus.

30. *Code of Canon Law*, can. 600 says: "The evangelical counsel of poverty in imitation of Christ who, although he was rich, was made poor for us, entails, besides a life which is poor in fact and in spirit and is to be led productively in moderation and foreign to earthly riches, a dependence and limitation in the use and disposition of goods according to the norm of the proper law of each institute.

once when a religious in initial formation was discussing his life. He talked about all sorts of things that he thought would interest the kids, and then he mentioned in passing that he no longer had a cell phone. He gave it up when he entered formation. The students were amazed at such astounding poverty. The young religious had forgotten that a cell phone was considered that important—as he came to see that he really didn't need it.

The ability not to be concerned in life about money and the like allows a man in love to dedicate his life more completely to God. Here are some examples, which should not be taken as exclusively and wholly how different religious communities view poverty. For a Benedictine monk, who professes a *conversio* or *conversatio morum* (conversion of the way of life) that would encompass poverty, poverty allows him to sanctify each part of the day in prayer through the Liturgy of the Hours in the choral office, and to spend time in personal prayer with *lectio divina*. For a Franciscan friar, poverty enables him to imitate the poor naked Christ, and have a special solidarity with those who are poor. For a Dominican friar, poverty makes it possible for him to spend more time in study and prayer in order to help the spiritually poor, such as those who don't know the Lord. Again, each community is allowed by the Church to have a different expression of poverty, according to its rule and legitimate customs.

Be prepared for the realities of poverty as lived in religious life today. Some communities are very strict in poverty, others not as much. Some religious are outstanding in following their charism regarding poverty, and, frankly, some religious have compromised their poverty with too many accommodations to the world. Sometimes young men may not find the poverty they were expecting when visiting with a religious community, but that does not necessarily mean that the religious are unfaithful to Jesus, who became poor for our sake. On the other hand, some young men may find that the religious community will not accommodate their special requests because of poverty. If you enter a community and hear "no" to a request because it is a matter of poverty, think about the reality of how that community lives poverty and offer it up to God. Be poor with Christ.

Chastity

Our experience is that young men have seen sexual corruption in the world and they want to flee from lust in order to have a pure and upright life. They want to escape "from the corruption that is in the world because of evil desire" (2 Pet 1:4). These men know the danger of evil desire, and many have at one time or another found themselves caught by that desire. Many young men have made mistakes in relationships with their girlfriends or in what they have seen on screens. They will be sorely disappointed if they think they will never have sexual temptation once they enter religious life. The counsel of chastity does not remove sexual temptation; it unites you to Jesus, who is the victor over every sin, including sins of unchastity.

Jesus was chaste and never married, but he certainly lived a full human life. Because Jesus wants us to share the fullness of life that he lived as the God-Man, he gives the opportunity to share his celibate chastity. Jesus Christ, the only begotten Son of God the Father, was fully God and fully man, and he shows us the way to live in this world. The love that Jesus has for the world is the same love that God the Father has for the world and the same love that God the Holy Spirit has for the world. In addition to this divine love, Jesus also loves with his full human nature.

Each person is individually precious in God's eyes. The love that flows from the heart of God the Father through Jesus Christ in the Holy Spirit is the grace of love (or charity) that is poured into our hearts. As St. Paul says, "the love of God has been poured into our hearts through the Holy Spirit that has been given to us" (Rom 5:5). Do you realize that God's love for you is unique? Sebastian, who hates making decisions about his life and is afraid that he might not have the strength to live chastity, can be reassured of God's love that sustains him. His love can sustain *you*.

Charity has different expressions. There is the love between husband and wife which we call marital love, and St. Thomas knows that marriage is "the greatest friendship" between two human beings on earth.[31] A proper use of sex within marriage can be called marital chastity. But even greater than marriage is the love that God has for each of us. Through the grace of God, we have the ability to love with the very love that flows from God himself. Giving up wife and children to live as a chaste celibate man consecrated to Jesus Christ is not something that is natural within this world. It is God's work within us—if he calls us, we should be confident that he will provide the means to live the calling. The Author of all life would not call you to a way of life that is impossible to live.

Chastity means more than saying "no sex." This self-denial is, of course, part of religious life. But chastity more fully means that, like Jesus, we live the gift of our sexuality as men in a way that includes loving everyone and desiring their salvation, even to the point of laying down our life.[32] This love is similar to marital love. In Ephesians 5:21-33, St. Paul describes marital love as showing forth the love that Jesus Christ the bridegroom has for his bride the Church. He loves her even to the point of laying down his life and shedding his blood for her.

The sexual drive that you experience is not meant to be suppressed. Rather, it is meant to be integrated into your emotional life and forged and disciplined with the assistance of God's grace until you become a man of full stature in Christ. This comes about over a period of time and through good choices; developing personal discipline with a combination of participation in the sacraments, prayer, and learning to deny yourself certain things. Eventually a man develops and matures to the point where he has integrated the gift of his sexuality in such a way that he can say yes and mean yes,

---

31. St. Thomas Aquinas, *Summa contra Gentiles*, Book III, chap. 123, no. 6.

32. The *Code of Canon Law*, can. 599 says: "The evangelical counsel of chastity assumed for the sake of the kingdom of heaven, which is a sign of the world to come and a source of more abundant fruitfulness in an undivided heart, entails the obligation of perfect continence in celibacy."

and say no and mean no, and begin to live with some freedom in choosing what is good and true. This is the virtuous life, and it is a great gift from God.

The energy that a man has in regard to his sexual drive, especially when he is young, might overpower him if he is not careful in directing it in rational ways, and for God's glory. We find the strength and courage to follow this way because Jesus Christ himself lived his life in this way. Where he has gone, we can, by his grace, follow.

But we must take care not to romanticize the challenges of living chastely. For example, everyone—even a married man trying to live the kind of chastity proper to the marital state—experiences loneliness, and it will not be absent from religious life. Do not think that in religious life the community or the ministry will automatically solve your problem of loneliness and temptations that arise from loneliness. By God's grace loneliness can be purified into a sense of being truly alone with God, just as Jesus spent the night in prayer alone (Luke 6:12). Be chaste with Christ.

Obedience

We have experienced men seeking to enter religious life who have a great desire to be completely obedient. That is very good. But at times their desire isn't conformed to the reality of human life. You may imagine yourself as falling prostrate at the approach of your superior every time he enters the room and surrendering every wish in a "holy indifference" where you never express by word or deed where you wish to sit or stand or how much you want to eat or drink. You may dream that you will need permission to cough or sneeze. Of course, that is ridiculous. Real obedience is not ridiculous. It's about wanting to share in the deepest desire of Christ's heart: to be lovingly obedient to his Father for the salvation of souls.

Yes, Jesus was obedient. Obedience is the most overarching of the three evangelical counsels, as it is directed to our own will, something more central than either poverty's concern for our material goods or chastity's concern for our sexual desire. Every religious community will have its own way of expressing the religious vow of obedience according to the founder's charism, but the foundation of any holy obedience is Jesus Christ and his perfect obedience to the Father. So, let's first take a look at obedience in the life of Jesus and see its importance for our salvation.

Jesus said: "I came down from heaven not to do my own will but the will of the one who sent me" (John 6:38). In his humanity, Christ conformed his human will to the divine will for our salvation. Jesus shows what it is to be the beloved Son, doing his Father's will. Our Lord says, "The one who sent me is with me. He has not left me alone, because I always do what is pleasing to him" (John 8:29). This perfect obedience—repeatedly manifested throughout his life—leads to Christ's Passion. In the Garden of Gethsemane, Jesus prays, "My Father, if it is possible, let this cup pass from me; yet, not as I will, but as you will" (Matt 26:39). As St. Paul says, "he humbled himself, becoming obedient to death, even death on a cross" (Phil 2:8).

Obedience in religious life has a deeply personal quality that should be stressed. Obedience is primarily about a personal bond and secondarily about rules; never forget that the personal bond is above all with God.[33] While it can be difficult for a religious to understand why he should be obedient in a particular situation, such as going to do a difficult assignment that he feels ill-suited for, he can look to Christ's obedience. All acts of obedience are taken up into the mystery of Jesus' obedience to the Father—the greatest act of obedience leading to the mystery of the passion and death of Jesus. The interior disposition of Jesus' obedience is personally doing the will of the Father, even in the midst of terrible suffering. Men who follow Jesus Christ in religious life are called to be obedient to

---

33. The *Code of Canon Law*, can. 601 says: "The evangelical counsel of obedience, undertaken in a spirit of faith and love in the following of Christ obedient unto death, requires the submission of the will to legitimate superiors, who stand in the place of God, when they command according to the proper constitutions."

persons, and most especially God, according to some religious rule or constitution.

Consider a scenario in which your superior asks you to organize a party for the oldest member of the community who is turning ninety. You say yes because your superior requested it. Alternatively, he could have assigned someone else in the community to organize the party and asked you to assist him. A third scenario could be that you asked your superior for permission to throw a party for the ninety-year-old, but the superior says that it's not appropriate to celebrate the ninetieth birthday because of circumstances that he doesn't need to explain to you. In each of these cases, what is said is different—and different tensions could arise in your heart—but the obedience to God and your superior is the same.

Making a religious vow is precisely an act of obedience. In the very act of professing, a religious isn't primarily performing an act of poverty or of chastity, but of committing his will. Do you now see how obedience is the supreme evangelical counsel, and how in religious life it involves the other counsels? St. Thomas teaches that acts done under vows are more meritorious than those undertaken without vows.[34] He gives three reasons. First, a vow is an act of the virtue of religion, which unites a man to God through worship. Think of chastity. There could be all sorts of reasons not to have conjugal relations. (After all, even the sinfully sexually active do not spend most of their day engaged in that activity.) It's only when that chastity is consecrated through the obedience of a vow that it attains the highest honor.[35] Second, a vow takes up not only the present time, but the future, and gives it to God. Third, a vow makes a man's will firm and permanent in a God-given goodness so as to perfect him in the virtuous life by rendering to God what is promised. Like a tree planted near the flowing waters, a vowed man is determined not to move from God's law (cf. Psalm 1).

Now, how can we do this? It is through the Holy Spirit. In the

---

34. St. Thomas Aquinas, *Summa Theologiae* II-II, q. 88, a. 6.
35. St. Thomas here follows St. Augustine, *On Virginity*, chap. 8.

next chapter we will look at how the Holy Spirit makes us holy. But right now, consider how Jesus Christ, the eternal Son of God made man for our salvation, was in his humanity filled with the Holy Spirit. Christ's own obedience to the Father is in the Spirit. The Letter to the Hebrews says: "how much more will the blood of Christ, who through the eternal Spirit offered himself unblemished to God, cleanse our consciences from dead works to worship the living God" (Heb 9:14). Christ on the cross offers himself to the Father through the power of the Holy Spirit, and he cleanses our consciences to offer right worship to God.

We do not have the capability to obey in this full religious sense, except by the Holy Spirit. This obedience is not only about the big matters of religious life, such as accepting assignments and duties. Obedience is also about the daily observances—religious practices mandated by each community that identify a way of life—for example, in the refectory (dining room), the common life together, the periods of silence, or the gestures used in prayer. All of these and other religious practices are to be done in obedience through a special gift of the Holy Spirit in the life of a religious priest or brother.

Moreover, a loving obedience will allow you to anticipate what is needed by the community and its superior—without specifically being told to do something. If you walk into a room and see that ninety-year-old brother of yours lying unresponsive on the floor, and it's past the normal time to make phone calls, don't wait for permission. Call 911 and a priest. Do what you need to do in an emergency. Someone who doesn't take action in that kind of situation doesn't have good sense and isn't authentically obedient.

Be prepared for the realities of obedience as lived in religious life today. You may think that chastity is the toughest of the evangelical counsels. Many older religious will tell you that it's obedience. In initial formation, religious need docility in small matters so as to be able to exercise obedience in great matters later in life. As a novice, if you won't clean the bathroom when you're told to do so, do you really think you'll obediently accept a very difficult assignment when you're in final vows? Religious are given all sorts of assignments that may be uncomfortable or even dangerous. Some religious are outstanding models of obedience, through whom Christ's obedience on the Cross radiates to the world today. Other religious, contrary to their Christian and religious state, imitate someone else in saying "I will not serve" (see Jer 2:20). Don't be like Lucifer. Be obedient with Christ.

Conclusion: Being with Jesus

We should never forget that the evangelical counsels are ways of being close to Jesus. We religious want to be with him. In the words of St. Thomas Aquinas, who knew Jesus as the Savior and Son of the eternal Father, Jesus is "our wisest and greatest friend." If you are like Sebastian, given as our example at the beginning of this chapter, and have trouble making decisions, recall that Jesus is here to help you. Be with him.

Even the world understands how important it is to go to an expert. But isn't it true that the Expert of all experts, in learning how to be a religious priest or brother, is Jesus Christ? In various studies, Catholic priests (both religious and diocesan) have responded as some of the happiest among all professions.[36] Part of the reason for such a response is that one's call to be a priest or a brother is not just a profession, but a special vocation. Those interested in religious life are often attracted by a community's joy in being with Jesus, the poor, chaste, and obedient One. A response to God's call—to say yes to God with one's whole life—gives testimony, by radical configuration to Jesus Christ (even beyond baptism), to who God is for the world. God is our happiness.

The evangelical counsels separate the man from the world, direct him to God, and bind him to live a contemplative and penitential life. He follows Jesus Christ as a disciple toward the goal of perfect charity in the Holy Spirit, who makes us like God: holy. It is to the Holy Spirit in Chapter 6 that we now turn.

---

36. Stephen. J. Rossetti, *Why Priests are Happy: A Study of the Psychological and Spiritual Health of Priests* (Notre Dame, IN: Ave Maria Press, 2011).

Holy Mother of God, pray that I may desire to be poor, chaste, and obedient.

CHAPTER 6

THE HOLY SPIRIT AND THE HOLINESS OF RELIGIOUS LIFE

"Avoid immorality. Every other sin a person commits is outside the body, but the immoral person sins against his own body. Do you not know that your body is a temple of the holy Spirit within you, whom you have from God, and that you are not your own? For you have been purchased at a price. Therefore, glorify God in your body" (1 Cor 6:18-20).

B randon wants to be holy, and he has been thinking about becoming a religious brother after his college graduation. At his Catholic college, his religious studies professor spoke one day at length against the idea that "holiness" was something that could be found in one way of life more so than another. The professor spoke like this: "It doesn't matter whether you get married, become a priest, or convert to another religion—God will still love you. God's love makes you holy and let nobody try to tell you anything different." The professor then went on to talk about the latest news of a religious brother, assigned to teach at the school his institute runs in that same city, being convicted of child abuse. "Who would want to become a religious, when we know that those who look so holy are frauds?" asked the professor right as class was ending. Brandon is now confused about what holiness is, and wonders whether he should just give up this idea of becoming a religious brother.

Everyone is called to holiness. Do not let the universal abstraction fool you. This means you. You are called to be holy. Do you want to be a saint? Seriously. If you don't want to be a saint, why would you consider religious life? To put it bluntly, if you are considering religious life because you need friends who can't leave you, want some respectable position, like to wear unusual clothes, or desire to hide from responsibilities that people have in the world, please pray that your motivations be purified—or simply drop the idea of religious life. If, on the other hand, you want to follow Jesus radically so as to be a sign of hope in this world, to lay down your life for others, to preach the gospel, to work out your salvation and be an instrument of salvation for many others, then come and join the ranks of the countless religious in heaven who are among the saints in light (Col 1:12).

What it means to be holy

Do you want to be like God? We read in Leviticus: "Since I, the Lord, am the one who brought you up from the land of Egypt that I might be your God, you shall be holy, because I am holy" (Lev 11:45). We are called to be what the Lord is: holy. One way of thinking about holiness is the idea of difference. "Holy, holy, holy is the Lord of hosts" (Isa 6:3) can be thought of as: "Different, different, different is the Lord of hosts." God is different from the world. When God makes us holy, he separates us from things that are not holy and makes us share in his own nature. We become different from the world, and our difference can be a means of salvation for the world.

Baptism is the flood of holiness that kills evil and brings new life in Christ, conferring the Spirit of adoption, and making us cry out to God, "Father!" This is God's work, not our doing. But isn't it true that inside each of us there is something that drives us to think that we can become holy merely by our own efforts? Holiness is the work of God, who so generously gives us grace to merit it. Brandon's teacher is right, in part. It is God's love that makes us holy. As St. Augustine says, and the liturgy repeats, our merits are themselves God's gifts to us.[37] Merits always presuppose God's gift of grace. God is the one who calls, God is the one who sustains, God is the one who grants perseverance. Do you believe this? This is all quite mysterious, but God grants us signs of his love—especially in his Church.

We love the Church. It's not coincidental that we speak of the Church in the Creed immediately after professing faith in the Holy Spirit. The Church is the Trinity's new creation, and the Holy Spirit is given to us in the Church precisely to make us like God: holy. The Spirit unites us to Christ, who is our way to the Father. The Holy Spirit cannot be seen, but he wants us to see his effects. The Church most especially shows forth the effects of the mission of the Holy Spirit. Because of the Spirit's work, the Church is one, holy, catholic, and apostolic. The Second Vatican Council teaches that all the activities of the Church are ordered toward our sanctification in Christ and the glorification of God.[38]

Now just because being "holy" has a preeminence among the four chief marks of the Church—one, holy, catholic, and apostolic—it does not mean that every Christian is in a state of sanctifying grace, the grace that makes one pleasing to God. The Church is God's way of calling people and conferring grace to them. We are called, as St. Paul says to the Corinthians, to glorify God in our body (see 1 Cor 7:20). But not everyone within the Church glorifies God. Not all in the Church accept the holiness offered through preaching and the sacraments. Still, the Church is holy and necessary for the salvation of the world. St. Cyprian affirmed, and others have often repeated: "Outside the Church, there is no salvation."[39] The *Cate-*

---

37. Preface I of the Saints, Roman Missal; St. Augustine of Hippo, *On Grace and Free Will*, chap. 15.

38. Second Vatican Council, *Sacrosanctum Concilium*, Constitution on the Sacred Liturgy, no. 10.

39. St. Cyprian of Carthage, Letter 72.21, to Jubaianus.

chism of the Catholic Church declares: "all salvation comes from Christ the Head through the Church which is his Body."[40]

Similarly, we can see that the Church's religious life offers something objectively holy. Listen to what Vatican II says that religious life offers within the Church:

> Indeed through Baptism a person dies to sin and is consecrated to God. However, in order that he may be capable of deriving more abundant fruit from this baptismal grace, he intends, by the profession of the evangelical counsels in the Church, to free himself from those obstacles, which might draw him away from the fervor of charity and the perfection of divine worship. By his profession of the evangelical counsels, then, he is more intimately consecrated to divine service.[41]

Religious are "more intimately consecrated" to worship God. But the Church does not claim that religious are necessarily holier than others. This distinction can be helpful to Brandon and his teacher—and to us.

One way of thinking about this objective holiness is to consider the sacred vessels used at Mass. These vessels have been set aside, and are thought of as different from other cups, bowls, and plates. They are used to hold the sacred Body and Blood of Christ. Now, inanimate vessels cannot be subjects of grace. But human beings are called to be vessels that hold Christ within them. We are vessels of grace. St. Paul gives us this image: "But we hold this treasure in earthen vessels, that the surpassing power may be of God and not from us" (2 Cor 4:7). Our lives are earthen vessels. We can be—so to speak—cracked, chipped, broken. But God is at work in us. Religious, even more than the rest of the faithful, are consecrated for the worship of God as his sacred vessels.

Every Christian not in a state of grace still bears an indelible

---

40. *Catechism of the Catholic Church*, no. 846.

41. Second Vatican Council, *Lumen Gentium,* Dogmatic Constitution on the Church, no. 44.

mark that he belongs to God in a special way. Even hell can't remove that mark on a Christian soul damned to suffer an everlasting just punishment for sin. Think of that. While religious don't receive a permanent mark at religious profession, every religious not in a state of grace still belongs to God through a total consecration which expresses, and is meant to intensify, the baptismal dedication. Just as sacred vessels set apart for divine worship should not be used for any other purpose, so the whole lives of the consecrated are meant precisely for the worship of God. If a religious is true to his name of being a religious, he is holy both in name and in fact—filled with the Holy Spirit. If a religious intentionally commits sins that directly oppose his identity as a religious, it is sacrilege. St. Thomas defines sacrilege as "the irreverent treatment of the sacred."[42] He gives the example of a virgin consecrated to God who fornicates, as she sins directly against the holiness of her state.[43]

Now we want to address an egregious form of sacrilege and advise how those considering religious life can respond to it—sexual abuse. Brandon's teacher brought it up, and we should face it head on. The sexual abuse of children and other vulnerable persons are not just sins, but crimes that should be punished. Their perpetrators should be prevented from contact with minors—ever again. Many people have been abused, and some of them have been abused by clergy, religious, and other authorities in the Church. Religious who abuse are committing terrible crimes. They should in no way be exempt from the civil system of prosecution. Rather, religious are to be held to a higher standard. There's a classical saying: "*Corruptio optimi pessima,*" which means, "The corruption of the best is the worst." Those who are called to religious life should realize how disastrous the crimes of religious are—not only for those sinful religious, but also for their victims, the Church, and the world. Because their very being has been consecrated to God for divine worship, their sin in this case is a most heinous form of sacrilege. They, con-

---

42. St. Thomas Aquinas, *Summa Theologiae* II-II, q. 99, a. 1.

43. St. Thomas Aquinas, *Summa Theologiae* II-II, q. 99, a. 3, ad 3.

secrated to God for his glory, have grossly violated the innocence of children, who are extolled by our Lord as those to be imitated if one is to enter the kingdom of heaven.

What can those considering religious life do about this problem? First, let the Holy Spirit draw you closer to the Lord Jesus, whose righteous anger overturned the tables of the money-changers in the Temple. Filled with the Spirit of Christ, you will be able to confront the abuse, lies, hypocrisy, and cover-ups that have occurred. By the grace of the Spirit you can live an authentic Christian life following the Gospel's first command: "Repent and believe in the Gospel" (Mark 1:15). All religious have sinned, and some have committed horrible crimes. But do not let the worst of religious life deter you from what the Church especially proclaims as radiant in holiness. Ask the Holy Spirit to purify all men who are thinking about joining the next generation of religious in the Church so that they might pick up their crosses manfully. Remember, we are talking about "a living sacrifice." Our religious life is meant to be, above all else, a holy life.

Never think lightly of the preciousness of holiness, of the grace of the Holy Spirit at work in the soul. St. Thomas says, "the good of grace in one is greater than the good of nature in the whole universe."[44] The grace of the Holy Spirit makes us pleasing to God, deifying our souls by healing and elevating us to be partakers of the divine nature, as St. Peter explains in 2 Pet 1:3-4. God dwells within us—makes his home within us—so that we might dwell within him and make our home within him forever in heaven. This grace allows us to experience the gifts of the Holy Spirit, the fruits of the Holy Spirit, the beatitudes, and many virtues beyond those commonly found in human nature. Let us now concentrate on a few key virtues pertaining to the call to religious life. After all, for us to become holy means that our souls are changed and have particular powers. The word "virtue" means, in fact, "power." The virtues make you powerful. Holiness is not for wimps.

---

44. St. Thomas Aquinas, *Summa Theologiae* I-II, q. 113, a. 9, ad 2.

The Theological Virtues

The theological virtues of faith, hope, and charity, infused into our souls by the Holy Spirit, place us into direct contact with God. The consecrated religious, like the layperson or the diocesan priest, freely chooses to order his life toward God through these theological virtues. Like other Christians, we religious are called to put all our faith in God, whom we cannot see. We are called to put all our hope in God, who is good in the midst of the troubles of this world. We are called to direct all our love toward God, whose love for us is greater than all other loves in this world. All Christians are called to the perfections of faith, hope, and love. But the religious man lives these virtues through a radical following of Jesus, who is poor, chaste, and obedient, as we saw in the previous chapter. What could be more important for your life than growing in faith, hope, and love?

We start with faith. Do you believe in God? You might think, "That's a funny question. I'm a Christian. Of course I believe. In fact, I'm thinking about religious life." Well, there are all sorts of people who have been baptized, but don't really believe. Very sadly, sometimes even religious don't have Christian faith. There's a merely natural way of believing, like "I believe Sam is telling us the truth" or "I believe that Topeka is the state capital of Kansas, but I'm not certain." The theological virtue of faith has a certainty that far exceeds merely naturally thinking that something is probably true, or that you're 99.99% sure. Faith is a gift from God that unites our minds to God, giving us knowledge of something revealed by God. We believe, because God is true. Faith is infused into us by God. By that supernatural gift, we will trust God who is most assuredly trustworthy in matters that we can't see or know by the gift of our natural reason alone. Because God has revealed himself, we are called to what St. Paul refers to as "the obedience of faith" (Rom 1:5 and Rom 16:26). We respond to God through acts of faith.

In thinking about religious life, you are in some way in the position of Abraham, "our father in faith."[45] God called Abram to leave his father and his land filled with idols and go to a land that God would show him (Genesis 12). Abram obeyed. God changed Abram's name to Abraham and promised to make him the father of many nations (Genesis 17). Do you think Abraham knew what would happen to him? No, not really. But he trusted God to take care of his life. God still calls men today to leave behind their families and receive a new identity in the faith lived in religious life. This is a tremendous call, and it makes men who become religious a blessing for the world. You can become like Abraham through the obedience of faith.

From faith, we turn to hope. Hope unites our will to God who is so good for us. If we could see God as he is, we wouldn't need faith. If we enjoyed God's goodness completely and without any obstacle, we wouldn't need hope. Hope is infused in us during our life in this valley of tears. Like faith, there's a natural sense of hope, such as "I hope my team wins tonight" or "I hope I will do well in my job this week." But when we speak of Christian hope, the theological virtue, we are talking about how those in need here and now cling to God's promise of goodness to us. We hope ultimately in God's power to raise us from the dead and conform our lowly bodies to Christ's glorious body (see Phil 3:21).

Two ways of going wrong with hope are the opposite errors of presumption and despair. In presumption, you think that because God is good, or because you are good, you will automatically go to heaven no matter what you do in this life. It's like getting on I-95 wanting to go from Washington, DC, toward New York City, but going south instead of north. No matter how long or how fast you go, you will never reach New York City. People with grave presumption are certainly on a journey. But they're going south. Without real hope to turn them around, they will never get to heaven.

The other sin against hope is even sadder than presumption: despair. In despair, you think that God will not save you, or that you

---

45. Roman Canon, also known as Eucharistic Prayer I, in the Roman Missal.

cannot be saved. It seems today that more and more suffer despair, and they do not enjoy God's goodness now or his promise of ever-lasting life. They are like the boy on the team who quits all sports because of bad experiences on the ballfield. But theological despair is far worse than giving up on sports; it's giving up on God and the life that he wants us to enjoy.

Are you tempted to presumption or to despair when thinking about religious life? Make acts of hope in God. See that God is good for you and think about how religious life is precisely a profound way of living out Christian hope. By its very nature, religious life points to an everlasting life. By our poverty in matters of this world, religious call all to think about the Kingdom that is to come because of who God is. The Holy Spirit is the "Promise of the Father" that Christ speaks of before his Ascension (Acts 1:4), and that Prom-ise is now at work in the Church's religious life so that we may be strengthened to rely upon God's goodness to us, a goodness that lasts forever.

From hope, we now go to the very top: love. St. Paul says, "So faith, hope, love remain, these three, but the greatest of these is love" (1 Cor 13:13). Someone might object by saying, "I need love too much to enter religious life." He might think religious life is throwing love down the drain. On the contrary, the teachings of the Church show how the motivations for entry into consecrated religious life fall especially under the virtue of Christian charity. The greatest expression of love is to lay down your life for your friends (see John 15:13). Jesus laid down his life for his friends, and he invites us to do the same. Men are called to religious life not because they don't need love. We come to religious life because of a deep sense of being immeasurably loved by God, and of wanting to give God our full love in return.

All authentic love goes back to God. We cannot authentically love God without loving our neighbor and we cannot authentically love our neighbor without loving that neighbor in God, for the sake of God. The evangelical counsel of chastity in religious life is cer-tainly meant to express that double love: a primacy of loving God, which also allows us to be free to love others as beloved brothers and sisters.

Let yourself be loved by God. Only by knowing that you are loved by the Lord, and by relying on his love, can you love as you are meant to love. Let your heart receive the love that we find in the Sacred Heart of Jesus Christ. He calls you his friend. Let your friend teach you how to love during this time of thinking about religious life. Love with all that you have, all that you are, now.

Prudence

For some people, prudence doesn't sound like an attractive virtue, or is thought of in a rather marginal way, if at all. But in the great tradition of reflection on human virtues, prudence is the queen of the other moral virtues: justice, fortitude, and temperance. Prudence is the virtue that oversees the actions to be done. If you choose to do anything, you need prudence to do it right.

Prudence is not as important as the theological virtues, because the theological virtues come from God, are sustained by God, and unite us to God directly. Our faith, hope, and love are in God.

To say our prudence is in God doesn't sound quite right, but after those theological virtues, prudence has the most important place. It is the ability to choose the right thing. Choosing religious life has eternal consequences for your life, and of course you want to make the right decision.

The word *discernment* has grown in popularity. It is used not only to talk about a vocation but also more mundane things: finding a job, choosing a school, or taking any course of action. Some people even discern whether they should go out to a movie with friends. We follow St. Thomas who has a more limited notion of discernment, and a more expansive view of prudence. Prudence helps in every kind of human action, and especially in the most important human actions.

Because prudence is seated in our intellect for making practical decisions about what to do, it deals with what is true. What do you know to be true? The infused virtue of prudence goes beyond the merely natural virtue of prudence, which works with natural truths, and is guided by the Spirit of truth. This is not merely some passing feeling. Feelings come and go. The virtue of prudence can make you strong in the truth to act on what is true. This shows that God allows us to really know him and his will for our lives.

Now prudence has many sides to it, so to speak. St. Thomas gives eight elements of prudence: memory, understanding, docility toward others, shrewdness in oneself, the good use of reason, foresight, circumspection, and caution. Let's apply these to pondering religious life. In each area, you can see your strengths—or your weaknesses. If you are weak in an area, you can pray and perform acts prompted by grace that will make you even more receptive to the Holy Spirit's action.

1. In **memory**, you can recall from experience what God has done for you and how God has been guiding your life—even when you were sinning against him. Again and again in the Bible, we hear about the importance of remembering, such as in Psalm 77: "I remember the deeds of the Lord, I remember your wonders of old, I muse on all your works and ponder your mighty deeds." Do you remember God's faithfulness to you in leading your life to this point?

2. Through **understanding**, you know what religious life is and is not. If you don't know what something is, you can't really make a prudent decision about it. Now is the time to understand what a commitment to religious life means for you. Do you understand?

3. In **docility**, you can be led by a spiritual director and a few others you trust. Docility to others is of great importance if you are interested in vowing obedience someday. Docility allows you to be taught, to be formed by wise recommendations. Can you be docile?

4. After docility to others, St. Thomas lists **shrewdness in**

oneself. That means you have it within yourself to make an assessment of what should or should not be done, such as in making a plan for religious life. It would not be fully human only to look to others about what to do. Some astute power of judgment needs to be inside of you to make a good decision about your vocation. Do you want to become shrewder?

5. By a **good use of reason**, you then can go from clear principles to considering less-clear matters. You can reason through such things, as, "I need to learn more about what it means to be a monk, and so I should go visit this monastery." This use of reason allows you to draw conclusions to act in a certain way. These steps of prudence are all about getting you out of your head to do what is good in real life. How can you use your reason to figure out what is unclear to do?

6. **Foresight** allows you to consider what might happen in your planned action, and to take that into account. You will be surprised by God in your vocation, but foresight allows you not to be surprised by things which naturally follow from a course of action. Take the example of thinking about how your family would react if you entered religious life. What do you expect their reactions would be? What can you plan to do to help your family adjust to your new identity, if you become a religious?

7. **Circumspection** means that you take into account the particular circumstances that bear on a decision. For example, you need to consider the circumstances of timing. Is this the right time to apply to enter religious life, or are there good reasons for you to wait, say another year, before applying?

8. **Caution** is an awareness that something evil could hinder a good action. Caution allows one to proceed, knowing that there is always some sort of danger when doing any action of great goodness. Do not forget that Satan hates all Christian vocations and will try to lure you away from any way of life

committed to God. Can you name what is evil in your life that would be an obstacle to your good actions at this time?

It's true—there's a lot in prudence. Believe us, St. Thomas has a lot more to say about that virtue.[46] Whether or not you go on to enter a religious community, using prudence will protect you from: doing things without thinking through what they mean; doing things simply because you feel like doing them; doing things simply because someone told you to; doing things without being sufficiently prepared; and doing things because of a superstitious understanding of what God wants. Yes, it's possible to be superstitious in matters of a vocation—and that's disastrous. For example, just because you have a dream that you were wearing a white habit does not mean that you need to email the vocation director of the first religious community you can think of with a white habit to avoid divine punishment. Religion is not superstition.

Chastity

If we were to name the highest and most important virtues in the Christian life, chastity would not be among them. It's not a theological virtue, like faith, hope, and charity. Chastity isn't even a cardinal virtue, but a virtue connected to the cardinal virtue of temperance.

So why discuss it now—especially since we already have been thinking about the evangelical counsels? There is a special need for the virtue of chastity for you considering the evangelical counsel of chastity. You need this virtue, this power, in order to accept the counsel. Chastity frees men to receive God's love and to love in return, and unchastity makes them slaves of their own passions. Pornography and other sexual sins do not prepare a man for any Christian state. Do you want the freedom to live according to the Spirit, and not according to the flesh? If so, grow in chastity.

St. Thomas gives advice about growth in chastity in connection

---

46. See St. Thomas Aquinas, *Summa Theologiae* II-II, qq. 47-56.

to the religious life. In the treatise *On the Perfection of the Spiritual Life*, he identifies various obstacles to a man's chastity, such as an effeminacy of life in seeking all sorts of bodily pleasures and dwelling on unchaste thoughts. He also shows what can help us.[47] Grow up and be a man! Do the work of applying St. Thomas's list of remedies to your own growth in the virtue of chastity. After each point he makes, we'll give an example to illustrate what it can mean for you now:

- Keep the mind busied in prayer and the contemplation of divine things, especially in praise of God. *When you're waiting in line, rather than reaching to text somebody, repeat some favorite short prayer: Lord Jesus, have mercy on me.*

- Study sacred scripture. *Read the Gospel for tomorrow's Mass and think about what it means for your life.*

- Occupy the mind with good thoughts, following St. Paul's words: "Finally, brothers, whatever is true, whatever is honorable, whatever is just, whatever is pure, whatever is lovely, whatever is gracious, if there is any excellence and if there is anything worthy of praise, think about these things" (Phil 4:8). *Have a healthy hobby of the mind—such as learning a foreign language, trying to memorize baseball players, or studying the different breeds of dogs.*

- Shun idleness and engage in bodily work. *Keep your room cleaned or volunteer on Saturday to help the poor.*

- Think about the problems that you have, as those thoughts about real difficulties in life can occupy your mind in place of lustful thoughts. *Do not avoid the real problems in your life but think about what they mean to you and how God can help you.*

---

47. For "aids to the preservation of chastity," see St. Thomas Aquinas, *On the Perfection of the Spiritual Life*, in *The Religious State, the Episcopate, and the Priestly Office*, trans. John Procter, O.P. (Westminster, MD: The Newman Press, 1950), pp. 32-40.

- Avoid constantly being with, and especially gazing at, women. *If you go to a football game, don't fix your attention on the cheerleaders.*

- Seek solitude, fast, and pray at night. *Rather than drinking alcohol on a Friday night, offer a decade of the rosary for the poor in the solitude of your room.*

If Aquinas were on earth today, we are sure that he would advocate the moderation of any electronic entertainment and, of course, decry the scourge of pornography. Today there exists a group especially dedicated to chastity under St. Thomas's patronage called the Angelic Warfare Confraternity, which can be found online. We highly recommend it to you.

Conclusion

Have you ever heard someone say, "I'm spiritual but not religious"? We believe that being spiritual demands a bodily worship of God. We are both physical and spiritual, both body and soul. We can't be truly spiritual without having bodily commitments during this life on earth. The Holy Spirit, the one who makes us spiritual, transforms our souls to be powerful in the virtuous life. You will see bodily effects.

For example, faith in your soul puts your body in the church. Think about it: "Glorify God in your body." That is what we read from St. Paul's First Letter to the Corinthians at the beginning of this chapter. Since your body is a temple of the Holy Spirit, know how to worship God in bodily ways—with acts of your hands in giving to the poor, with acts of your feet in going to daily Mass, with acts of your eyes in studying the Holy Bible. That is our spiritual worship, a spiritual worship now that could lead you to give your whole life to God, giving your body as a living sacrifice, in the holiness of religious life.

Think back to the story at the beginning of this chapter. Rather than being confused by what his religious studies professor said, Brandon can become more certain of how the Holy Spirit makes

Christians holy. By the grace of the Holy Spirit, we are transformed to be virtuous—to be powerful. Because of God's love for us, we become like God. In the holiness of religious life, Christians are offered an intense experience of living for God alone. It is true that some religious have rejected God, just as some married people have rejected their spouse and God. But religious life is still a great gift, a unique blessing for the Catholic Church that communicates the mystery that God is worthy to receive all that we have and all that we are in our worship.

If you have been challenged like Brandon about the truths of your faith, rely more on the Holy Spirit to lead you to all truth (cf. John 16:13). God has set religious life as a distinctive sign of the Church's holiness—a gift to be cherished by all Christians and a way of life for some who are chosen.

All-holy Virgin Mary, teach me how to accept the Holy Spirit
in my life and so be holy.

—PART THREE—

RELIGIOUS LIFE'S DISTINCTIVENESS

CHAPTER 7

DIOCESAN PRIESTHOOD, RELIGIOUS BROTHERHOOD, RELIGIOUS PRIESTHOOD, AND DISCERNING THE DIFFERENCE

*"There are different kinds of spiritual gifts but the same
Spirit; there are different forms of service but the same Lord;
there are different workings but the same God who produces
all of them in everyone" (1 Cor 12:4-6).*

Ryan is a college sophomore majoring in mathematics. After helping with a retreat for high schoolers last summer, he believes the Lord might be calling him to a religious vocation. He knows that his university is served by Augustinians but he couldn't tell you much about them, other than they have something to do with St. Augustine. In fact, he went to that university because his dad went there, and because it's a very good school with a winning men's basketball team. Now that he's thinking about a vocation, he's wondering about the differences between being a parish priest back home in the Diocese of Harrisburg and being a religious priest or brother.

It's easy to tell the difference between a married layman and a Carthusian monk. But other states of life may be more difficult for you distinguish. You may want to forego the good of marriage and family for the sake of the Kingdom of God. But you may feel pulled in different directions and not fully understand the differences between being a religious brother and a religious priest. Similarly, you may feel very strongly called to be a priest, but unsure whether you should enter a diocesan seminary or a religious community. You may simply want a quality formation in the Christian life so as to be prepared to serve God wholeheartedly.

This chapter is meant to help you discern the differences among diocesan priesthood, religious brotherhood, and religious priesthood. Sometimes men feel a mysterious attraction to religious life, but they have known only diocesan priests and a few religious sisters. They have not yet visited a community of religious men, and they have a rather stereotypical or otherwise ill-formed understanding of what religious do (or don't do). Sometimes men think they're called to serve God in a special way, but don't have a clue about where to go or what to do. Sometimes they think that diocesan priests and religious all belong in the same category. This chapter is to equip you with a sort of vocabulary and grammar to think about these vocations and discuss them in prayer with God and with people you trust. We begin with the diocesan priesthood.

Diocesan Priesthood

Although the term is not commonly used today in America, a diocesan priest has been customarily called a "secular priest," such as in the Church's *Code of Canon Law*. This is not meant as a put-down, as if diocesan priests were living worldly lives not devoted to holiness. Rather, it means that they spend their lives in the world (*saeculum* in Latin means "world" or "time") and not within a religious consecration. Immediately before ordination to the diaconate, diocesan seminarians make a promise of celibacy—but they do not thereby enter religious or consecrated life. Rather than living by a profession of the evangelical counsels of poverty, chastity, and obedience according to a rule/constitution, diocesan priests live by a promise of obedience to their bishop and serve the sheep of God's flock who themselves live in the world. Most commonly, these diocesan priests have the pastoral care of the souls within a specific geographical territory of a diocese.

When we speak of being a parish priest, we are typically speaking of the diocesan priesthood, although many religious priests also serve in parishes and can be pastors, as we will see below. Occasionally, you do also find some diocesan priests who, with the support of their bishop, intentionally choose to live together in some kind of community or have some special assignment other than parochial or campus ministry.

A diocesan priest commonly serves as a parish pastor, and he may have parochial vicars (also known as assistant or associate pastors) who assist him. The pastor is the spiritual father of the parish community to which he has been assigned by his bishop. During his assignment to a particular parish, he has pastoral responsibility before God for each person. Many diocesan priests serve a parish and live alone in a rectory. They handle their own finances and receive a simple salary for the parish ministry they do. Because they don't take a vow of poverty, they need to be concerned about personal taxes and other financial matters.

If you are thinking about becoming a diocesan priest, we urge you to read Father Brett A. Brannen's excellent book *To Save A Thousand Souls: A Guide for Discerning a Vocation to Diocesan Priesthood* from Vianney Vocations. Father Brannen will assist you in thinking about how to respond to God's call, understanding what diocesan seminary is like, and anticipating what to expect in the ministries of the diocesan priesthood. Above all else, you should contact the diocesan vocation director.

The Consecrated Life of Religious

Diocesan priests, like the laity who have been baptized but have not made a profession of consecration, are not in the consecrated life. The other two groups we are considering, religious brothers

and religious priests, are in the consecrated life. Before we distinguish between a religious brother and a religious priest, it would be
good to think about what the consecrated life means. So, you may
be asking, what exactly is the consecrated life if it doesn't include
diocesan priests?

The profession of the evangelical counsels of poverty, chastity,
and obedience distinguishes the consecrated life from other forms
of Christian life. It is true that other Christians practice poverty,
chastity, and obedience, but those who are consecrated profess and
live these counsels in a public way. For a beautiful overview of the
consecrated life, including women's consecrated life, read St. John
Paul II's *Vita Consecrata*. There St. John Paul II observes:

> [Christ's] way of living in chastity, poverty, and obedience
> appears as the most radical way of living the Gospel on this
> earth, a way which may be called divine, for it was embraced
> by him, God and man, as the expression of his relationship
> as the Only-Begotten Son with the Father and with the Holy
> Spirit. This is why Christian tradition has always spoken of
> the objective superiority of the consecrated life. [48]

Do you want to be radical? The consecrated life of poverty,
chastity, and obedience is "the most radical way of living the Gospel." We repeat this idea in this book, because some people shrink
from the language of objective superiority. Not so, says Pope St.
John Paul, who himself was a diocesan priest for many years before
becoming a bishop.

The consecrated life has many different forms, which can be
confusing. So we want to make things simple. We think it would
be good to call upon two authoritative sources for the meaning of
religious life. The first is from the *Catechism of the Catholic Church*:

> Lived within institutes canonically erected by the Church, it is
> distinguished from other forms of consecrated life by its litur-

---

48. St. John Paul II, *Vita Consecrata*, no. 18.

gical character, public profession of the evangelical counsels, fraternal life led in common, and witness given to the union of Christ with the Church.

Notice the key elements here. Religious have institutes which have been erected and are running according to the established laws of the Church. They have a liturgical character, meaning that they are worshiping God in a public way through the official prayers of the Church. They make a public profession of the evangelical counsels. They live a common life as brethren to one another, and they give witness to Christ's own abiding presence in his Church.

Our second source is the *Code of Canon Law.* The Code begins its law on religious life in this way:

Can. 607 §1. As a consecration of the whole person, religious life manifests in the Church a wonderful marriage brought about by God, a sign of the future age. Thus, the religious brings to perfection a total self-giving as a sacrifice offered to God, through which his or her whole existence becomes a continuous worship of God in charity

§2. A religious institute is a society in which members, according to proper law, pronounce public vows, either perpetual or temporary which are to be renewed, however, when the period of time has elapsed, and lead a life of brothers or sisters in common.

§3. The public witness to be rendered by religious to Christ and the Church entails a separation from the world proper to the character and purpose of each institute.

Notice that religious life is "a total self-giving as a sacrifice offered to God." The Church profoundly recognizes that religious are called to be "a living sacrifice," as St. Paul urges in Rom 12:1. If you become a religious, your very identity will be "a continuous worship of God in charity." This manifests a sublime beauty. Religious show in their lives a marriage that does not end at death: the marriage of the Lord with his Church.

Regarding the obligations and rights of institutes and their members, the *Code of Canon Law* states:

> Can. 662 Religious are to have as the supreme rule of life the following of Christ proposed in the gospel and expressed in the constitutions of their own institute.

> Can. 663 §1. The first and foremost duty of all religious is to be the contemplation of divine things and assiduous union with God in prayer.

> §2. Members are to make every effort to participate in the Eucharistic sacrifice daily, to receive the most sacred Body of Christ, and to adore the Lord himself present in the sacrament.

> §3. They are to devote themselves to the reading of sacred scripture and mental prayer, to celebrate worthily the liturgy of the hours according to the prescripts of proper law, without prejudice to the obligation for clerics mentioned in can. 276, §2, n. 3, and to perform other exercises of piety.

> §4. With special veneration, they are to honor the Virgin Mother of God, the example and protector of all consecrated life, also through the Marian rosary.

> §5. They are to observe faithfully an annual period of sacred retreat.

> Can. 664 Religious are to strive after conversion of the soul toward God, to examine their conscience, even daily, and to approach the sacrament of penance frequently.

Notice how this section of the Code begins. The supreme rule of life is following Christ himself, according to the Gospel and as expressed in the constitutions of an institute. Jesus is the standard of our life. Every religious, like everyone else in the Church, first follows Jesus Christ. But each religious follows our Lord according to a way of life officially approved by the Church.

While some religious are active in the spread of the Gospel through outside apostolates, and some are contemplative through prayer and study of the Word remaining inside their monasteries, the *Code of Canon Law* clearly states that contemplation is of greater importance to religious. It's worth repeating: "The first and fore-most duty of all religious is to be the contemplation of divine things and assiduous union with God in prayer." All religious priests and brothers are bound to this intense life of prayer.

Most communities of male religious have both priests and brothers. Some have only priests and those in formation for the priesthood. Some have only brothers. We will look at the different forms of religious life in the next chapter, but sometimes people are confused about the basic distinction between a religious ordained to the priesthood and one not ordained.

Now, a monk can be either a priest or a brother. A man may enter a monastery and be a brother, but later be ordained. He does not cease being a monk. "Monk" simply designates a man in the monastic life. Or take the example of a friar. The word friar comes from the Latin word *frater* which means brother. All friars are brothers, by definition, but some are ordained and some are not. So, for example, you might hear, "The Franciscan brothers will be at the Holy Hour tonight," even though some are brothers and some are priests.

While considering many details, don't neglect what is most important: all of religious life is ordered to charity in the worship of God. With the evangelical counsels, material things (removed by poverty), marriage and family (removed by celibate chastity), and the preference of one's own will (removed by obedience) give way so that a man may more easily strive for the perfection of charity in being undividedly devoted to God. That's the meaning of being "religious." St. Thomas Aquinas says, "If a man devotes his whole life to the divine service, his whole life belongs to religion. Thus, by reason of the religious life that they lead, those who are in the state of perfection are called religious."[49]

Now that we have this background on being a religious in the consecrated life, let's look first at religious brothers and then at religious priests.

Religious Brotherhood

Whereas many religious in formation for the priesthood are called "brothers," here we are referring to those who are not preparing to be priests. So what is a religious brother? A brother is consecrated to God through the profession of the evangelical counsels. The religious brother lives out his community's charism through a faithful public following of the vows of poverty, chastity and obedience according to his rule. The religious brother's life of consecration should always be stressed. Being has precedence over doing.

Religious brothers are found in clerical institutes (composed mostly of priests and having a clerical mission and governance), mixed institutes (having both priests and brothers), and institutes of religious brothers (composed only of brothers). In 2016, more than one in four male religious in the world was a brother.[50]

Many religious communities naturally emphasize the fraternal life, the brotherhood in Christ by baptism and by religious consecration. Jesus says, "You have but one teacher, and you are all brothers" (Matt 23:8). From this fraternal communion springs the mission of the religious institute. Sometimes it is said that brothers are free to do work that priests cannot do. Whereas priests may be completely immersed in sacramental ministries (especially where there is a shortage of priests), brothers may be able to reach people in ways quite different from priests. Brothers can have assignments that are external to the community or internal, or both.

External ministries are of course dependent upon the gifts of

---

49. St. Thomas Aquinas, *Summa Theologiae* II-II, q. 186, a. 1, ad 2.

50. 52,625 religious brothers and 133,138 religious priests in the world in 2016. https://cara.georgetown.edu/frequently-requested-church-statistics/

that individual brother. Many brothers are wholly committed to the works of mercy: both the corporal works of mercy, such as feeding the hungry or visiting the sick and imprisoned, and also the spiritual works of mercy, such as instructing the ignorant and counseling the doubtful. These ministries can be found in many parishes, schools, hospitals, universities, prisons, centers for the poor, etc.

Ministries internal to the community depend upon what that community needs. An institute comprised entirely of religious brothers would certainly have brothers as their superiors and formators, whereas mixed or clerical communities would have different laws and practices. The list of traditional community roles of brothers would be quite long, depending on the community. Being porter, guest master, or procurator (bursar or treasurer) for a community entails a great amount of contact with the outside world. On the other hand, some jobs are more intensely focused on the brethren of that particular community, such as serving as cook, sacristan, sexton (chapel maintenance worker), gardener, tailor, records keeper, archivist, librarian, liturgist, cantor, organist, barber, or infirmarian.

You may have heard the Benedictine dictum *ora et labora*, which means "pray and work." Interestingly, when you speak to brothers about their lives, many will tell you that their prayer is serious work; for example, it's difficult to stay concentrated while chanting the Divine Office, day after day. Conversely, even their work becomes a prayer, meaning that manual labor can open the soul to God.

To be frank, there is a special need for religious brothers. The numbers of diocesan priests, religious brothers, and religious priests have all declined over the past fifty years in the United States, but religious brothers have taken the hardest hit. In the United States, there has been a marked drop of men entering religious life to be brothers. In 1970, there were 11,623 brothers in the United States. In 2017, there were only 4,007.[51] During this same time period,

---

51. Center for Applied Research in the Apostolate, "Frequently Requested Church Statistics," https://cara.georgetown.edu/frequently-requested-church-statistics/

the population of self-identified Catholics in the United States has grown from 51 million to 71.3 million.

Of course, different regions of the world have different challenges and opportunities. One sign of a healthy renewal of this vocation in the universal Church is the first document from Rome pertaining only to religious brothers which appeared in 2015: *The Identity and Mission of the Religious Brother in the Church*, from the Congregation for Institutes of Consecrated Life and Societies of Apostolic Life (CICLSAL). If you are thinking about becoming a religious brother, we highly recommend that you read that document, which can be found online. It can also be ordered in book form in English and Spanish, in a study format.

Religious Priesthood

With few exceptions, religious priests were religious before being ordained to the priesthood. In fact, a religious is to make a final profession of vows before being ordained to the diaconate. This final profession effects a stability in the consecrated life which is important to have before undertaking ordained ministries.

At ordination, a religious priest, like his diocesan counterpart, receives an indelible mark on his soul. A man is ordained a priest forever. Unlike his diocesan counterpart, a religious priest is not incardinated, i.e., placed under the jurisdiction of a bishop in a diocese. Rather, his ordinary is his religious major superior (such as a provincial or an abbot).

Some religious communities ask applicants to indicate whether they intend to become priests or remain brothers. In some communities, the novitiate may be the same in either case, but the formation after the novitiate would be quite different. Religious studying to be priests would normally need, unless there be some special privilege, the education that the Catholic Church requires for others in priestly formation, although there may be approved adaptations for a particular institute's charism. In some communities, a man in the vocation process does not indicate whether he is to be formed to be a brother or a priest. For example, an abbot may decide whether a monk should be placed in priestly formation well after the monk's solemn profession.

In any case, after his ordination to the priesthood, a religious does what is assigned to him. Under obedience, like a religious brother, a religious priest may have different assignments all in the same location or, depending upon the charism of his institute, be sent far away. Many religious orders and congregations are world-wide and are divided into regional provinces. A religious priest may be assigned to work within a province to which he is bound in a special way. Or, he may be sent far away for missionary purposes or for assignments given by the supreme moderator, the head of that worldwide religious institute.

Now what exactly do religious priests do in these assignments? There's usually more variety than what you find among diocesan priests because of the variety of religious charisms. But broadly speaking, a religious priest, like the diocesan priest, serves the people of God in ordained ministries and, like a religious brother, serves according to his community's charism.

As noted above, when people think of priests today, they often think of those who serve in parishes, who tend to have the greatest direct influence on people's lives. They offer the Mass at their parish church, baptize, hear confessions, witness marriages, and anoint the sick. They also offer spiritual counseling and guidance in various matters, in addition to praying for them in a particular way. Whereas some mission lands still have more missionary religious than diocesan priests, the majority in the United States and Canada experience diocesan priests in their parishes.

A religious priest assigned to parish ministry may do many of the things a diocesan priest does. But the religious priest is conse-crated in a way that one outside of consecrated life is not. Some-times people notice that religious priests generally live in commu-nity and that their lives are governed by a rule, with a local superior. Typically, a religious priest would share the responsibility of parish ministries with other members of his religious community. When a community of religious runs a parish, we typically say something like, "St. Anthony of Padua Catholic Church is run by the Franciscans. It is a Franciscan parish." Usually by a longstanding agreement with the diocese, the religious community is expected to take care of the parochial ministry. The pastor is installed by the bishop of that diocese, but the pastor's name is proposed by the major superior of the religious community. Religious priests are not allowed to have parishes independent of the authority of the local bishop. Rather, religious priests cooperate with the local bishop and his diocesan priests in parish ministries.

But there are so many more ministries for religious priests than parish assignments. It all depends on the charism and traditions of the religious institute, just as with religious brothers. We will look at this in more detail in the next chapter. Some religious priests are contemplatives, that is, they are exclusively devoted to the sacred liturgy and other prayer; they may not have active apostolates among the people of God but pray for all people through their contemplative life. Some religious priests teach and administer schools. Some religious priests are missionaries, whether foreign or domestic. Some may not have parishes of their own but may specialize in giving parish missions and retreats. Some priests are needed to do internal ministries within their religious communities, serving as superiors, formators, procurators (bursars or treasurers), fundraisers, and the like. Some of these works may be done by religious brothers, but others may pertain more to the priestly identity in sacramental ministry and governance. Since a religious priest is first of all a religious, all sorts of ministries appropriate for that religious community may follow—just as we saw regarding a religious brother.

In the United States, the numbers of religious priests have declined considerably in the past fifty years. There were 21,920 religious priests in the United States in 1970, and in 2017 there were 11,424. For another point of comparison, diocesan priests in this country declined from 37,272 to 25,757 during the same time span.[52] Keep in mind that the Catholic population has risen considerably.

If you look seriously at a religious institute, you may find that the community's size has been reduced from decades ago. But then again, there are challenges for all the states of life in the Church. For a quite different example, consider marriage in the Church. In 1970 about three in four Catholics who married did so in the Catholic Church. In 2016, the percentage was only 29%.[53] Do not be discouraged by what you see. Instead, be encouraged by our unseen Lord who calls us by faith to follow him and to convert the world.

Conclusion

Do you want to commit your life totally to God? Every Christian's life is meant to be totally dedicated to God—whether that Christian is a Carthusian monk or a layman who is a married father—as different as their lives may be. The diocesan priest certainly commits his life to God for the sake of the people under his charge. The diocesan priesthood is a great gift to the Church. We so often count on our diocesan priests, who promise obedience to their bishop at their ordination, and bear the brunt of the ordained ministries. Diocesan priests need to be better appreciated by all the Church, including religious. But it should be plainly known that the Church does not consider diocesan priests to be in consecrated life. Both the religious brother and the religious priest are in consecrated life, having professed public vows of the evangelical counsels, and living in the state that the Church has always been promoted as having "objective superiority" in holiness.

In our next chapter, we will explore the great complexity and beauty of different forms of men's religious life, especially as they developed in God's providence over the course of the many centuries of Church history—and are present here and now.

---

52. https://cara.georgetown.edu/frequently-requested-church-statistics/

53. Center for Applied Research in the Apostolate's research blog: http://nineteensixty-four.blogspot.com/2018/03/a-dip-in-adult-catholic-population.html

Ever-virgin Mary, you always did the Lord's will. Pray that I may always do the Lord's will in my life.

CHAPTER 8

CHARISMS AND COMMUNITIES

"Consider your own calling, brothers. Not many of you were wise by human standards, not many were powerful, not many were of noble birth. Rather, God chose the foolish of the world to shame the wise, and God chose the weak of the world to shame the strong, and God chose the lowly and despised of the world, those who count for nothing, to reduce to nothing those who are something, so that no human being might boast before God. It is due to him that you are in Christ Jesus, who became for us wisdom from God, as well as righteousness, sanctification, and redemption, so that, as it is written, 'Whoever boasts, should boast in the Lord'" (1 Cor 1:26-31).

Matthew thought he was going to become a lawyer, get married, and raise his family in the Los Angeles area. He thought he had everything figured out. One day, though, while attending Mass, it hit him that he could be a priest. A great desire rose up in his heart. He imagined himself as a priest next to the altar in union with Jesus. Moreover, after a few months, because of the Franciscan friars in his home parish, the Jesuits at his college, and a recent private retreat he made at a Benedictine abbey, he has been thinking strongly he should be a religious priest. He has begun to read about various religious orders, but he still really doesn't know much about the differences among the different communities. Which one should he enter?

We can't tell Matthew, or you, which religious community to enter. But we can offer some basic principles when weighing the possibilities. The first rule is to start where you are. Which religious communities do you find attractive right now? Which religious are you already in contact with? For example, if the Franciscans run your home parish, and you are attracted by their witness, set up an appointment to meet with them. If the Jesuits run your campus ministry, and you want to be a "man for others" by joining their company, make a vocation weekend with them. If you come across the website of an abbey that evokes a holy desire that you can't shake, schedule a visit. If a priest you highly respect has suggested that you consider a particular community, look into it. In other words, start your investigation by delving deeper into a community that, by God's providence, has already crossed your path.

When you do make contact, pay special attention to your interactions with men in that community. You will not come to know God's plan alone. Ask to make an appointment with the community's vocation director (or simply one of the priests or brothers) and sit down for a one-on-one conversation. Ask his advice. Use your holy prudence and put into action such elements of prudence as docility, shrewdness, circumspection, and foresight. Trust the Lord is guiding you through this interaction.

There is a second, broader path to discovering the community to which you may be called. It's entirely possible you may not know any religious (or none you find attractive). In that case, we recommend that you research the broad spectrum of communities available and see what appeals to you. That is precisely the purpose of this chapter: to provide a brief, broad overview of the hundreds of communities in the Church today, particularly in the United States. You may be surprised that a particular community seems like a perfect fit for you (at least on paper).

After describing what a "charism" and "a form of life" are, the following pages give a sketch of the major movements in the history of religious life, with examples that can be seen today. In other words, the communities that you will read about—founded in distant times and places—have addresses in the United States. You could call them up, email them, or knock on their door. They will answer!

But before you dig into this chapter, we offer a caveat. These pages are dense with proper names, dates, and historical details, which may excite some readers and bore others. Either way, don't be overwhelmed by the tremendous variety of religious life in the Church. Perhaps you need only skim this chapter to get a sense of the variety of religious life. The towering Cistercian Doctor of the Church, St. Bernard of Clairvaux, is said to have commented on the variety of religious orders in his day: "I admire them all. I belong to one of them by observance, but to all of them by charity. We all need one another: the spiritual good which I do not own and possess, I receive from others."[54] We want his sentiment to be our own.

Charism: What Makes a Community Distinct

"Consider your own calling, brothers," says St. Paul. Always remember that the call comes from God, not from our merits—if there be such. Holiness, we think, is the bottom line about why you should enter religious life (or any other kind of life, for that matter). Every Church-approved community offers an authentic path of following Jesus Christ and living the Gospel. But each community has a different path.

At its core, what makes each community distinct is its *charism*. Broadly defined, a charism is an extraordinary gift of the Holy Spirit, given to a community's founder, which expresses the unique call to holiness and mission of a religious community. Authorities in the Church, the local bishop or the Holy See, then investigate the authenticity of the charism as lived by the community and give approbation (approval) to a community's rule and constitutions.

While charisms entrusted to founders and lived out by their

---

54. St. John Paul II, *Vita Consecrata*, no. 52.

communities vary widely, St. John Paul II teaches that they all have a Trinitarian dimension. First, the charisms lead to the Father. "The charism of each Institute," says St. John Paul II, "will lead the consecrated person to belong wholly to God, to speak with God or about God, as is said of Saint Dominic, so that he or she can taste the goodness of the Lord (cf. *Ps*34:8) in every situation."

Second, the charisms lead to the Son: "consecrated persons are enabled to take up the mission of Christ, working and suffering with him in the spreading of his Kingdom."

Third, the charisms lead to the Holy Spirit, for a charism "prepares individuals to let themselves be guided and sustained by him, both in their personal spiritual journeys and in their lives of communion and apostolic work, in order to embody that attitude of service which should inspire the true Christian's every choice."[55]

Because of the great importance of the charism, a community's spiritual health can be best gauged by its fidelity to the charism—not by numbers of members, popularity, or institutional assets. A very impressive building does not equal a holy religious community. Having encountered a great number of religious from long-established communities, we have tremendous respect for those that have stayed true to their charism and produced many holy men. But just because a community has been around for centuries doesn't mean it will last forever. Likewise, we respect newer communities that seem to be gifted with new charisms, while recognizing that their newer approaches do not supersede the old. Whether ancient or new, what matters is fidelity to their particular gift from the Holy Spirit.

Forms of life in the history of religious life

A charism becomes embodied in what could be called the "form of life" of a religious community. The form of life expresses what is unique in the charism that the founder received, communicates the purpose for the community's existence, and can be known in

---

55. St. John Paul II, *Vita Consecrata*, no. 36.

the community's rule/constitutions as well as in the saints (past and present) it has produced.

Each form of life thus expresses the Gospel for a particular purpose. What do you want the purpose of your life to be? What do you want to live for? Think about the end, or purpose, of a particular religious community. Then ask yourself: "Can I be known as that? Can I lay down my life for that? Would the purpose of that religious community make me, with all my gifts and failings, holy?" Your life will be lived for that purpose. People may not know who you are personally, but you will be known as a Cistercian monk, a Capuchin friar, an Oblate of St. Francis de Sales, a Passionist, a Marian of the Immaculate Conception, or whatever religious you may become. Each religious community has defining characteristics. Can you accept those characteristics as defining your life? If you don't want to teach, don't enter a teaching community. If you don't want to be a missionary, don't enter a missionary community. This may seem obvious, but not everybody thinks about matching a religious community's end or purpose with what they want their end or purpose in life to be.

Put simply, the most important thing for your religious community should be the most important thing for you. Otherwise, it's not a good match, and you won't really feel at home in the community. Let's now look at this history of holiness present here and now—and perhaps you'll find a place that you'll want to call home.

Monastic Orders

Do you want to be a monk? If so, you're thinking about a very old form of religious life. To understand it, we first need to look at the tradition of ancient hermits, which expresses the earliest monastic life.

The word monastic comes from a Greek word, *monos*, that means "one." A hermit lives alone, away from others. People can still enter a consecrated life of becoming hermits, but this is exceptional in practice today. More commonly, certain monastic communities will offer the option for their men to live as hermits or have characteristics of this eremitic (hermit-like) life.

The Camaldolese have an eremitic tradition that stretches back to St. Romuald, who founded the hermitage of Camaldoli in 1023. In the United States, different Camaldolese traditions are represented by the New Camaldoli Hermitage in Big Sur, CA, and by the Holy Family Hermitage in Bloomingdale, OH. The Carthusians, founded by St. Bruno in 1084, also live a life that emphasizes the hermitage for the monk. In the United States, they can be found at the Transfiguration Charterhouse in Vermont. Several other communities, those many centuries old and some new communities, emphasize the oneness of being alone with God. In some sense, every religious needs to develop a sense of being alone with the Lord.

Most monasticism today is not eremitic but based on the community. This idea of monasticism emphasizes that the "oneness" comes from living together as one, being of one heart and mind, as the community of believers was described in the Acts of the Apostles (Acts 4:32). The special word for this kind of monasticism comes from the word *coenobium*, the common life: cenobitic. In the fourth century, St. Pachomius in Egypt and St. Basil of Caesarea in Cappadocia (within modern-day Turkey) provided influential forms of cenobitic monasticism. In extolling life in a community, St. Basil famously contrasted that life with that of a hermit living alone, while meditating on the scene of Jesus washing his apostles' feet (cf. John 13:1-20). St. Basil says to an imagined hermit:

> For, behold, the Lord for the greatness of his love of men was not content with teaching the word only, but that accurately and clearly he might give us a pattern of humility in the perfection of love he girded himself and washed the feet of the disciples in person. Whose feet will you wash? Who will you

take care of? To whom do you make yourself inferior and last of all, since you live alone?[56]

"Whose feet will you wash?" Monks in the cenobitic form of life emphasize the community, where they help one another every day. The community life is usually under the command of an abbot. The word abbot comes from a word that means "father," and so the abbot is the father of the community. All the men live by a common rule. In the Christian East, the great majority of monasteries have traditions that stem from St. Basil's *Rules.* An example of this Basilian tradition in the Ukranian Catholic form in the U.S. is St. Josaphat's Monastery in Glen Cove, NY. But other traditions, both contemporary to Basil and those developed after the fourth century, can be found still today. For example, St. Maron, a younger contemporary of St. Basil from Syria, has a monastic tradition that continues to the present, such as in its intensely Eucharistic expression at the Most Holy Trinity Monastery in Petersham, MA.

The *Rule of St. Benedict* is the most widespread of the Western rules of life. Because of its foundational role in Western religious life, it is recommended that all those thinking about religious life should read it. For 1,500 years it has helped people find their vocation. The early Benedictine monks of Europe, as well as the Celtic monks who left Ireland to evangelize in Britain and on the continent of Europe, saved Western civilization from barbaric depravity through their love of learning and desire for God.

Benedictine monasteries still live the *Rule of St. Benedict* today. Monks living by St. Benedict's *Rule* have a vow of stability (meaning they stay in the same location), and so it is said that a man really has a vocation to a particular monastery, not to the Order of St. Benedict as a whole. Men who are thinking about the Benedictine way of life need to consider what monastery could God be calling them to join. Monasteries are grouped together into congregations,

---

56. St. Basil the Great, *Longer Rules*, q. 7, translation altered. See *The Ascetic Works of Saint Basil*, trans. W. K. Lowther Clarke (London: Society for Promoting Christian Knowledge, 1925), p. 166.

each with a distinctive history and customs, within the Benedictine Confederation of the Order of St. Benedict. That confederation, headed by an Abbot Primate, is a modern structure to group together the many different families of Benedictine monasteries. It is customary that monasteries begin as monastic foundations of abbeys, and so you will find family trees of religious lineage. To take two examples, St. Vincent Archabbey in Latrobe, Pennsylvania, for the American Cassinese Congregation, and St. Meinrad Archabbey in St. Meinrad, Indiana, for the Swiss American Congregation, have particular prominence within their congregations. But there are many abbeys and even smaller monasteries that do not have the full "abbey" status.

In addition to Benedictine monasteries, many other monastic communities live by St. Benedict's *Rule*. To take just one example of a medieval reform movement, the Cistercians have their three holy founders who were the first abbots of the original Cistercian abbey called Cîteaux: Saints Robert of Molesme, Alberic, and Stephen Harding. Today you can find both Cistercians who are O.Cist. and those who are O.C.S.O., that is, of the strict observance. The monks of this latter reform, begun in the 17th century, are commonly called Trappists. An example of an O.Cist. monastery is Our Lady of Dallas Abbey, which has a clerical, teaching apostolate in service to Cistercian Preparatory School and to the University of Dallas in Texas. Examples of Trappist monasteries in the U.S. include the Abbey of Gethsemani in Kentucky, the Abbey of Genesee in New York, and Holy Cross Abbey in Virginia. Sometimes Trappists are known for their edible products, such as bread and beer. They are also known for their demanding horarium, or community schedule, with the first communal prayers dark and early, such as at 3:30 a.m. These examples make manifest a life dedicated to prayer and work.

Orders of Canons

Would you like to dedicate your whole life to the liturgical praise of God in a particular church? Religious canons have a clerical religious life dedicated to sacred worship. Canons typically follow the *Rule of St. Augustine*. Augustine died in the year 430, 50 years before Benedict of Nursia was born. But Benedict is named Patriarch of Western Monasticism, not Augustine. (We don't think they're fighting in heaven over titles.) Augustine's *Rule* is known especially for its brevity and emphasis on being of one heart and soul in God through charity. In the Middle Ages, there were many groupings of canons that followed the *Rule of St. Augustine*.

The Order of Canons of St. Augustine, known in English sometimes as the Austin canons (not to be confused with the Augustinian friars discussed below), continue the tradition of priestly life established by St. Augustine. For one American expression of this tradition, know that the Abbey of Klosterneuburg in Austria established the Canonry of St. Leopold in Glen Clove, NY, in 2011.

The Order of Canons Regular of Prémontré, the Premonstratensians, also lives by the *Rule of St. Augustine* in this form of life. They're more commonly called the Norbertines, because St. Norbert of Xanten, the Apostle of the Eucharist, founded them in the early twelfth century. The Norbertines are devoted especially to worshiping God in the sacred liturgy of the Church. Some communities run schools, and their men also assist in the pastoral administration of the sacraments. Examples of Norbertine communities include St. Michael's Abbey in Orange, CA, St. Norbert Abbey in De Pere, WI, and Daylesford Abbey in Paoli, PA.

The Order of Canons Regular of the Holy Cross, commonly known as the Crosiers and founded by Bl. Theodore de Celles, also represent this religious tradition. Their devotion to the Holy Cross arose at the time of the Crusades, and their traditional habit has the red and white crusader cross. With a strong emphasis on the Augustinian-inspired unity, Crosier communities can be found in Phoenix, AZ and Onamia, MN.

Newer forms of this Augustinian-inspired life of canons are found in the Canons Regular of St. John Cantius in Chicago, and Canons Regular of the New Jerusalem in Charles Town, WV. Both groups offer the extraordinary form of the liturgy, the latter exclusively so.

Orders of Friars

In the late twelfth and thirteenth centuries, a number of religious movements emphasized apostolic renewal, the fraternal life, mobility, mendicant poverty, fervent Marian piety, intellectual training, and outreach to people, especially those in the growing cities. Because they wanted to be known as brothers, *fratres* in Latin, these orders are called orders of friars. Would you like to be a friar? Friars have many monastic observances, but they're not monks. Their lack of stability seemed to make them like the "gyrovagues," monks who roamed from place to place, which is condemned in the first chapter of the *Rule of St. Benedict*. Their arrival in the history of religious life caused some to think that the end of the world was coming, as their form of life was so revolutionary. We're serious.[57]

The largest community of friars was founded by St. Francis of Assisi. St. Francis, who was a layman for much of his life before acquiescing to become a deacon, wanted to live the Gospel in utter simplicity and poverty. His Friars Minor (Minor meaning lesser, out of humility) quickly became established throughout Europe and in other parts of the world. St. Anthony of Padua and St. Bonaventure, two Franciscan Doctors of the Church of the thirteenth century, give shining testimony to the Gospel.

The Franciscan friars have four major branches in their 800-year history. The first three given below come from the "first order" friars of the Franciscans; while the fourth arose out of the "third order" traditions. (The "second order," if you are curious, are cloistered nuns.) Let's just say that the Franciscans in the thirteenth century weren't always united in their interpretation of their found-

---

57. For a vehement argument against the friars by a university professor and secular priest at the University of Paris in the 1250s, see William of Saint-Amour, *De Periculis Novissimorum Temporum*, trans. G. Geltner, Dallas Medieval Texts and Translations, vol. 8 (Leuven: Peeters, 2008).

er—especially about how to live poverty. Gradually, more and more differences among Franciscan groups came about.

- In 1517, Pope Leo X recognized the Franciscan Observants, who became known simply as the Order of Friars Minor (O.F.M.). They were reorganized by Pope Leo XIII in 1897. The Order of Friars Minor has more friars than any other Franciscan order.

- Also in 1517 the Order of Friars Minor Conventual (O.F.M. Conventual) was recognized. The Conventual Franciscans emphasize within their name the coming together as brothers in the fraternal life. Friars live in convents, which in the U.S. are normally called friaries.

- The Order of Friars Minor Capuchin (O.F.M. Cap.) developed through a reform of Franciscans in the 1520s. These friars became known for their long capuche, or hood, and other reforms in their living out the Franciscan rule of life.

- Besides these three communities of the first order friars, we should also mention the Franciscans Friars of the Third Order Regular (T.O.R.), which developed from the medieval lay penance movement, but are priests and brothers living according to the Franciscan charism.

All of these Franciscan orders have provinces in the United States with many friaries and ministries of parishes, shrines, colleges, retreat centers, centers for direct care for the poor, chaplaincies, etc. In addition to these major branches of the Franciscan tree, there are many additional offshoots. The Friars of the Atonement, the Franciscan Friars of the Renewal, and the Franciscan Missionaries of the Eternal Word are some of many separate communities that embody forms of the Franciscan charism.

Parallel to the dramatic start of the Franciscans in the Middle Ages is the rise of the Order of Preachers founded by St. Dominic and approved by Pope Honorius III in 1216. Dominic's preachers replaced the traditional emphasis on manual labor with a greater emphasis on clerical study, in order to preach the truth of the Gospel—especially against heresy. Two Dominican Doctors of the Church from the thirteenth century are St. Albert the Great and his even more illustrious student, St. Thomas Aquinas, known as the Common Doctor or the Angelic Doctor.

Perhaps because St. Dominic bequeathed the *Rule of St. Augustine* (which he had observed as a canon in Osma, Spain) and his legislative concern for practical constitutions to govern the life, the Dominicans have always stressed unity and obedience in the Order. Unlike the Franciscans, the Dominicans have not broken off into multiple separate orders. The Order of Preachers is found throughout the world. In the United States you can consider the Eastern Province of St. Joseph (founded in 1805), the Western Province of the Most Holy Name of Jesus (1850/1912), the Central Province of St. Albert the Great (1939), and the Southern Province of St. Martin de Porres (1979), each with its own distinctive expression of the one order.

Also quite popular through the centuries have been the Carmelite friars. The Carmelites started as hermits on Mount Carmel, the place especially famous for the prophet Elijah's victory over the prophets of Baal (cf. 1 Kings 18:1-46). They have a strong contemplative tradition with a special place for devotion to the Blessed Virgin Mary. St. Albert of Jerusalem gave them a rule in the early thirteenth century, and they became known as an order of friars. Perhaps the most famous Carmelite of the thirteenth century is the English Prior General St. Simon Stock, hailed in tradition for receiving the Carmelite scapular (brown scapular) from Our Lady. In the sixteenth century, St. Teresa of Avila and St. John of the Cross, two Doctors of the Church renowned for their teaching on prayer, led a Carmelite reform in Spain. After that reform, two separate Orders of Carmelites existed: the Order of Carmelites (O.Carm.) and the Order of Discalced Carmelites (O.C.D.), the latter of which was the product of this Spanish reform. Discalced means without shoes. Both Carmelite Orders are present in many places in the United States.

Like the original Carmelites, the Augustinian friars started as hermits. Living in the region of Tuscany, Italy, they were brought together to be the Order of Hermits of St. Augustine and became known as an order of friars. Today's Order of St. Augustine is the same order as that formed in the 1240s. The Augustinians have had various developments and off-shoots over the centuries, including the Augustinian Recollects, founded in the sixteenth century and present in the United States. The more numerous Augustinian friars have many friaries, churches, and schools in their three provinces in the United States.

Still other medieval orders of friars continue after these many centuries.

- Like the Trinitarians, who were founded by St. John de Matha and St. Felix of Valois for the rescue of Christians held captive by non-believers, the Mercedarian friars were founded by St. Peter Nolasco (with the help of the Dominican St. Raymond de Penyafort) to redeem Christians from their Muslim captors. The Mercedarians are officially the Order of the Blessed Virgin Mary of Mercy and live today in such places as Philadelphia and Cleveland.

- The Servite Friars (the Order of the Friar Servants of Mary) also continue a deep devotion to Our Lady, especially to her title of Our Lady of Sorrows. In the U.S. they are centered in the Chicago area.

Societies of Clerics Regular

In the early modern period various societies of *clerics regular* arose. These societies received charisms that stressed the apostolic dimensions of religious life. They distanced themselves from traditional monastic observances of praying the Divine Office in choir and wanted to be identified primarily through their pastoral ministry, such as sacramental ministries, education, missions, and other services. How does that sound to you? If you want to be a religious committed to a ministry, but don't want what are traditionally called monastic observances, one of these societies and many later congregations may be a good fit.

The most famous of these is the Society of Jesus, which was founded by St. Ignatius of Loyola and received papal approval in 1540. With over 16,000 priests, brothers, scholastics, and novices on six continents, the Jesuits form the largest male religious community in the Catholic Church (if you do not count all the Franciscan friars as a single order). After he was injured in battle, Ignatius was given a book of the life of Christ and a book of the lives of the saints. He turned from his worldliness and was inspired by the examples of Francis and Dominic and wondered if he could live as they did. Ignatius began his company in 1534 with a small band of men, including St. Francis Xavier and St. Peter Faber. The Society of Jesus has a fourth vow of obedience to the Pope for their mission, which members may be invited to take.

The Jesuits have an enormous presence in the United States through their recently restructured five provinces: Maryland, Northeast, Central and Southern, Midwest, and West. They have many ministries. To take one kind of ministry as an example, consider their educational institutions. They have twenty-eight colleges and universities and about sixty high schools in the United States.

We want to mention four other societies of clerics regular founded in the sixteenth and early seventeenth centuries. We list them not so that they be memorized, but so that you continue to see the reality of the diversity in religious charisms in Church history present for you.

- The Theatines, founded by St. Cajetan of Thiene and others in 1524, form the Congregation of Clerics Regular of Divine Providence. They were founded in a spirit of asceticism, reform, and the apostolic work of the clergy. Within the United States, they have a seminary and several parishes in Colorado.

- St. Anthony Mary Zaccaria's Barnabites, who are the Clerics

Regular of St. Paul, were approved in 1533. The Barnabites strive for a reform according to the inspiration of the Apostle Paul, and can be found in such places as Pennsylvania, New York, and California.

- The Camillians, or Clerics Regular, Ministers to the Sick, were founded by St. Camillus de Lellis in the late sixteenth century, and have a U.S. presence in Wisconsin. They receive, through their founder, a charism of ministry to the sick poor, including the resolve to risk their own life.

- The Piarists, Order of Poor Clerics Regular of the Mother of God of the Pious Schools, were founded by St. Joseph Calasanz in 1617. Whereas the Camillians are devoted to the sick, the Piarist charism concentrates on education. The Piarists can be found in several places in the eastern United States and Puerto Rico.

All of these societies of clerics regular continue the sixteenth and seventeenth century-concern of Catholic reform today.

Religious Congregations in Modern Times

After these societies of clerics regular, many congregations were founded for various particular needs in the Church. Both the older religious orders and the newer religious congregations are called "religious institutes" by the Catholic Church's Magisterium. Religious congregations may be either of diocesan or of pontifical right. The pontifical right denotes that the community is immediately and exclusively subject to the Holy See for matters of internal governance and discipline.

Special mention should be made of the many congregations devoted to foreign missionary service. Let's put this in a historical perspective. Many religious communities have evangelized and re-evangelized the world throughout the ages. Think of the monks in the early Middle Ages or the friars who led missions into non-Christian lands in the thirteenth century. In the sixteenth century, the Jesuits became outstanding for their missionary work, such as through St. Francis Xavier, patron of the foreign missions. Older forms of religious life continued their missionary service, as exemplified by the many Franciscan missions established between 1769 to 1833 in California. And newer forms of religious life in congregations came about for the sake of the missions. The Second Vatican Council recognizes with appreciation the unique position of religious in the Church's missionary outreach: "Religious institutes of the contemplative and of the active life have so played, and still do play, the main role in the evangelization of the world."[58] That is an astounding fact that should be better known.

In addition to service in foreign missions, sometimes the missionary spirit of the congregation is expressed in the domestic mission of renewal: specializing in the mission of education, parish renewal, or concentrating on a certain population, such as youth. Would you like to join one of these congregations? The following are but a few of the religious congregations founded after the seventeenth century with a presence in the United States:

- Congregation of the Holy Spirit (Spiritans), founded by Fr. Claude Poullart des Places in 1703

- Congregation of the Passion (Passionists), founded by St. Paul of the Cross in 1727

- Congregation of the Most Holy Redeemer (Redemptorists), founded by St. Alphonsus Liguori in 1732

- Congregation of Priests of Mercy (The Fathers of Mercy), founded by Fr. Jean-Baptiste Rauzan in 1808

- Missionary Oblates of Mary Immaculate, founded by St. Eugene de Mazenod in 1816

---

58. Second Vatican Council, *Ad Gentes*, Decree on the Mission Activity of the Church, no. 40.

- Oblates of the Virgin Mary, founded by Ven. Bruno Lanteri in 1816

- Congregation of Holy Cross, founded by Bl. Basil Moreau in 1837

- Missionary Sons of the Immaculate Heart of Mary (Claretians), founded by St. Anthony Mary Claret in 1849

- Salesians of Don Bosco, founded by St. John Bosco in 1857

- Comboni Missionaries of the Heart of Jesus, founded by St. Daniel Comboni in 1867

- Society of the Divine Word (Divine Word Missionaries), founded by St. Arnold Janssen in 1875

- Oblates of St. Francis de Sales, founded by Bl. Louis Brisson in 1875

- Consolata Missionaries, founded by Bl. Joseph Allamano in 1901

- Congregation of Marian Fathers of the Immaculate Conception of the Most Blessed Virgin Mary (Marians of the Immaculate Conception), founded by St. Stanislaus Papczynski in 1670, but re-founded in its present form by Bl. George Matulaitis in 1910

Some religious congregations were founded exclusively for religious brothers, without clerics. Would you like to be a brother in a teaching congregation of brothers? Here are some examples:

- In France, St. John Baptist de la Salle, himself a priest, founded the Institute of the Brothers of the Christian Schools, which received papal approbation in 1725.

- Bl. Edmund Ignatius Rice, a brother himself after becoming a widower, founded the Congregation of the Presentation Brothers *and* the Congregation of Christian Brothers in early nineteenth-century Ireland.

• Theodore James Ryken founded the Xaverian Brothers, under the patronage of St. Francis Xavier, in 1839 in Belgium, before he came to the United States.

Each of these congregations of brothers has a presence in America today.

Societies of Apostolic Life

In addition to religious congregations, the centuries after the Protestant Reformation have also the seen the rise of many apostolic societies that resemble religious life. The *Code of Canon Law* states:

> Can. 731 §1. Societies of apostolic life resemble institutes of consecrated life; their members, without religious vows, pursue the apostolic purpose proper to the society and, leading a life in common as brothers or sisters according to their proper manner of life, strive for the perfection of charity through the observance of the constitutions.
>
> §2. Among these are societies in which members assume the evangelical counsels by some bond defined in the constitutions.

Would you like to enter one of these societies? The following lists some of them:

• Congregation of the Oratory of St. Philip Neri (Oratorians), founded by St. Philip Neri in 1575

• Congregation of the Mission (Vincentians), founded by St. Vincent de Paul in 1625

• Society of the Priests of Saint Sulpice, founded by Fr. Jean-Jacques Olier in 1641

• Congregation of Missionaries of the Most Precious Blood of

Our Lord Jesus Christ (Precious Blood Missionaries), founded by St. Gaspar del Bufalo in 1815

- Missionary Society of St. Paul the Apostle (Paulist Fathers), founded by Fr. Isaac Hecker in 1858

- Missionaries of Africa (White Fathers), founded by Archbishop (later Cardinal) Charles Lavigerie in 1868

- St. Joseph's Society of the Sacred Heart (Josephite Fathers and Brothers) formed in 1871 from the Mill Hill Missionaries in the U.S., becoming its own society in 1893

- Catholic Foreign Mission Society of America (Maryknoll Fathers and Brothers), founded by Fr. James Anthony Walsh and Fr. Thomas Frederick Price in 1911

- Pontifical Institute for Foreign Missions (PIME Missionaries), founded by Pope Pius IX in 1926

- Priestly Fraternity of the Missionaries of St. Charles Borromeo, founded by Fr. Massimo Camisasca in 1985

- Priestly Fraternity of St. Peter, founded by Fr. Josef Bisig and others in 1988

All these societies of apostolic life have a presence in the United States. Often, some societies concentrating on missions in Africa, Asia, and Latin America will still have some communities in the United States especially to assist their missions abroad.

Secular Institutes

In 1947, Pope Pius XII in the apostolic constitution *Provida Mater Ecclesia* recognized a new form of consecrated life: the secular institute. Whereas the societies of apostolic life are not strictly religious in the most proper definition of the Church today (as understood by Rome's Congregation of Institutes of Consecrated Life and Societies of Apostolic Life), secular institutes are institutes of the consecrated life (like religious institutes), but have their setting properly in the world. The *Code of Canon Law* defines in this way: "A secular institute is an institute of consecrated life in which the Christian faithful, living in the world, strive for the perfection of charity and seek to contribute to the sanctification of the world, especially from within."[59]

Would you like to have that form of consecrated life in the world? One example of a male secular institute is the community of the Schoenstatt Fathers, founded by Fr. Joseph Kentenich in 1965. Like many other communities, they are within a broader family. The Schoenstatt movement, which has a charism devoted to the Blessed Virgin Mary, was founded by Father Kentenich in 1914 and is expressed in various ecclesial forms. Schoenstatt Fathers can be found in such places as Wisconsin and Texas.

New Communities

Communities continue to be founded in the Church. Are you thinking about entering a new community? If so, take care to find out what the canonical status of the community is. Many new communities aspire to be religious but are still public associations of the Christian faithful. Some have not yet achieved that status even within their diocese. Some new communities do not desire to be religious communities, but societies of apostolic life or secular institutes. Some of these communities may be recent manifestations of an ancient or medieval charism, rather than a product of a completely new charism. Yes, the array of communities can be bewildering. Therefore, we think it's important for you to know what a community actually is.

Do not let appearances fool you. A Jesuit priest in khaki slacks and blue button-down shirt is a religious, but a man in a medieval-looking habit without a public profession of vows of the evangelical counsels and without belonging to a religious institute, is not a religious. New communities, marked by their initial zeal, are

59. *Code of Canon Law*, can. 710.

welcomed with caution by the Catholic Church; they need to prove themselves before receiving some form of approbation.

If looking at a new community, consider these questions. Has the Church given approval to this community? If so, what kind of approval is it? What does the community aspire to be? Is the founder still alive? Is there a healthy dynamic within the community, or is the founder treated as a guru or cult leader? Are the formators and superiors themselves well formed? Does the community know its own identity, or is it still in search of an identity?

Without beginning as a seed, a new community cannot exist as a promise of new life from the Holy Spirit, who is the Lord and giver of life. The Holy Spirit entrusts a charism to a founder, who imparts that gift to the community, which always begins quite small. Some founders have been outstanding in holiness; the first generations of the community benefited from that blessing in a profound way. Some founders have had serious psychological and moral problems, and the community members suffered greatly at their hands. The bottom line: keep your eyes wide open and use the virtue of prudence when investigating *any* community.

Conclusion

This historical guideline, with references to their ongoing presence, can be useful in situating communities within the Church's life—but this survey is far from complete. Much has been omitted for the sake of brevity.

At times, a community may not fit neatly into this rather sweeping timeline. For example, the Alexian Brothers, a religious community dedicated to the care of the sick, date their foundation to 1334, an age known for the beghards and beguines (male and female semi-monastic laity especially in Germany, the Netherlands, and Belgium). Or consider Opus Dei, which is not a religious community. Its name means "Work of God," and is the same expression as the traditional Latin term for the monastic Divine Office (Liturgy of the Hours). St. Josemaría Escrivá conceived the idea for Opus

Dei in 1928 as a means for Christian holiness in the world. In 1982, it became the only "personal prelature," which is a structure of a prelate, clergy, and laity banded together for pastoral activities.

Also, we did not explore the various third orders, monastic oblates, laity of religious families, and associates that participate in the charisms of communities, but are themselves not religious institutes, apostolic societies, nor secular institutes. Religious charisms work many benefits in people's lives beyond the religious themselves. For example, sometimes a man finds he's not meant to be a Benedictine monk, but he becomes a married man and father who, as an oblate, lives out aspects of monastic life in the world.

The Liturgy of the Hours has the invitatory antiphon for the Common of Holy Men: "Come, let us worship God, wonderful in his saints." The holy communities described in this chapter are expressions of how wonderful God is. Every community approved by the Church, by its charism, communicates an aspect of God's manifold holiness proclaimed in the Gospel. In the following chapter, we will highlight a few of the greatest saints in religious life. By drawing close to these saints, we can draw close to God, wonderful in his saints.

Queen of the apostles, you have a tender love for all who
follow your Son. Pray that I may follow him in the way that
makes me most pleasing to God.

CHAPTER 9

STORIES OF THE SAINTS IN RELIGIOUS LIFE

"Be imitators of me, as I am of Christ" (1 Cor 11:1).

Austin grew up knowing that his name was an English form of Augustine. When he was in junior high, he was fascinated by the story of St. Augustine of Hippo, the unmarried teenage father who eventually became one of the greatest religious, bishops, and theologians in Church history. In his sophomore year of college, he read Augustine's *Confessions* and loved it. His patron's words spoke to his soul. Unfortunately, alcohol also spoke to his soul. During a period of intoxication, he hooked up with a woman, and that began a long, unchaste relationship. He drifted from the faith, no longer going to Mass. After college graduation, he struggled to find a job. His girlfriend dumped him for a friend of his who had a lucrative job. One day he found his copy of the *Confessions* and read it again. That experience changed his life. He went to the sacrament of confession, gave away his stockpile of liquor, found a successful job in the tech industry, and realized that he desired to enter religious life. Now at the age of 29, he wants to be like St. Augustine—after Augustine's conversion, that is.

We need heroes. Think about the heroes people admire today: sports figures, movie stars, presidents, grandparents, humanitarians, billionaires, and the list goes on. When you were little, did you have a favorite superhero? At some point, most kids have some sort of hero, real or imagined. In Austin's case, he was blessed to know that his name honored St. Augustine as his baptismal patron. Fortunately, after many years of sin he was able to draw on the example of that childhood spiritual hero.

In our brief scriptural quotation at the head of this chapter, we see that St. Paul made bold to give himself as an example for imitation. Why? Because he imitated Jesus Christ. When we consider the lives of the saints, we see images of Christ, who is "the image of the invisible God" (Col 1:15). The Church is both the communion of holy things (the sacraments) and the communion of holy ones (the saints). In the saints, we see how sinners are transformed through the sacramental life to be holy, as the Lord himself is holy. All the faithful can turn to the saints for their intercession, example, and communion in friendship. This companionship is more powerful than the bonds of death. Heaven comes to help us.

Because religious life belongs to the holiness of the Church, it should not be a surprise to find that so many saints and blesseds admired throughout the Church were religious. Go through the universal calendar of the Church, and you'll see one religious after another. Take August as an example and consider the male religious who are commemorated:

- St. Alphonsus Liguori (Aug. 1)

- St. Peter Julian Eymard (Aug. 2)

- St. Dominic (Aug. 8)

- St. Maximilian Kolbe (Aug. 14)

- St. John Eudes (Aug. 19)

- St. Bernard of Clairvaux (Aug. 20)

- St. Joseph Calasanz (Aug. 25)

- St. Augustine of Hippo (Aug. 28)

We highly recommend that you take some holy male religious as powerful patrons and models. From our experience, many men who enter religious life have a deep bond with at least one male religious saint. Be inspired by the lives of saints in making decisions about your future. For example, if you are thinking about becoming a Jesuit, look not only to St. Ignatius of Loyola, the founder of the Society of Jesus, but also to the many Jesuits renowned for their holiness, such as St. Peter Canisius, St. John Berchmans, St. Isaac Jogues, St. Peter Claver, St. Francis of Jerome, Bl. Miguel Agustín Pro, and Bl. Rupert Mayer. The list of Jesuit saints and blesseds goes on and on.

In addition to "All Saints" on November 1, some communities celebrate all the saints of their community on another day. For instance, the Carmelites honor "All Carmelite Saints" on November 14. If a community that you are considering for entrance is not blessed with a long history of men beatified and canonized, we still think it would be wise for you to be inspired by some holy male religious in history. Get to know them. Read about them. Better yet, if they have left writings, read what they have left behind. Have images of them in your room. Ask for their intercession each day. If you enter religious life, you will enter the great stream of religious life's sanctity. Desire to swim in that kind of holiness—with all its dangers, sorrows, blessings, and joys.

Here are six stories of male religious outstanding in holiness. Perhaps one of these six saints will stand out for you, or perhaps you have some in mind we don't list in this chapter. But we think it very important that you concentrate on examples of renowned religious as heroes for your life. Some never draw that connection to religious life's distinctiveness in holiness. For example, lots of people study St. Augustine of Hippo, but do they realize that he's a religious founder who left a Rule that has been lived by hundreds of religious communities for over 1600 years? Know the holy religious men more and more, love them more and more—and you will be drawn closer to Jesus Christ.

St. Anthony of Egypt (251-356)

Demons pulling on his beard and beating him, violence all around, tempting images of lust, greed, and gluttony... Artists have loved to portray the life of St. Anthony of Egypt, also known as St. Anthony the Great. He lived to age 105 before dying in the middle of the fourth century and is hailed as the "Father of Monks." We know him especially through the written portrait given by St. Athanasius, Bishop of Alexandria, Egypt. Monks far from Egypt heard about Anthony's life, and wanted some record of it for their growth in virtue. After Anthony's death, Athanasius was happy to oblige. He writes: "I received your directive with ready good will. For simply to remember Anthony is a great profit and assistance for me also. I know that even in hearing, along with marveling at the man, you will want also to emulate his purpose, for Anthony's way of life provides monks with a sufficient purpose for ascetic practice."[60]

Just as athletes and soldiers practice what the Greeks call *askesis* (discipline or asceticism), with all sorts of physical training, strict dietary regimen, sleep suppression, and mental practices, so Anthony shows a religious how to be disciplined in control over his bodily movements, his fasting, his vigils, and his demanding schedule of prayer. A monk becomes a soldier for Christ, fighting the powers of evil—especially in his own mind. Don't you realize that the greatest battleground on earth is your mind?

Anthony's ascetical life began when he had powerful experiences of hearing Sacred Scripture proclaimed in church. He was about nineteen years old, and his parents had both passed about six months earlier. While going to church he was meditating on how the apostles left everything to follow the Savior. In the church he heard the Gospel in which the Lord says to the rich young man: "If you wish to be perfect, go, sell what you have and give to the poor,

---

60. *Athanasius: The Life of Antony and the Letter to Marcellinus*, trans. Robert C. Gregg, Classics of Western Spirituality (Mahwah, NJ: Paulist Press, 1980), Introduction, p. 29. The spelling of the name has been changed from Antony to the more common English rendering of Anthony in our quotations of this book.

and you will have treasure in heaven" (Matt 19:21). Immediately, he knew that his thoughts about the saints and his hearing about this Gospel were providential. He sold almost everything and gave to the poor. When returning to the church soon afterwards, he heard: "Do not worry about tomorrow" (Matt 6:34). He then left everything, entrusted his sister to the care of a convent, and was free to begin the monastic life. Such is the power of the Word of God for religious life! St. Anthony became resolute, deciding not to turn back even to think about his former way of life.

St. Anthony can be a model for you to become resolute, never turning back from following Jesus. Anthony realized he needed help. He sought the counsel of the old religious men wise in their ascetical practices and imitated them. He worked with his own hands and prayed constantly. Even though he was illiterate, his memory of hearing the Scriptures read to him served him in place of books.

Anthony was the first to go deep into the Egyptian desert, a place known for demons, to be alone with God there as a hermit. But so popular was he that others flocked to the desert to be like him and imitate his combat against the evil one. Athanasius writes that Anthony urged everyone who came to him "to prefer nothing in the world above the love of Christ."[61] Athanasius continues:

> And when he spoke and urged them to keep in mind the future good and the affection in which we are held by God, *who did not spare his own Son, but gave him up for us all* [Rom 8:32], he persuaded many to take up the solitary life. And so, from then on, there were monasteries in the mountains, and the desert was made a city by monks, who left their own people and registered themselves for the citizenship in the heavens.[62]

This *Life of Anthony* was written in Greek and was soon translated into other languages. Fewer than fifteen years after its author's

---

61. *Life of Anthony*, no. 14 (Gregg, p. 42). The *Rule of St. Benedict*, chap.4 will later have something similar: "Prefer nothing to the love of Christ."

62. *Life of Anthony*, no. 14 (Gregg, pp. 42-43).

death, its Latin translation would alter forever the life of Augustine of Hippo, who heard about Anthony just before receiving his grace of conversion. The life of Anthony continues to inspire many.

St. Bernard of Clairvaux (1090-1153)

The most popular man of his time. That's how St. Bernard of Clairvaux could be described. He had a magnetic personality. When he went to become a monk, about the age of twenty-three, he didn't come alone. It's a wonderful thing to see, even today, that when one enters religious life, someone close to him does the same. In Bernard's case, he brought with him about thirty young men from his extended family and friends. They entered the first Cistercian abbey, at Cîteaux itself. Only three years after his arrival, he was sent to found a daughter house at Clairvaux and became its first abbot. It is said that his own father and brothers joined that monastery.

Many people loved listening to Bernard. He was so convincing that when he came to preach, people would hide their loved ones lest they be tempted to join the monastery. We have about 330 sermons, about 500 letters, and 13 treatises from him, and so we too can hear his thoughts. The Church calls him "the Mellifluous Doctor," a fancy expression that means his teaching flowed sweetly. We could say that it was like music to his listener's ears.

Bernard wanted his monks to experience God's love. People don't want just some dry academic information; they want experience. He writes in his treatise *On Loving God*, "The more surely you know yourself loved, the easier you will find it to love in return."[63] Bernard's preaching on the Song of Songs from the Old Testament exemplifies the Cistercian emphasis on experiencing God's love for us. He preaches:

> This sort of song only the touch of the Holy Spirit teaches
> (1 John 2:27), and it is learned by experience alone. Let those

---

63. St. Bernard of Clairvaux, *On Loving God*, III.7 in *Bernard of Clairvaux: Selected Works*, trans. G. R. Evans (New York: Paulist Press, 1987), p. 179.

who have experienced it enjoy it; let those who have not burn with desire, not so much to know it as to experience it. It is not a noise made aloud, but the very music of the heart. It is not a sound from the lips but a stirring of joy, not a harmony of voices but of wills.[64]

Have you experienced the greatness of God's love in your life? If you haven't, do you want to experience it? Bernard could help you, especially now as you consider the vocation to religious life.

Ironically, even though he was the greatest promoter of Cistercian vocations, constantly encouraging men to retreat from the world in prayer, Bernard also dealt with many problems in the Church and in the world. Whether within the monastic cloister or in his frequent travels, he prayed and spoke about the Christian mission in the world. He was a papal adviser, such as in his famous *On Consideration,* to his admirer (and fellow Cistercian) Pope Eugene III. He also was commissioned to preach the Second Crusade—which turned out to be a disaster in the Middle East for Christians. He was greatly concerned with the rights of the Church against hostile political powers in Europe. Within theology, he hated with a passion the approach of Peter Abelard, whose use of philosophy in matters about God and the things of God seemed heretical. St. Bernard defies the stereotype of what a monk "should" do and say, and he can lead you to be true to yourself while being true to God.

St. Francis Xavier (1506-1552)

Thousands of miles from his homeland, St. Francis Xavier is said to have cut out the signatures of his dearest friends who wrote him letters so as to keep the scraps of paper on his own person in his travels. He always wanted those he loved close to his heart—even though he would never see them again in this world. Such is the power of religious friendship.

---

64. St. Bernard of Clairvaux, Sermon 1 on The Song of Songs VI.11 in *Bernard of Clairvaux: Selected Works*, pp. 214-15.

Do you want to be a missionary in a far-off land? If so, know that the Church places the foreign missions under the patronage of the great Jesuit missionary to the Far East St. Francis Xavier. He serves this patronage in heaven alongside the cloistered Carmelite nun St. Thérèse of Liseux. Francis Xavier was one of the original companions in the Society of Jesus, when Ignatius of Loyola and six others offered themselves to God in Montmartre, Paris in 1534. Ignatius wanted to send a couple men to evangelize Asia. His first choice, Nicholas Bobadilla, became ill and could not go. Francis was his replacement. It sometimes happens in religious life that the first man selected by a community for a duty does not ultimately get the assignment, but God can still do great things through a religious who is an afterthought.

Francis had been ordained a priest in 1537, and in 1540 set out for an assignment which would never allow him to return. He went first to Lisbon, Portugal to sail with the Portuguese to India. They set sail on April 7, 1541, Francis's 35th birthday, and arrived in Goa, India more than a year later after a lengthy stay in Portuguese Mozambique, in the southeast of Africa.

Francis had many missionary adventures not only in India but throughout Asia, including many islands, because he wanted to preach the Gospel there. He died on December 3, 1552, on an island just off the coast of China. He preached, baptized, and catechized with the strength of God. It is said that he baptized about 100,000 people during his missionary work. Because of this, his right forearm is kept in the Jesuit Church of the Gesù in Rome—except when on another mission. That arm has recently been on tour in Canada.

While the Church is amazed by his wondrous missionary zeal, you should also keep in mind what Francis would repeatedly tell his fellow Jesuits thousands of miles away. He told them in so many words that he missed them, and loved them, and longed to hear news of them. He wrote many letters, and he would sign a letter to his brethren: "The least and most lonely of your brothers, Francis."[65] The greatest of religious saints, those who are zealous to convert the world, still have human needs, desires, and loves. God doesn't obliterate our humanity in religious life.

St. Martin de Porres (1579-1639)

"Too dark-skinned"—that's what St. Martin's father, Juan de Porres, thought when his baby boy was born of an illegitimate union with Ana Velázquez, a free African woman from Panama. Martin was born on December 9, 1579 in Lima, Peru, and his father would not claim Martin because he was black. Martin began life in misery. Juan later repented of abandoning Martin, as well as Martin's little sister, born two years after Martin. For a few years, he had the children with him in Ecuador, but later separated them sending Martin back to his mother in Lima. Martin knew what it was like to come from poverty, a broken family, and racial prejudice—aspects lived in different ways by so many people today. Can you identify with him in some way? Juan did give some money to Ana to make sure that Martin would be able to continue an education in a trade. Martin learned how to be a barber, which at that time included training in medical services.

Of quick intelligence, Martin grew up with great faith. Many stories are told about his devotion to the Cross of our Lord Jesus Christ. He prayed constantly. He was outstanding in humility, and his love for the poor knew no bounds. At age fifteen, he sought to live and work in the Dominican priory of Our Lady of the Holy Rosary. The Dominicans had many traditions of rosary devotions, and just eight years before Martin was born, the third Dominican to be Pope, St. Pius V, proclaimed a feast to recall the rosary's importance in the battle of Lepanto on October 7, 1571. This is now known

---

65. Letter 44, To the Society at Rome, trans. in Henry James Coleridge, S.J., *The Life and Letters of St. Francis Xavier*, vol. 1, 2nd ed. (London: Burns and Oates, 1874), p. 284.

as the Feast of Our Lady of the Rosary. Martin prayed the rosary fervently and frequently.

Martin began life at this large Lima priory dedicated as a lay servant, but later professed vows as a "religious donatus"—a status that made him a consecrated lifelong member of the religious community, though neither a priest nor brother in the usual sense. Brother Martin's outreach to the poor and the sick made him renowned in the city and beyond. People repeatedly testified to miracles he performed during his lifetime and after his death.

His dark skin, which caused his father to abandon him, allowed him to show forth God's grace in a way that overturned unjust social conventions in both the world and the Church. Three years after he died, the General Chapter (or worldwide gathering) of Dominicans included special notification of Martin's death and passed legislation striking down laws in the worldwide Order of Preachers that forbade admission to "mestizos, Indians, and Africans, through one parent or both."[66] In the United States, devotion to Martin in the mid-twentieth century through statues and images helped break down racial prejudice where African Americans suffered from injustices. St. John XXIII canonized him in 1962, and St. Martin de Porres is hailed as patron of social justice.

Martin is sometimes depicted with animals, especially mice by his feet, as he had a tender care for all God's creatures. He frequently appears carrying his broom, a sign of his humble duties of sweeping the priory's floors. (Religious life gives many opportunities to take care of the place where religious live.) For some religious devoted to study, the wood of the desk is the wood of the Cross. For some who are devoted to cleaning, the wood of the Cross is the wood of the broom. If you enter religious life, you'll find the Cross though some work of humility—and there you will also discover the Lord's power.

---

66. Quoted in Augustine Thompson, O.P., *Dominican Brothers: Conversi, Lay, and Cooperator Brothers* (Chicago: New Priory Press, 2017), p. 158.

St. André Bessette (1845-1937)

Alfred Bessette's earliest years were in a one-room cabin about thirty miles southeast of Montreal, Quebec. As a child he was of poor health and he did not receive a proper education. In fact, he never learned to write; his letters were all dictated. He always wanted to be a religious and was renowned among his family members and friends for his piety. But he needed to work for a living. Over the course of several years, he worked at different trades and moved to different towns in Canada and the United States. A priest by the name of Father André Provençal took notice of Alfred's piety, and Alfred said to him, "I want to enter religion to serve the Good God and sanctify myself. I want to be able to pray more easily. It is only among the priests at church and at devotions that I feel happy." Can you identify with his feeling of happiness? Father Provençal recommended Alfred to become a brother in the Congregation of Holy Cross and wrote the Congregation's superior at the College of Saint-Laurent in Montreal, "I'm sending you a saint."[67]

There Alfred received the religious name of Brother André, but his health posed terrible problems in the novitiate. In fact, when he petitioned to make temporary profession of vows, he was denied due to ill health. As you can imagine, he was devastated. A new novice master replaced the old one and recognized Brother André's devotion to prayer. Brother André had gifts of constancy in prayer—praying always when he worked. He made his appeals to make profession as a Holy Cross brother, and a vote was taken again, allowing him to make profession on August 22, 1872. Because his superiors were concerned that he couldn't do much manual labor, he was assigned to be porter. He joked, "My superiors showed me the door and I stayed there." He also used to say, "I was

---

67. Both quotations come from sources cited in C. Bernard Ruffin, *The Life of Brother André: The Miracle Worker of St. Joseph* (Huntington, IN: Our Sunday Visitor, 1988), p. 23.

at the door forty years without going out."[68] As you can see, a good sense of humor is needed in a religious vocation.

As porter, he greeted the many people who came and helped them. He often directed them to go to St. Joseph. Brother André always had a tender devotion to St. Joseph, the Spouse of the Blessed Virgin Mary and Guardian of the Redeemer and wanted others to know of St. Joseph's protection. Over time, the poor and sick reported miracles after visiting with Brother André and praying to St. Joseph. They credited Brother André. He was alarmed, saying, "How stupid people are to think that Brother André makes miracles. The Good God makes the miracles, St. Joseph obtains them, and I am only the wire which transmits their blessings." In another image for his humility, Brother André said, "It is with the smallest brushes that the Artist paints the most exquisitely beautiful pictures."[69]

Through Brother André's prayers and fundraising St. Joseph's Oratory was built on the high mount of Montreal. What began as a tiny chapel in 1904 became plans for a magnificent church. The basilica's roof was still not complete when Brother André died on January 6, 1937. Its interior was completed in 1967, and it stands above the city of Montreal as the world's largest shrine dedicated to St. Joseph. The basilica beckons pilgrims who come from distant lands.

Brother André, who was such a sickly child from a very humble family, lived to be over ninety-one years old, and became famous throughout the world. He was the first canonized member of the Congregation of Holy Cross, a community renowned for foreign missions, parishes, and education (such as at the University of Notre Dame). Keep in mind that he himself had no prestige in education, did not do parochial ministry, and was based largely in his home area of Montreal. Most importantly, he expresses the holiness at the

---

68. Both quotations come from sources cited in Ruffin, *The Life of Brother André*, p. 30.

69. Both quotations come from Ruffin, *The Life of Brother André*, p. 46.

heart of his religious institute's charism. When Pope Benedict XVI canonized him on October 17, 2010, he said:

> [Brother André] demonstrated boundless charity and strove to relieve the distress of those who came to confide in him. With very little education, he had nevertheless understood where the essential of his faith was situated. For him, believing meant submitting freely and through love to the divine will. Wholly inhabited by the mystery of Jesus, he lived the beatitude of pure of heart, that of personal rectitude. It is thanks to this simplicity that he enabled many people to see God.[70]

St. André continues to inspire some to enter religion, and to enable many others also to see God.

St. Maximilian Kolbe (1894-1941)

Raymond Kolbe was born to a German father and a Polish mother on January 8, 1894, and became an extraordinarily devout boy who wanted to become a religious. One night when he was wondering what would happen in his life, he saw a vision of the Blessed Virgin Mary. He later recounted this experience in this way:

> That night, I asked the Mother of God what was to become of me, a Child of Faith. Then she came to me holding two crowns, one white, the other red. She asked me if I was willing to accept either of these crowns. The white one meant that I should persevere in purity, and the red that I should become a martyr. I said that I would accept them both.[71]

With this vision in mind, he left his family to enter the Conventual Franciscans and received the name Maximilian in 1910. He applied himself thoroughly to formation and advanced studies, earning doctorates in philosophy and theology. As a young priest,

---

70. Pope Benedict XVI, Canonization Homily on Sunday, October 17, 2010.

71. Quoted in Benedict J. Groeschel, C.F.R., *The Saints in My Life: My Favorite Spiritual Companions* (Huntington, IN: Our Sunday Visitor, Inc., 2011), p. 181.

he expressed a very fervent devotion to Our Lady and formed the Militia of the Immaculata to fight for her honor. He and some other Franciscans founded the "City of the Immaculata" in Poland, which became a huge friary with several hundred friars and a major publishing center. Their monthly publication reached about a million readers.

In 1930 Maximilian was sent to be a missionary in Japan and founded another "City of the Immaculata." In 1933, when away from Japan for his community's business, he wrote the Franciscan brethren in Nagasaki an important principle about sin: "Whenever you feel guilty, even if it is because you have consciously committed a sin, a serious sin, something you have kept doing many, many times, *never let the devil deceive you by allowing him to discourage you.* Whenever you feel guilty, offer all your guilt to the Immaculate, without analyzing nor examining it, as something that belongs to her.... My beloved, may *every fall*, even if it is a serious and habitual sin, *always become for us a small step toward a higher degree of perfection.*"[72] After his assignment in Japan, he returned with tuberculosis to Poland, and continued his amazing work. He was there when Germany invaded Poland in 1939.

During the Second World War, Maximilian and the Franciscan friars provided shelter to refugees, including about 2,000 Jews. Against the madness of what he saw around him, Maximilian wrote in his community's publication, "No one in the world can change Truth. What we can do and should do is to seek truth and to serve it when we have found it. The real conflict is the inner conflict. Beyond armies of occupation and the hecatombs of extermination camps, there are two irreconcilable enemies in the depths of every soul: good and evil, sin and love. And what use are the victories on the battlefield if we ourselves are defeated in our innermost personal selves?"[73]

---

72. St. Maximilian Kolbe, *Stronger than Hatred: A Collection of Spiritual Writings,* trans. Edward Flood (Brooklyn: New City Press, 1988), p. 104.

73. Quoted in Groeschel, *The Saints in My Life,* pp. 183-84.

Soon after that publication, the Franciscans were severely punished for their goodness and truthfulness. Maximilian himself was taken to the Auschwitz concentration camp, where horrible atrocities were being committed. When the guards prepared to execute a man for what another prisoner had done, the man pleaded that they spare him for the sake of his wife and children. Maximilian asked if he could take the family man's place and the guards agreed. This heroic Polish priest died two weeks later from a lethal injection after having ministered to other prisoners left together in a cell to starve. It was August 14, 1941, the Vigil of the Solemnity of the Assumption of the Mother of God.

In 1971, St. Paul VI beatified Maximilian Kolbe as a "confessor," i.e., non-martyr, as it was not clear at that time that he was killed as a martyr by his persecutors. In 1982, St. John Paul canonized St. Maximilian with the special designation as a "martyr of charity." Maximilian was offered two crowns by the Immaculate Virgin Mary. He indeed received both of them.

Conclusion

You can't do justice to the memory of these saints without keeping in mind the religious life that supported them. Can you imagine St. Anthony of Egypt as a married man or St. Martin de Porres as a diocesan priest? We can't. They wouldn't be the saints that we know them to be. Also, it's not accidental that St. Bernard was a Cistercian or that St. Maximilian Kolbe was a Conventual Franciscan. Do you see the connection between each saint and his religious life? Some people don't see the connection, but each religious saint expresses his religious community's charism to be holy. The religious saints most powerfully show the distinctiveness of religious life in the Church. That is very important for you to keep in mind when considering religious life.

In the next part, we guide you through a process of application to a religious community, then an examination of the life and stages of initial formation, and finally what you can expect from God, others, and yourself.

> *Mary, you are the queen of the saints. Set my heart afire*
> *to burn always, like the tabernacle light in the church's*
> *sanctuary, so that I may always give witness to the presence of*
> *your Son in my life.*

—PART FOUR—

APPLYING, ENTERING, AND EXPECTING

CHAPTER 10

THE APPLICATION PROCESS

"Glory in his holy name; let hearts that seek the Lord rejoice!
Seek out the Lord and his might; constantly seek his face"
(Psalm 105:3-4).

G arrett grew up as an only child to parents who were both lawyers in Florida. He is a senior in college, and after spending the previous summer on a mission trip to Haiti, he is preparing to ask the vocation director of a Benedictine abbey about how to apply. He told his parents about this idea and they brought up many good questions he had not considered. Now he has some fear about what the application process entails.

If, like Garrett you are interested in applying to a religious community, you will have to work closely with the vocation director. There is no substitute for that. Some religious communities will have on their website, or will openly tell inquirers, how their application process works. Other communities won't have much online and expect candidates to bring it up of their own accord—almost as a litmus test to demonstrate the seriousness of their interest.

If you want to enter, do exactly what you are told by the vocation director. If you are not willing to be docile to his instructions, you will not be able to survive religious formation.

This chapter gives some advice on the application process to help men like Garrett who have some apprehension. In addition to some matters that are self-evident, we want to share with you some spiritual insights to guide your heart as you apply. As the Psalmist says, "let hearts that seek the Lord rejoice!"

A firm intention to enter religious life

In order to reach a destination, especially when the travel is difficult, you need a plan. If you don't, you're not going arrive. That sounds reasonable, right? If you live in Nebraska and want to visit New York City, you need to have a firm intention and carefully consider the details. How are you going to get there? How long will it take? Do you already have the money and time for the trip? After you have your plan, with precise dates and movements in mind, you can depart. Without preparation, you may wish to visit New York but you aren't going to make it. A wish isn't the same as a firm intention expressed through a plan. As the saying goes, people do not plan to fail, they fail to plan.

Applying to a religious community is so much more than planning a vacation. If you have a sense that the Lord is inviting you to follow him by living out the evangelical counsels, then with the help of a spiritual director, act on this invitation. Make what certain traditional spiritual authors call in Latin a *propositum religionis*—a firm intention to embrace the religious state.[74] It doesn't mean that you will necessarily stay in the religious community, or even that the community will accept your application, but it does mean that you have a serious resolve to attempt it.

This *propositum religionis* is not just an emotional sentiment. It is an act of your will arising out of an intense devotion for the Lord. It begins before you enter religious life, and if you profess final vows, it can persist for a lifetime. Feelings may come and go, but an act of the will can last all through life. You may have good days and bad days, but you can always remember that you made a willful, lifelong commitment. That act of the will can begin now.

This firm intention to embrace the religious state will help you

---

74. St. Thomas Aquinas, *Summa Theologiae* II-II, q. 189, a. 10, ad 1.

when you will be tempted (and you *will* be tempted) to give up the idea without giving it a fair try. All sorts of obstacles will come your way. You will need the virtue of fortitude, that manly courage to forge ahead, in following the Lord wherever he goes. Just as you would have to carefully plan a visit to New York City, so too do you need to know what is necessary to enter a religious community's initial formation—and then do what is necessary.

Purifying motivations

For the young man who wishes to enter religious life, it's important for him to reflect on why he desires to enter. "I like the habit" may be a way the Lord initially catches your attention for a certain religious community. But the striking appearance of clothing should not be your reason for coming. When St. Benedict writes in his *Rule* about those beginning life at the monastery, he emphasizes that the first quality to be considered is whether a man "truly seeks God."[75]

Now, before you enter, is the time to ask yourself the tough questions. You are going to have to answer the question: "Why do you want to do this?" No one can answer that question for you. Yes, such a choice would be pleasing to the Lord. That is a good answer. But in your life at this time, here and now, what has the Lord done for you to lead you to seriously consider this? Why do you think he has called you?

Be honest about the motivation to apply. Bring it to prayer and discuss it with your spiritual director. Many times, a man may have great motivations mixed with not-so-perfect motivations. Remember that you don't enter religious life because all things (including your motivations) are perfect. You enter because you desire to be perfected in charity. Also, realize that your motivations can be purified over time. It is not uncommon to find that men's reasons change from the inquiry process to the application, from application to the novitiate, from the novitiate to first profession,

---

75. *Rule of St. Benedict*, chap. 58.

from first profession to final profession, and in the perseverance from final profession to death. For example, you may know more of a community's reputation than its members before you enter the novitiate. You may feel at some point that certain members of the community are so impressive that they help you stay—but then later find that you're not staying for them, but for Someone else.

As we discussed earlier, Thomas Aquinas says that religious life is ordered to the perfection of charity. Do you want to be loved by God and to love God fully in return? "What shall I render to the Lord for all his goodness to me?" (Psalm 116) If you want a life of love that is out of this world, religious life provides a specific training for this. All are called to holiness, but the "regular life," lived according to a rule (in Latin: *regula*), provides a tried and proven way of striving toward perfect charity. In the prologue to his *Rule*, St. Benedict says that he has established "a school of the Lord's service."[76] Religious life is a school of love, a school of holiness, a school of living life to the fullest in God's sight. You go to school to learn, not because you are already knowledgeable.

Having thought about your firm intention to enter a community, and the need to purify motivations in this process, let's turn to more practical details about the application process.

The application paperwork

If a holy desire arises in you which becomes a firm commitment to try religious life in a particular community, ask that community's vocation director what you need to do in order to apply. He may have you wait. Some say that a hasty entrance prepares for a hasty exit. Make sure that you listen very carefully to what the vocation director says to you. He may advise you to do any number of things: pray more or pray in a particular way; volunteer; grow in some human virtues; lose weight; visit with more religious in the community; stay close to Christ in frequent confession and daily Mass. Do not be afraid to ask the vocation director questions about how to

---

76. Prologue to the *Rule of St. Benedict*.

be docile to the working of the Holy Spirit in your life, but also do not treat the vocation director like a spiritual director. A vocation director works in the external forum, and reports as is prudent to the officials in his community.

If both you and the vocation director think it would be prudent for you to apply, then consider what needs to be done during the application process. There should be a list of biographical, factual, and canonical questions for you to answer. In the paperwork, you will need to demonstrate that you are healthy. Health is one of the traditional areas of concern for suitability to religious life. If the community admits you to formation, they will be investing a lot in you on various levels. They want to make sure you have what it takes, and that you are strong, healthy, and ready to go. You may have medical paperwork that needs to be filled out by your primary care doctor, dentist, and perhaps other health professionals.

A part of the application may be an autobiographical essay, or series of essays, in which you respond to basic questions about your life. We find this to be an important part of the process—so important that you could write something even before you complete the rest of the application. Putting on paper your "vocation story" can help you understand how God is the ultimate author of your life. It can allow you to "connect the dots" to see what kind of picture is being drawn. So often people lead lives where the "dots" are all over—things seem random, disjointed, in some ways even senseless. But the narrative of Scripture gives us a different vision: "We know that all things work for good for those who love God" (Rom 8:28).

You will need recommendations from others in the application process. Think about the people who could recommend you. The vocation director will give them a form or questionnaire and may also call them to follow up. It may be important for the community to receive one recommendation from a family member. You may be asked for three, four, or five other recommendations. You could ask priests, religious, friends, employers, teachers, or co-workers to testify to your character, depending on what the community's application policy is. Often people are honored and delighted to give a letter of recommendation for religious life. You will put the vocation director in touch with those people, and you'll never see what they wrote about you.

If you decide to ask an employer or a co-worker for a recommendation, proceed with caution. Once your boss knows you're thinking about leaving the company, in his or her mind, there's a danger you will become a "lame duck" and merely somebody to replace—whether or not you even enter religious life. Also be reluctant to tell your co-workers, or anybody who could pass along the information to your place of employment; word travels fast. The last thing you want to do is sabotage your job before being accepted. Even if you are accepted, generally it's best to avoid communicating the news to your boss until the moment you hand in your resignation notice. Also, be sure your boss is the first in the company to know. As a general guideline, never make known your thoughts on possibly leaving your company until you absolutely know that you are definitely leaving and know when you want your last day to be.

You will also need to submit your official sacramental records, affirming that you have been baptized and confirmed. If you have only recently been received into full communion with the Catholic Church, you will need to show what you have been doing during that time to grow in your Catholic faith. The consecration of religious life presupposes full initiation into the sacramental life of the Church. If you are also called to Holy Orders, then you would prepare for that sacrament, being ordained first to the diaconate and then to the priesthood.

You will need to submit transcripts. Some religious communities expect applicants to have at least a bachelor's degree and to demonstrate that they can undertake studies as appropriate to formation. If you are thinking that you are called to be a priest, the Church requires a lengthy program of philosophical and theological studies, usually a total of at least six years of studies. A community wants to make sure that you have the ability to complete the studies required in a demanding program of priestly formation.

The vocation interviews and psychological assessment

In addition to the paperwork, typically you will have a series of formal interviews. (There are also "informal interviews" during the community visits—which we'll discuss next.) In the formal interviews you probably will have an extensive conversation with the vocation director. He may ask you a range of questions about your family, doctrinal and devotional patterns in your life, your history regarding observance of chastity, understanding of the evangelical counsels, your education, your work, your friendships, etc. As you probably suspect at this point, he may ask you some uncomfortable, personal things. Your transparency is important. If you evade certain questions it will be a red flag for the vocation director. Be as forthcoming as possible.

Because psychological health is so important, another formal interview will be with a psychologist who will administer an extensive battery of examinations. He will probe a great number of areas regarding family life, thought patterns, sexual history, personality issues, intelligence, etc. You will be asked about matters pertaining to sexual orientation, pornography, and child abuse. Why is this important? Because a community wants to make sure that, as far as can be known, you have the prerequisite psychological health to live a demanding religious life that has all sorts of pressures and challenges. This is for your sake, the sake of the community, and the sake of the wider Church and world.

Certain psychological illnesses have a range regarding what is acceptable and what is prohibitive. For example, if someone has an obsessive-compulsive disorder that prevents him from performing daily tasks in freedom, then that person should not enter religious life. Others may have a bit of obsessiveness that can be managed. Other psychological illnesses should be considered prohibitive, such as dissociative identity disorder. With a psychological assessment, the counselor will have you sign a release form. All of the results will need to be given to the vocation director, who will share those results with the admissions committee/vocation council and superior.[77]

It is highly likely that you will have formal interviews with members of some sort of admissions committee or vocation council. They may already have access to your autobiographical writing or perhaps even to your complete application. They may ask all sorts of questions about your life and your motivation to seek entrance into their community. Some of them may appear extremely kind; others may appear quite severe.

You may find this process more emotionally straining than what you were expecting. After all, you may think, this community should thank me for wanting to enter. Communities should express proper thanks to God for the gift of vocations. But they must find satisfying answers to important questions. Are you sent by God to this community, or is there something else that is motivating your application? Will you be a good fit for the community? Are you capable of persisting in your vocation? Communities must do their due diligence at every stage of a man's interest in pursuing a religious vocation. Would you want to enter a community that would accept just anybody? Remember, the community desires what is best for you in your journey with the Lord and also what is best for the Church. In the end there is a lot at stake.

The community visits

Notice what the community does and does not do in each of your multiple visits to a religious community. Ask God for the grace to see if you can call this community "home." In *Death of a Hired Man*, Robert Frost writes:

Home is the place where, when you have to go there,

They have to take you in.

---

77. For more on psychology in admissions as well as in formation toward the priesthood, see the Congregation for Catholic Education's *Guidelines for the Use of Psychology in the Admission and Formation for Candidates for the Priesthood* (2008), available online.

As an applicant coming to visit a community, know that you don't have to go there, and they don't have to take you in. If you enter and someday make final profession, you have found a home forever.

During this time of application, you'll be praying, eating, and chatting with the community. These times are no less important than the "formal interviews." Community members not on the admissions board may give feedback to the vocation director from their interactions with you in the external forum. It is possible that you'll be meeting certain community members for the first time during this application process. As the saying goes, you never have a second chance to make a first impression. Here are some practical pointers for these informal visits, which will also serve you well during the times of formal interviews.

Be friendly. Smile. Look like you're happy to be in the community, and express gratitude for the opportunity to be there, for the prayer, for the food, for the conversation. If you're not happy to be there or grateful for their hospitality, why would you continue in the application process? If you are happy and grateful, let it be heard and seen. Before their departure, some men will write a letter to the community via the vocation director, thanking them for their hospitality. The superior may post the letter on the community bulletin board for the members of the community to read.

Be humble. Do not brag about what you have done, or focus on yourself. People will ask you questions about your life. Be honest and straightforward with them. In return, ask them questions about their lives and about their community. Without appearing like you are interviewing them, ask them such things as what brought them to the community, their assignments over the years, what advice they have for you, etc. Even if you are quiet by nature, it is very important to have meaningful conversations during your visit. Conversely, if you are normally very talkative, be sure to listen at least as much as you speak.

Have the clothing and comportment that wouldn't get in the way of social interactions. For example, in many cases, business casual dress is appropriate attire when visiting a religious house. Give a proper, confident handshake. Look people in the eye, without staring, when talking with them. Let people see that you can be yourself, as someone who is real and not putting on an act. A good sense of humor can be helpful. Relax when you enter a community's house. It is a moment of grace for you to learn first-hand about religious life. Sometimes men are so desperate to be accepted by a community that they pretend to be something they aren't.

It is clear when a man comes to visit how serious he is by the way he presents himself. Even if you don't join that community, you will still be a better Catholic man as a result. Religious want what is best for you, for their community, and ultimately for the Church. If something about your visit or interviews does not make sense to you, have the courage to speak openly but humbly with the vocation director about it.

The community's decision regarding your application

Many men express interest in a religious vocation but don't make it to the application process. This can happen for all sorts of reasons: being led to a different state of life such as marriage; being caught in a sinful pattern of behavior prohibitive to religious life; losing a holy desire for religious life; having debt; having unsuitable physical or psychological health; being bound by commitments to the world or to persons in the world. Some of the reasons may be good reasons, some may not be so good. In any case, lots of men don't even apply. If you do apply, you will hear one of three replies: no, not now, or yes. Let's consider each of these decisions.

If you apply and are not accepted, it can be very difficult. Just as there's a range of reasons for not applying, there's also a range of reasons for not being accepted. It may be something about not being the right fit with that religious community. A community considers only whether it is right to accept an applicant to their way of life, at this time and place. It is not considering whether you are going to heaven, or even whether you have a religious vocation. Sometimes great saints are told no when they go to one religious community but are accepted in another. It's possible that this is what is happening in your case. It's also possible that something surfaced during your application process that communicates it would be best for you not to be in religious life. It's possible that the vocation director or the community's superior simply has a gut instinct that says "no." If you want to ask the vocation director a question about this decision, do so right then and there, and then move on. His work as vocation director is done, and so is yours with that community. Talk with your spiritual director about what not being accepted to the community means for your life. He can help you and offer some possibilities for the future. Re-dedicate your life to God and to thinking about where God wants you to be: striving toward holiness. Never give up on God, as he never gives up on you. Remember that the Lord has a wonderful plan for your life, regardless of the answer from a particular community.

Another answer you could hear is: not now. In fact, this is a common answer. The community might want you to make more progress in certain areas of your life, such as growth in human virtues, a longer period of chaste living, more time to get to know the community, more work, a completion of an academic degree, payment of loans before entrance into the community, or simply more life experience and maturity. You can take such an answer as a formative opportunity for your life by talking with your spiritual director about it. Feel free to ask the vocation director to be honest with you as to why he believes now is not the time for you to enter formation. Ask if there's some clear benchmark to achieve, such as the completion of a degree or the payment of loans, or something else. Perhaps it is again something of a gut instinct on the part of the vocation director or his community's superior. If the vocation director is encouraging you, put together a tentative plan of action with him. Then make a detailed plan and timeline with your spiritual director. Feed your holy desires. If you are not enthusiastic in your desire to enter, the community may slow you down.

If you are accepted, ask the vocation director what steps need to be taken. Talk with your spiritual director about what is advised and see how in the recesses of your heart God is preparing you to receive great graces—often through suffering. Remember, you are being invited to offer your body as a living sacrifice in a religious community. Stay focused as you prepare to take the next step in your life of entering formation.

Conclusion

If you are thinking about the possibility of one day applying to a community, even if you are not ready to apply, it's a good idea to have a serious conversation with its vocation director. Some men make the mistake of waiting until the last minute to ask difficult questions about whether they should apply. They might learn of some obstacle in that conversation that could have been handled appropriately six months earlier. Just because you ask about the application process does not necessarily mean that you're going to apply. Normally when a man asks the vocation director good questions about the application process and what would be involved if he applied, it shows that he wants to prepare himself.

Some men find the application process to be a demanding spiritual experience. It's true that your vocation director may test you. He's not a mere recruiter, after all. A vocation director must function as a sort of gatekeeper, and a community begins its scrutiny of you before the application process. Yes, the community *begins* its scrutiny there. More testing will come your way, if you enter the community. Look at the application as a process that many thousands have gone through before you, a process that allows the Church to think with you what the Lord has planned for your life.

Our chapter began with the story of Garrett, who has some fear about the application process. If you have some fear, think about how the Lord at this time can purify your fears. Sometimes people will talk about the purification of loves, as our loves can be easily disordered and need to be put in proper order. But our fears also need to be ordered. Once they are purified, we can see that the first stage of wisdom, the first of the gifts of the Holy Spirit, is fear of the Lord. Once we have the proper fear of the Lord, nothing—not even a daunting application process and an intimidating vocation director—can make us afraid. Do not be afraid!

Always keep God in mind, despite the all-too-human aspects of the process such as travel and paperwork. If God wants your application to be accepted, it will be accepted. It's possible, however, that you may learn that you need to follow Jesus in some vocation other than religious life. Resolve now to serenely accept the Lord's will for your life.

Mary, my mother, pray for me so that I may know what God wants and then apply myself completely to doing it.

CHAPTER 11

ENTERING THE LIFE AND STAGES OF FORMATION

*"This is how it is with the kingdom of God; it is as if a man
were to scatter seed on the land and would sleep and rise night
and day and the seed would sprout and grow, he knows not
how. Of its own accord the land yields fruit, first the blade,
then the ear, then the full grain in the ear. And when the
grain is ripe, he wields the sickle at once, for the harvest has
come" (Mark 4:26-29).*

When Daniel was growing up at St. Mary's parish in a west Texas town, he knew that a young man from his parish entered a monastery somewhere far away. The parish prayed frequently for the man, who took the name Brother Angelus. Daniel always thought "Brother Angelus" was an unusual name. For some reason, although Daniel barely knew Brother Angelus, his story made a deep impression on him. He had only a vague memory of the fellow before he left for religious life. He rarely came back, but each time he did Daniel thought it was good to see a monk in a habit. (He had thought only nuns in old times wore habits; he didn't realize that habits are worn by some religious men today.) After about ten years, it was announced that Brother Angelus was now Father Angelus. He had been ordained a priest and was going to offer a Mass of Thanksgiving at St. Mary's. Now a college student, Daniel is wondering what happened to Brother Angelus during those years. Daniel himself has become interested in the possibility of being a religious who goes off to a distant country to be a missionary. He can't shake what he calls his "crazy idea." He's wondering what would happen to him if he entered a religious community.

What is it like to be in religious formation? It's a bit like the seed in the parable from Mark 4 given above. Something inside begins to grow, and you know not how. Those who are growing toward spiritual maturity don't know all the details of what happens in their spiritual life; it is a mystery beyond full comprehension even to the saints themselves. Religious formation is the soil where the seed can grow.

Whereas Daniel was initially fascinated by Brother Angelus's habit and change of name, he is now learning that the most significant change is internal—the internal transformation of a man walking the path toward perfect charity. That path is long; it lasts a lifetime. No wonder, then, that initial formation takes several years. Its duration ensures that a man knows what path he is on, its dangers and opportunities, and how it is meant to lead to a perfection of love.

Twenty-five years after the close of the Second Vatican Council, the Congregation for Institutes of Consecrated Life and Societies of Apostolic Life (CICLSAL) issued an instruction called *Directives on Formation for Religious Institutes* (1990), available online. It's a goldmine of information on the life and stages of formation. While some things will always be holy mysteries, such as the life of grace; other things can be known with clarity, such as how one goes from being a novice to temporary profession. The Church provides a standard, and each community has its appropriation. Religious communities have vast differences among them, but the Church does give general expectations about what their formation should have in common.

Some institutes post their rule/constitutions online and are eager for people to read them. If you enter a community, you'll be studying that community's legislation closely in formation. Sometimes people wonder why one community does something differently from others. It could be that they have an approved proper law (legislation particular to a community). Approved proper law is to be followed, even when there's a conflict with the more universal norm of law, unless it is expressly forbidden.[78] For one example, the Jesuits have proper law regarding profession that is different from the *Code of Canon Law*.[79]

We'll now consider the life of formation in the evangelical counsels. In religious life we never tire of concentrating on poverty, chastity, and obedience, because the profession of the evangelical counsels most especially expresses how we follow Jesus.[80] That's our life. Then we will take a tour through the stages of formation: postulancy, novitiate, temporary vows, formation after a final profession, and ongoing or permanent formation.

Life of Formation in the Evangelical Counsels

Every form of religious life expresses the evangelical counsels, as recognized by the Church in approving the rule/constitutions of

---

78. Universal law's deference to particular law is called the principle of subsidiarity. Cf. *Code of Canon Law*, can. 20.

79. A man called to be a Jesuit priest makes a profession after a two-year novitiate, and the next time he may be invited to a profession follows a tertiaship after some years of priestly ministry.

80. *Code of Canon Law*, can. 598: "§1. Each institute, attentive to its own character and purposes, is to define in its constitutions the manner in which the evangelical counsels of chastity, poverty, and obedience must be observed for its way of living. §2. Moreover, all members must not only observe the evangelical counsels faithfully and fully but also arrange their life according to the proper law of the institute and thereby strive for the perfection of their state."

each institute.[81] If the Church has approved the rule/constitutions, then you know the Church has said that this is an authentic way of following the Lord according to the Gospel. This formation in the evangelical counsels occurs in every phase of formation, although one should note the significant difference between "not yet in vows" and "in vows." When you're not yet in vows, you prepare to make a vow by living out aspects of the evangelical counsels. We'll now consider each of the three counsels, focusing on what the Church teaches for structuring religious life and providing some real-life commentary.

We begin with poverty. The Church expects all religious to be "poor in fact and in spirit" and so to have a life "foreign to earthly riches."[82] We want to quote in full two points given on poverty by the 1990 *Directives*, and then provide some illustration.

- There are young people who, before entering the religious life, enjoyed a certain amount of financial independence and were accustomed to obtain by themselves all that they wished. Others find themselves at a higher level of life within a religious community than they had in their childhood or during their years of study or work. Instruction in poverty should take account of the history of each one. It should also be remembered that among certain cultures, families expect to gain by what appears to them to be an advance for their children.

- It is of the nature of the virtue of poverty to be engaged in a

---

81. An institute's book of constitutions is usually prefaced by a letter of the Church's official approval of the legislation. The Order of Preachers updates its *Book of Ordinations and Constitutions* at every General Chapter (now celebrated every three years). By exemption, the Dominicans are excused from submitting its legislation to the Holy See for approval. (The patron saint of canon law, St. Raymond of Penyafort, was the third Master [Supreme Moderator] of the Order of Preachers.)

82. *Code of Canon Law*, can. 600: "The evangelical counsel of poverty in imitation of Christ who, although he was rich, was made poor for us, entails, besides a life which is poor in fact and in spirit and is to be led productively in moderation and foreign to earthly riches, a dependence and limitation in the use and disposition of goods according to the norm of the proper law of each institute."

life of work, in humble and concrete acts of renunciation, of divestiture, which render religious freer for their mission; to admire and respect creation and the material objects placed at their disposal; to depend upon the community for their level of life; to desire faithfully that "all should be in common," and "that to each one is given what is needed" (Acts 4:32, 35).

Within the same religious community, you can have someone who comes from a family with many millions of dollars in investments and someone whose family struggled after immigrating to this country to provide the basics of food, clothing, and shelter. More men entering religious life today in the U.S. were born outside this country, and some of them come from cultures that perceived the religious life as a means of gaining social respect and advancement. Others come to a religious community without the emotional support of their parents, who think their sons are throwing away their opportunities for a comfortable and secure life. Some become religious after giving up six-figure salaries, and others come to religious life after begging to have their college loans paid off.[83]

In the U.S. before the Second Vatican Council, some men's communities that were urban had rural novitiates—and required their men to do some farm work. Today it is still common for men to do work that emphasizes humble obedience. It is said that the novitiate really begins when you start painting walls (or scrubbing floors, or sweeping stairwells, or doing dishes, or chopping wood, or pulling garden weeds). If the novice master tells you to paint walls which you have painted before and don't think need painting again, don't tell him that. Trust us. It most likely won't go over well.

Also, religious communities will often make sure that those in initial formation work with and for the poor. If you find yourself griping (vocally or just in your heart) about how your religious

---

83. If you need academic loans paid off, ask the institute that you're considering what is recommended. There exist societies founded to help people pay off their loans before entering religious life. To take two examples, consider the Labouré Society and the Mater Ecclesiae Fund for Vocations, both with information available online.

house doesn't have your favorite cereals for breakfast, sometimes being with the poor who are hungry or who do not eat nutritious meals can give you a reality check. The involuntary poor can't get a daily order at Starbucks.

The Church also provides detailed instruction on formation in chastity. The Church wants communities to provide a formation regarding "the obligation of perfect continence in chastity."[84] According to the 1990 *Directives*, formation in chastity includes such principles as:

- preserving joy and thanksgiving for the personal love in which each one is held, and is chosen, by Christ

- encouraging frequent reception of the sacrament of reconciliation, recourse to regular spiritual direction, and the sharing of a truly sisterly or brotherly love within the community, which is brought about by frank and cordial relationships

- explaining the value of the body and its meaning, acquiring an elementary physical hygiene (sleep, exercise, relaxation, nourishment, etc.)

- giving basic notions on masculine and feminine sexuality, with their physical, psychological, and spiritual connotations

- helping in matters of self-control, on the sexual and affective level, but also with respect to other instinctive or acquired needs (sweets, tobacco, alcohol)

Now what does all this mean? The Church wants religious communities to have a comprehensive formation plan regarding chastity. Some aspects deal with strengthening the virtue of temperance (the virtue that moderates our use of pleasures) and practical matters of properly eating, drinking, resting, and socializing.

---

84. *Code of Canon Law*, can. 599: "The evangelical counsel of chastity assumed for the sake of the kingdom of heaven, which is a sign of the world to come and a source of more abundant fruitfulness in an undivided heart, entails the obligation of perfect continence in celibacy."

Limits and boundaries are important. You may need to go to bed at a certain time and get up at a certain time. You may have restrictions regarding snacks—whether that be a community policy, an initial formation policy, or something that your formator tells you as an individual. You may not be able to have your preferred brand of beer, not only because of poverty but also because of chastity. Limiting your alcohol intake can help you have a stronger virtue of temperance to help in matters of chastity.

Of great importance is having a regular confessor who can not only absolve you of sin, but also provide counsel amid your temptations to unchastity. Also, there are some basic matters in the external forum that you would need to discuss with your formator. A formator needs to hear from a man, in so many words, that he is relying on God, desires to live religious life, and can—with God's help—lead the chastity of religious life. If a man finds that he is not called to live the chastity expected in religious life, he should leave the community. By the way, the young St. Thomas More of Tudor England loved the Carthusian life and spent much time with the Carthusian monks—but knew he was meant to be married. After his first wife died, he quickly married another woman, a widow, who became the step-mother for his children.

A man in initial formation needs to have a healthy sense of his masculinity, the meaning of sex as the marital act, and marriage and family in a world increasingly hostile to the chaste life. Usually men have seen disasters regarding the misuse of sex, in their own lives or in lives of those very close to them (such as parents, siblings, or friends). A man who learns in initial formation to have real chastity can experience freedom—even though he should not expect temptation will simply disappear. He needs what the church calls "affective maturity," in which he can deal virtuously with both men and women as an adult man whose heart is set on God, ready to accept the call to live chaste celibacy for the sake of the kingdom. The affective maturity of a religious will allow him to exercise a spiritual fatherhood of others.

Although not explicit in the *Directives on Formation for Religious*

Institutes, we also want to touch upon the question of homosexuality and religious formation. The Congregation for Catholic Education says that the Church "cannot admit to the seminary or to holy orders those who practise homosexuality, present deep-seated homosexual tendencies or support the so-called 'gay culture.'"[85] Rome's teachings on the priesthood bind equally those in diocesan formation and religious formation toward the priesthood. While this document does not pertain to religious brothers, the Church's concern also is to be prudently applied to religious formation in general.

After considering poverty and chastity, the same document turns to obedience. The Church wants religious to imitate Christ, who was obedient until death (Phil 2:8), and so submit their will.[86] Sometimes men might be frightened about what obedience entails, especially if they have heard strange horror stories of what some young brothers were required to do. The Church is concerned about protecting rights and does not want communities to become cults with cult leaders who take the law into their own hands and play mind games on community members, forcing them to do acts inappropriate to human dignity. For an example of a person's rights in a religious institute, the *Code of Canon Law* says:

> Members are to approach superiors with trust, to whom they can freely and on their own initiative open their minds. Superiors, however, are forbidden to induce the members in any way to make a manifestation of conscience to them.[87]

Now consider a couple of the 1990 *Directives'* goals of formation in obedience:

---

85. See *Instruction Concerning the Criteria for the Discernment of Vocations with regard to Persons with Homosexual Tendencies in view of their Admission to the Seminary and to Holy Orders* (2005), no. 2.

86. *Code of Canon Law,* can. 601: "The evangelical counsel of obedience, undertaken in a spirit of faith and love in the following of Christ obedient unto death, requires the submission of the will to legitimate superiors, who stand in the place of God, when they command according to the proper constitutions."

87. *Code of Canon Law,* can. 630 §5.

• that to give oneself in obedience, it is first necessary to be conscious of one's existence. Candidates need to leave the anonymity of the technical world, to know themselves as they are, and to be known as persons, to be esteemed and loved.

• that for obtaining obedience, the witness of the elder members in a community has greater influence on the young than any other theoretical consideration. Still, a person who makes the effort to obey as Christ did, and in Christ, can succeed in overcoming less edifying examples.

As for the first point, it may sound strange to hear "it is first necessary to be conscious of one's existence." What does that mean? Some men find that in religious formation they get to know the real meaning of life. Computers, puppets, and trained dogs don't go into religious formation; it's only for people with immortal souls who think and love. Only a self-possessed man can give himself away to God. You need to know who you are in order to be formed. You may not like your formator or superior, but you still need to do the dishes, learn to be cantor, sit in the same spot for an hour to be social, or whatever else you're asked to do—as long as it is not a matter of sin. Always remember that obedience, like the other evangelical counsels, is primarily about your relationship with the Lord.

Another point from the *Directives* mentions "less edifying examples" of religious life which you are likely to encounter. They too will be important for your formation, as you'll need to be able to rely more and more on God to be formed for holiness. Just don't completely discount "the less edifying examples" of persons who live religious life, as that would be unfairly judging your brethren. Sometimes a grouchy brother can surprise you with a profound spiritual insight.

Stages of Formation

Now that we have reviewed some structural basics of formation in the evangelical counsels, let's address the stages of formation with the help of the *Directives on Formation for Religious Institutes,* other teachings and laws of the Catholic Church (especially the *Code of Canon Law*), and some common sense gained from living religious life and doing formation work. Keep in mind that this is a general overview, and religious communities have, at times, different terminology or ways of doing formation.

Here is a basic chart showing a typical progression of formation:

STAGE	TIME
Postulancy	0-3 years[88]
Novitiate	Usually 1 year[89]
Temporary Vows	3-6 years[90]
Initial Formation after Final Profession	0-3 years[91]
Permanent Formation (after Initial Formation)	Until death

Postulancy (a.k.a. Pre-Novitiate, Candidacy, Affiliation)

Postulancy is an "exploration phase" when you get to know the religious community. Some institutes accept men for this postulancy stage and have them live in community while taking classes. Some take philosophy classes at a university especially if they hope to be clerical candidates. Other classes may be offered in-house, such as instruction on the institute, its history and charism, its spirituality, and its liturgical practice. Often concurrently with taking classes the man will be engaged in some sort of ministry. If the man is already

---

88. Typically, a few months, depending on the institute's proper law.

89. Must be at least one year and may (rarely) be as long as two years, before first profession.

90. Must be at least three years, and there may be multiple temporary professions for a man.

91. For clerical candidates, there must be further formation in preparation for ordinations to the diaconate and the priesthood. For religious brothers, there may be further formation akin to the formation before final profession. All religious after initial formation are in permanent, or continuing formation, until death.

living with the community, he can see close-up for himself what the community is and does. This also allows the community to see who the man is and what he does in his new religious environment in preparation for the novitiate.

The *Code of Canon Law* lists a few requirements regarding entrance into the novitiate.[92] The major superior of the institute must admit him. He must have "the health, suitable character, and sufficient qualities of maturity to embrace the proper life of the institute." Maturity is of great importance. If you don't have the maturity to receive the proper formation of the novitiate as the Church intends, you will have serious difficulties if you continue in religious life. The candidate for the novitiate must be at least seventeen years old, not in a bond of marriage and normally not in a bond to some other religious or apostolic community. He must not be induced by force, grave fear, or fraud, and the superior who received him must likewise be free. The Code continues that a superior should not admit "secular clerics" (diocesan priests) without consulting their "proper ordinary" (their bishop), nor those so burdened by debts they cannot repay. A candidate must show proof of being baptized, confirmed, and free to enter religious life. If a man was previously in formation, then documentation needs to be obtained from the bishop, major superior, or seminary rector—depending upon the man's personal situation. It is common that a man who has been in formation elsewhere, will have that experience influence his perception of the new formation experience—whether that be good or bad. An institute's proper law may give additional impediments or simply conditions that should be fulfilled before novitiate.

If a community has a postulancy, formally speaking, then that community most likely has a postulancy director. The director might also have some sort of formation team or council, and the director, after consulting others, would need to advise the major superior of the institute on what should be done regarding a postulant's promotion to the novitiate. Depending on the community,

---

92. *Code of Canon Law*, cann. 641-45.

a postulant may automatically become a novice, or he may need to petition further to enter the novitiate. The word postulant comes from the Latin verb *postulare*, to ask. A postulant asks to enter the community as a novice.

Just to be explicit about a pattern in formation: in every step of the process, it is the major superior of the institute who has the final word about acceptance of a petition. That major superior is the "ordinary" of the institute and has "ordinary" power over the institute; similar to how a bishop of a diocese has "ordinary" power over his diocese. Thus, the major superior has final authority on everything from a vocation application, to a petition for vows, to a petition for Holy Orders. For an abbey, the major superior is the abbot. For a religious institute structured by provinces, the major superior is the provincial. A religious institute also commonly has a supreme moderator or superior general. Normal matters of vocation and formation usually do not go to the attention of the supreme moderator, as the major superior has proper authority in these cases.

If a man has been approved to the novitiate, and he still wants to proceed, he enters the novitiate. If one of these two conditions is absent, he does not—and so goes elsewhere. An age-old custom regarding all the levels of formation is that if there's a serious doubt about whether a man should be advanced, it is better that he not be approved for the next step.

Novitiate

Whereas the Church allows for great variety of postulancy experiences (and even does not require a formal postulancy), the Church expresses considerable expectations regarding the novitiate. The Church gives this careful definition:

> The novitiate, through which life in an institute is begun, is arranged so that the novices better understand their divine vocation, and indeed one which is proper to the institute, experience the manner of living of the institute, and form their

mind and heart in its spirit, and so that their intention and suitability are tested.[93]

Notice how this is the stage when "life in institute is begun." Even if you had a three-year postulancy (which is rare for religious institutes), life in the institute hasn't yet properly begun. Also, you are not a religious until you profess vows. The novitiate is the time for you to be immersed in the life and prepare for profession, if that is what you and the community think God wants at the end of the novitiate.

An institute's novitiate typically lasts one year and it may not last more than two years.[94] Novices must spend twelve months in the community of the novitiate, although the major superior may allow novices to spend some of that time in another house of the institute.[95] The care of novitiate formation is given to one director, sometimes called the master of novices or novice master. He may have an assistant and may also have a formation council or team to give further assistance within the community. The wider religious community is also called to support this novitiate formation. A novice may freely leave the novitiate at any time to return to the world, and a religious community has its proper law on how a novice may be dismissed from the community.

The Church has the following expectations concerning novices:[96]

- they are to be led to cultivate human and Christian virtues

- through prayer and self-denial, they are to be introduced to a fuller way of perfection

---

93. *Code of Canon Law*, can. 646.

94. *Code of Canon Law*, can. 648 §3: "The novitiate is not to last longer than two years."

95. *Code of Canon Law*, can. 648 §1.

96. *Code of Canon Law*, can. 652 §2.

- they are to be taught to contemplate the mystery of salvation and to read and meditate on the sacred scriptures

- they are to be prepared to cultivate the worship of God in the sacred liturgy

- they are to learn a manner of leading a life consecrated to God and humanity in Christ through the evangelical counsels

- they are to be instructed regarding the character and spirit, the purpose and discipline, the history and life of the institute

- they are to be imbued with love for the Church and its sacred pastors.

Religious generally find their novitiate to be a very intense experience. Many religious will tell novitiate stories for the rest of their lives. Some love the formation director. Some don't like him. Some think he's a saint—regardless of whether or not they like him. Others think he's far from a saint, especially if they don't like him.

Novitiate is like boot camp: an intensive immersion designed to launch you into religious life. It will either whet your desire to continue in the community through a temporary profession, or reveal to you (and/or the community) that you should pursue God's call to be holy elsewhere.

Temporary Vows

At the end of novitiate, a man makes temporary vows which normally last for one to three years. A man needs to be in temporary vows at least three years before making final profession, but the time varies depending on the community's practice and the individual circumstances.[97]

The Church requires individual institutes to have a complete

---

97. A final profession may be anticipated by three months short of a period of three full years. See *Code of Canon Law*, can. 657 §3. The time of temporary profession may be extended by the competent superior, to a maximum of six years, or—if permitted by proper law—even nine years, which is rare. See *Code of Canon Law*, can. 657 §2.

plan of formation whereby the men can lead the proper life of the institute in a systematic manner. It is common for men in temporary vows to pursue a degree or certification.

If a man is preparing for the priesthood in the religious community, then he will experience the extensive priestly formation prescribed by the *Program of Priestly Formation*.[98] Regarding studies, the Church expects two years of pre-theology, mostly philosophy, and four years of theology. A man preparing for Holy Orders needs to make a final profession of vows before ordination to the diaconate. In some communities, there will be a celebration of final vows one day and ordination to the diaconate the very next day. In other communities, a man does not proceed to priestly studies until having professed final vows—and so the time in temporary vows is not a time for study toward the priesthood. Community practices vary widely among religious institutes. If you hope someday to be a religious priest, you should ask the vocation director of a community what is involved in preparing for professions and ordinations.

This period of temporary vows has great importance because you are, in fact, a religious, but you haven't yet made a permanent commitment. You could leave the institute after your temporary vows. Or, for grave reason, you could petition to be dispensed from the remainder of time in temporary vows.[99] You could be asked to leave, or even be the subject of a process of dismissal, but you also have canonical rights that need to be respected by the community.[100]

What sort of religious you are during temporary vows will be an indicator of what sort of religious you will be in perpetual (i.e., final) vows—if you take that definitive step in a religious community. Are you one who puts on a show to jump through hoops and please the right people at the right time, or do you live by the law of the Lord to please him? In the midst of this very important time of

---

98. At the time of this book, it is still the fifth edition of the *Program of Priestly Formation* (available online) for both diocesan and religious formation toward priestly ordination.

99. *Code of Canon Law*, can. 688 §2.

100. *Code of Canon Law*, cann. 694-704.

testing, take your delight in the Lord. Lean on him during this intense experience of prayer, study, community work, and apostolate. We pray in Psalm 37: "If you find your delight in the Lord, he will grant your heart's desire."

Further Initial Formation After Final Vows

Just as there's a petition for temporary vows, there's a petition for final vows (vows until death). This requires many detailed steps, involving a formal petition, examination, recommendation, votes, and approval from the major superior. Depending on the institute and its observance of poverty, it is before final profession that you may need to dispose of all monies and goods, for example, cashing out a 401k. That final profession would bind you to the observance of the full life of the institute. In some monasteries, a funeral pall is placed over the man lying prostrate to symbolize his death. Some other religious lie in a cruciform position on the floor. Various dramatic gestures are made to signify giving one's whole life to God as a living sacrifice.

In some communities, once a man professes perpetual or final vows he is no longer in initial formation within his community. In other communities, a clerical student is in initial formation until his ordination to the priesthood (or even for a time afterwards), and so he still has more initial formation as a religious—not just considered as a clerical candidate. Communities have different laws and customs. Ask the vocation director of a community what that community sees as the end of initial formation. Obviously, ordination to the priesthood has great significance for religious in clerical formation, and the period between diaconate ordination and priesthood ordination is very formative in how the religious exercises ordained ministry.

Ongoing or Permanent Formation

The Church has this law: "Throughout their entire life, religious are to continue diligently their spiritual, doctrinal, and practical formation."[101] Initial formation begins religious life, and ongoing or permanent formation in the virtues, prayer, study, ministry, and the religious observances of community life continues until death. Because formation is classically understood as what forms a religious at the beginning, the word formation still commonly refers to initial formation.

Now why does the Church have this stress on permanent formation in strengthening the life of religious? Because there's need. We don't stop learning—or at least we don't stop needing to learn. God continues to call in new circumstances, and we need to respond to that call. Besides, all sorts of ways of life need a boost to help people stay on the right track. You shouldn't be complacent about what matters most to you. Religious life is meant to be intense, an intense way of love. Because there's no limit to love during this life on earth, we can always be formed more and more in our path toward perfect charity. Also, at special times in the life of a religious after final vows, some serious formation about an aspect of the life, such as obedience, chastity, or poverty, needs to occur.

The 1990 document on formation for religious speaks of "a severe crisis" that can occur at any age as a result of external factors or directly personal factors. Can you think of what could make a crisis for a religious after final vows? It could be an unexpected or unwanted change of assignment, a failure, a terrible injustice committed against the religious, a grave problem in the community, lack of comprehension about natural things or lack of faith about things revealed, severe temptations, patterns of sin, illness, addiction, falling in love—and not receiving God's love and loving him in return through the evangelical counsels. Yes, some religious have terrible problems because they don't receive love and give love virtuously. If you become a religious and at some point, experience a severe crisis, recall how you have become "a living sacrifice." Nearly everyone

---

101. *Code of Canon Law*, can. 661.

experiences crises in life. The question is what would you do if you experience a crisis after professing final vows.[102]

We want you to be realistic. Do not think that living religious life is easy. There are all sorts of difficulties in being a man, in being a Christian, and in being a religious. A religious formation doesn't remove all problems in your life. It forms you to be a man among men, bonded together in the fraternal life, to pick up the cross and follow Jesus wherever he goes by living the evangelical counsels with him.

Conclusion

Just as a farmer doesn't know all the scientific details of the growth of a seed to a plant, so a Christian doesn't know all the mysterious details of the growth of the Kingdom of God in the soul. Religious life is an intense experience of the Kingdom. Changes occur within a religious during formation, and sometimes the changes are undetectable even to those religious.

Yet, with all the mysteriousness of religious life, we want you to think about the life and stages of formation. Some elements can be learned without much difficulty. The novitiate may feel like three years. But, as you can see from what we said in this chapter, that's a canonical impossibility. This chapter has been full of facts so you can be prepared for what the Church wants in formation. In the next chapter, we'll explore what to expect, and not to expect, in religious life.

> *Queen of mercy, you were most docile to the working of the*
> *Holy Spirit in your life. Pray that I may also be docile to the*
> *formation God wants me to have.*

---

102. Religious should not have quick recourse to petitioning for what the Church calls "exclaustration," a temporary time away from the community whereby one is freed from some obligations but is still under the care of superiors, or for definitive departure from your institute. See *Code of Canon Law*, cann. 686-87.

✠

CHAPTER 12

WHAT TO EXPECT
(AND NOT TO EXPECT)
IN RELIGIOUS LIFE

"If anyone wishes to come after me, he must deny himself and take up his cross daily and follow me. For whoever wishes to save his life will lose it, but whoever loses his life for my sake will save it" (Luke 9:23-24)

A senior in high school, Noah is thinking about entering a religious community in a few years, but he has very little idea of what to expect. He is imagining that it will be tough, but that he will have lots of friends, get to wear some cool clothes, and will become a saint—even if the world around him is becoming more confused. It will be a relief from the craziness that he daily experiences in his broken family and in his high school. Surely, religious life will be different, thinks Noah. But how?

St. Luke records our Lord's call to follow him as taking up the cross *daily*. Every day we are to pick up our cross and follow Jesus. People can have all sorts of beautiful things to say about it, but we want to emphasize one obvious thing about this daily experience. The cross is painful. Crosses were not made for comfort, but for suffering and death. To be "a living sacrifice" as St. Paul enjoins is to be conformed each day to the cross of our Lord Jesus Christ.

This pattern of sacrificial living in service to the Lord is already spoken in the wisdom of Ben Sira:

> My child, when you come to serve the Lord, prepare yourself for trials. Be sincere of heart and steadfast, and do not be impetuous in time of adversity. Cling to him, do not leave him, that you may prosper in your last days (Sirach 2:1-3).

The whole second chapter of that Old Testament book is a realistic account of religious life, and we encourage you to meditate on it. If you apply to a religious community and are accepted, you will be tested and tried. Here are some things to expect—and not to expect.

What to expect from God

The first thing to expect is to encounter God himself.

"Wait for the Lord with courage. Be stouthearted, and wait for the Lord" (Psalm 27). Never forget that a vocation is a call from God, and that if your call is authentic, you will have a deep sense of God in your life—his presence, his absence, his goodness, his strangeness, his truthfulness, his beauty, his promise, his providence, his love, and his mercy. If you do not expect God in entering religious formation, please do not enter formation. Yes, God is everywhere, but consecrated religious life clears certain things away, allowing us to be with the Lord in an extraordinary way. Expect God himself. What else matters? You should expect God especially in the sacred liturgy, as religious live an eminently liturgical life. In living out any authentic Christian state of life, a man could make St. Catherine of Siena's prayer his own: "What more could you have given me than the gift of your very self?"[103] Religious are blessed to expect God himself in a profound way.

---

103. St. Catherine of Siena, *The Dialogue*, trans. Suzanne Noffke, O.P., Classics of Western Spirituality (New York: Paulist Press, 1980), no. 167, p. 365.

Expect God to give joy.

Religious communities that attract young men radiate joy. Joy is the effect within your soul when you have present in mind some wonderful good you love. Ultimately, this joy is about God and is meant to be uninterrupted. As St. Paul says, "Rejoice in the Lord always" (Phil 4:4).

Religious life affords opportunities to enjoy many other gifts from the Lord. Chief among these are the other brothers. Some men walk into a religious community expecting a rather grim atmosphere and are stunned to find laughter, lightness of heart, humor, thoughtfulness, smiles, hospitality, and graciousness. When a man chooses to live his life in truth combined with charity, it is joy that binds the two together. If you don't have a sense of joy in a community, there's a problem either in you or the community or both. Joy can exist in great austerity and terrible suffering—so long as there is charity. Without charity, there is no spiritual joy. But if you have charity, you can have joy even when the sacrifice of religious life hurts. Make St. Paul's words your own: "Now I rejoice in my sufferings for your sake, and in my flesh, I am filling up what is lacking in the afflictions of Christ on behalf of his body, which is the church" (Col 1:24).

Expect God to ask you to make deep personal sacrifices beyond what might be obvious.

Yes, living religious life will bring all sorts of objective demands. Beyond what can be seen, God invites you to be a living sacrifice in the depths of your being—in ways that others would not see. You may have some cherished sin or misconception in your heart of which you are unaware, which you eventually realize must be transformed.

Through living religious life, you grow in self-knowledge. A faithful brother discovers things about himself such as persistent, deep-seated selfishness. These and other faults can be made glaringly apparent in your life—many times with the help of your brothers and your formators. Such transformative growth is frequently painful. Expect religious life to offer endless opportunities to be generous and offer your life in sacrifice for the common good, out of love for the Lord. Religious life provides daily opportunities to die to self.

Don't expect God to preserve you from temptation.

Temptations can be so frustrating. If you enter religious life, you may think that you will be freed from certain temptations that strike against your core identity as a Christian man. The early Desert Fathers communicate otherwise. Listen to this: "Abba Anthony said to Abba Poemen, 'This is the great work of a man: always to take the blame for his own sins before God and to expect temptation to his last breath.'" Listen to what is written next: "He also said, 'Whoever has not experienced temptation cannot enter into the Kingdom of Heaven" He even added, 'Without temptations no one can be saved.'"[104] This idea is sometimes expressed in the pithy form: "No salvation without temptation."

Our Lord was tempted after he was baptized. Christians are tempted after their baptism. Religious are tempted after their vows. We're in good company. But why would God allow temptations? St. Thomas Aquinas teaches, "By fighting against concupiscence and other defects to which he is subject, man may receive the crown of victory."[105] In other words, the grace of God will always be sufficient to assist each person in times of temptation. God will not allow you to be tempted without the grace needed to resist the wiles of the enemy. When you face temptation in religious life, be a man and fight for that crown of victory with expectant faith.

Don't expect God to give you allocutions of what to do.

Sometimes men expect to receive some sort of audible call: "Hey, Noah. It's me, God. Kaitlyn is a great young woman, but you

---

104. *The Sayings of the Desert Fathers: The Alphabetical Collection*, rev. ed., translated with a foreword by Benedicta Ward, SLG (Kalamazoo, MI: Cistercian Publications, 1984), p. 2.

105. St. Thomas Aquinas, *Summa Theologiae* III, q. 63, a. 3.

should stop dating her. Join the Franciscans after you graduate from college. Okay?" They tell themselves if they don't hear that, they won't enter a community. No, it doesn't work like that. Yes, the Lord has done some remarkable things to reveal a man's vocation, but normally the Holy Spirit will give you promptings (inspirations) showing you the way without a distinct voice. Similarly, in formation, do not expect something like: "Noah, it's God speaking to you again. Yes, I know you find the novice master difficult. I find him difficult too. Go ahead and make your petition for first vows." Chances are the same absence of allocutions will continue twenty years after first vows. Do expect, however, to grow in your ability to "hear" the Lord within your heart through prayer.[106]

What to expect from others

Expect fraternity.

An only child is not a brother. When you enter a religious community, you should expect brotherhood. Even if you are the only one in formation in your community, you should have a sense of a broad brotherhood. For almost all institutes, this brotherhood is not only about the brethren you see within your community. A brotherhood may stretch well beyond the confines of the walls of a house. Even a Benedictine monk vowed to stability in one monastery has brethren around the world and inherits a tradition that has been in place for 1500 years. This fraternity will be the source of some of your life's most memorable joys and most memorable sorrows, if you continue in religious life.

---

106. "The voice of the Lord in summons, however, is never to be looked for as something which will be heard...in an extraordinary manner. It is rather to be detected and weighed in the signs by which the will of God is customarily made known to prudent Christians." Second Vatican Council, *Presbyterorum Ordinis*, Decree on the Ministry and Life of Priests, no. 11.

Expect correction.

Some people are rarely corrected in their youth. You may on one level know that you're not perfect, but you may be shocked to find out how you are repeatedly corrected in religious life. You will have many opportunities to be corrected by superiors, formators, and peers. Here are some examples from different aspects of religious life, especially from initial formation:

Showing up late and disrupting the community. Singing off-key. Smelling bad. Saying things that amounted to gossip. Talking too much to the beautiful women visitors after Mass on Sundays. Talking too little to the older religious in the community. Being lazy. Receiving a ticket for speeding. Not studying enough. Staying in your room to study too much. Being with the same brother or group of brothers to the exclusion of others. Not being diligent in your house job. Forgetting to clean the bathroom. Not finding time to set the tables right. Being perceived as rude in your ministry. Not smiling. Laughing too much. Not knowing how to shake hands properly. Using ironic humor inappropriate to religious life. Causing a disturbance in the community. Looking like a space-cadet in the sanctuary. Not being hospitable to the community's guests. Showing disdain for work. Staying up too late at night. Looking like you crawled out of bed without any attention to self-care before showing up in the chapel. Doing the right thing, but at the wrong time, in the wrong way, or in the wrong place.

From our years of experience, trust us, the list of corrections could go on and on. Learn now not to be easily offended when someone corrects you. You must trust the process of religious life. It has been around a long time. It works, and there is a centuries-proven wisdom within it. Be a man, and trust that religious life will slowly and gradually bring you to be that man come to full stature in Jesus Christ (cf. Eph 4:13).

Don't expect that you will naturally like everyone in your community, and that they're all wondrous saints.

Frequently when a man makes a vocation weekend he is struck

by the attractiveness of the life and perhaps how far he is from where the members of the community seem to be. From a distance, everyone in your desired living community may look so holy and you might think that you will naturally like them all. You won't need more than a few days as a community member to find out otherwise. Community members typically find others in the community annoying at times. Even saints can be difficult to live with. Members of your community are a work in progress, just like yourself.

Don't expect that you will be understood and accepted in all your ways by your superiors, formators, spiritual director, peers, and senior members of your community.

Many young men have a strong desire to be accepted and appreciated. They will seek ways—consciously or not—precisely to get what they think they deserve. It can come as a shock to them to find out that some in their community think that they really don't belong. Do not expect that everyone is 100% in support of you staying within the community. Believe it or not, this is a normal occurrence within religious life. Your vocation will be tested by fire, including by the fire of community life.

For example, a brother may think you should not remain in initial formation for a specific reason you find difficult to accept. Listen to his concerns, as he deserves to be heard. Those concerns may come to you through a formator, who may or may not agree with that brother. Such listening to others in your community is part of the dynamic of religious life that has been around for centuries and has made many a saint. Your spiritual director has a privileged role in the internal forum to help you grow in holiness. Those in the external forum, too, are also part of your formation. Superiors, teachers, and other community members may have observed things that you, with limited self-knowledge, don't even know about yourself. When these things are brought to light, you must listen.

Isn't it true that everyone has a deep desire to be understood and accepted? This is human nature. The best Christian communities seek a balance between accepting different personalities and challenging men to grow. One example is a man who is over-the-top narcissistic. Every conversation somehow seems to go back to him. He will be asked to look closely at the problem. He should be docile and accept the feedback, even if it comes as a surprise, realizing that correction is an act of charity. "The Lord chastises those whom he loves" (Proverbs 3:12). In this case, the Lord is using others to address the man's narcissism. Religious life, if one surrenders or is docile to it, can hasten personal transformation and help you to grow in holiness. Once again, think about what it means to be "a living sacrifice."

Don't expect that everyone will appreciate the sacrifice that you are making.

Many people do not appreciate the sacrifice of religious life or the contradiction it presents to the world. You will most likely have family members and friends who do not think very highly of what you are doing. Do not be deluded to think that the whole world will thank you for going into religious life. Think of what the world did to the Lord Jesus. Is the servant exempt from what happened to the Master (cf. John 15:20)?

What to expect from yourself

Expect lingering questions, some confusion, disappointment, and loneliness.

You may think that once the novitiate begins God will set everything in order that you may walk on dry ground through the Red Sea, with the waters of chaos walled up to your right and to your left. Would that it were that way! Instead, expect at times to be more like Job—wondering where God is when things are not going as you planned—and you feel empty and alone. God makes his presence known from the whirlwind, and you may have even more questions than answers as you move through religious life.

Expect failure and mercy.

We all fail in various ways. Do not think that because you have entered the life of perfection, that everything will be perfect. The religious life is a path toward perfect charity, but this doesn't mean that you and others in your community will love perfectly, at all times. Religious life is a school of charity—and classes continue through your whole life. You will need repeatedly to ask for mercy, and you will need repeatedly to give mercy.

Expect to be stretched through annoyance.

The Israelites grumbled in the desert. One of the most common faults in religious life is complaining when patience runs low.[107] Isn't it true that it is easier to tear down than to build up? When you find yourself irritated because of your unreasonable formator, your know-it-all classmate, your difficult studies, or your senseless ministry, think about the areas where you need to change. This is the virtue of penance; whereby out of love of God we have sorrow for our past sinfulness and rely on his help to amend our lives. Without the virtue of penance, you will be miserable in religious life. With the virtue of penance, you can be joyful and be set on the road to become a saint.

Expect to be GRACED.

Since you can expect to encounter God, you can also hope for his holiness in your life. Grace transforms the soul especially through the virtues. In Chapter 6, we considered some virtues, especially the three theological virtues: faith, hope, and love. Now let's consider very briefly six other virtues important in religious life. They can be remembered through the acronym GRACED: generosity, responsibility, attentiveness, compassion, engagement, and docility.

> Generosity: Some men get exasperated by how much work they have to do in religious life. Younger men are expected

---

107. See *Rule of St. Benedict*, chap. 5.

to do more manual labor around the house. Guess what? The more senior members of the community have all been there. Work is not only about the many tasks concerning study, the liturgy, ministry, and other house jobs, but also about the work of thinking and talking about all sorts of problems and difficulties both in the community and also in our world. If you become overwhelmed by work during formation, don't "play the victim." Instead, discuss your problems with your superior or formator. But yes, be prepared to grow in generosity in many ways.

Responsibility: You may have had a six-figure income before entering, with major responsibilities for the lives of others; or you may be coming straight from a school which was completely paid for by your family, with little responsibility of your own. In any case, know that you will have responsibility in community life. The first responsibility is for your own formation. Who will be primarily responsible for your formation? You. That's the traditional wisdom of the Church. Yes, formators, superiors, and the community as a whole all have necessary parts to play. But you could be in the holiest, most observant, most loving, best all-around community in the whole world—and not be formed well. Why? Because you did not take adequate responsibility for your formation. Taking responsibility means taking matters to heart, being formed inside-out, praying without ceasing, being honest, and asking questions properly when you don't understand something important. In addition to taking responsibility for your own formation, you'll discover many other responsibilities in work, prayer, community life, and ministry.

Attentiveness: This virtue allows you to know what is needed and do it at the right time and place. Formators want you to notice what is needed and quickly volunteer to do something about it. A man in formation cannot go through life being passive but must be active and be aware of the needs of the wider community. If he is attentive to small matters, he will most likely be attentive to larger matters that affect both his community and the Church in the world. Religious life demands attentiveness.

Compassion: Religious life should inculcate a sense of deep care and concern for others. Many institutes state clearly that they were founded, in one form or another, for the salvation of souls. Have that compassion for the institute's mission and for the brethren within that community. Be ready to forgive. Charity begins at home. If you are compassionate to those in your own community, the Lord will empower you to be compassionate to the world.

Engagement: Some men entering religious life are not accustomed to excel in engagement. They find it easier to withdraw, and sometimes they'll even make prayer or study an excuse for not engaging properly. Don't be a submarine that goes underwater and isn't seen for long stretches of time. Engage in the life that is being given to you, and also have the proper social bearing within your community. For example, if you have meals where people are expected to talk, do not be silent throughout the meal. Think of things to say that would build others up. Communities commonly have a time for silence and a time to talk. Respect such traditions that are formative for you in living the life, but don't use them as an excuse to be withdrawn. Most men need the guidance of the senior members of their community to find the way of virtue in proper engagement.

Docility: This virtue is greatly needed in religious formation. Be teachable. Formation brings about a type of change. If your community notices that you aren't changing while in formation, you will most likely not continue in religious life. Pray to see why docility is so much needed. As St. Paul says, God "encourages us in our every affliction, so that we may be able to encourage those who are in any affliction with the encouragement with which we ourselves are encouraged by God" (2 Cor 1:4).

Don't expect that you will become some other human being.

We don't care if you take on a new name, always wear a religious habit, lose weight (which rarely happens in religious life), become proficient in certain skills, have lots of new friends, and get to do cool things—you will be the same person. Even if you look to an outsider like another St. Francis of Assisi or St. Bruno, you'll be the same person as you were before you entered—with all sorts of personality strengths, weaknesses, temptations, desires, foibles, emotions, and anxieties. You will have the same family at home. Yes, don't forget that you still belong to your family in a profound way that no religious life can alter. You're always your parents' son, even if they are a thousand miles away or are deceased. In being graced, you can have docility and change—but you cannot be changed into different person. As St. Thomas Aquinas teaches, God's grace perfects our human nature; it doesn't destroy nature.[108]

If you find blonde college cheerleaders attractive before you enter a religious community, you will find them attractive when you are in religious life—both in initial formation and years later. If you remember some sexual sin with a girlfriend before you enter, you will remember that sin after you enter. If you have a desire for a wife and children before you enter, you will have a desire for wife and children afterwards, too. Sexual desires have rather significant patterns, and don't expect yourself to change to be someone else. But these sexual desires can also be redeemed and molded for greater zeal and love for the Lord. Even though we all come to religious life with a certain history, for better or for worse, the Lord can and will transform those histories to be points of grace and mercy in helping us to understand ourselves and to show compassion to others.

If the laziness of others gets on your nerves before you enter,

---

108. St. Thomas Aquinas, *Summa Theologiae* I, q. 1, a. 8, ad 2.

guess what will drive you crazy in religious life? If you have a health problem before you enter, yes, it's not that difficult to realize that you will have that same health problem, and it might become worse over the years of formation. If you are a perfectionist, you will be tempted to interpret the command to be perfect even in little things that don't matter much. (Who really cares if the spoon is a half inch or one inch from the knife at a dinner place setting?) If you are a narcissist and do things (consciously or not) to get people's attention or make them like you, your narcissism will persist in religious life—even if it is more masked or subtle.

Don't expect that you will get to do what you want to do.

There's something obvious about giving up the will in religious obedience. Obedience is rather prominent in religious life. But you may be fooling yourself. Even those with a pious mentality of self-denial think deep down that they will be able to do what they want. For some, they think they will be able to live poverty as they would like—but they're wrong. For better or for worse, they will live poverty as their community lives poverty. You may have grandiose dreams of being a great itinerant mission preacher or retreat master, but your community will want you to do parochial work at the same parish for a long time. You may want to be a savvy media evangelizer, but you'll have an assignment in campus ministry. You may want to be a profoundly respected liturgical theologian, but you're needed simply to serve as sacristan. We have found that while our original hopes and dreams in entering religious life have been dashed at one time or another, the Lord is full of surprises in the assignments. In some mysterious way, the Lord purifies, and his grace fills those who say yes in obedience to what they would not have originally chosen to do.

Don't expect that you will have lots of time to pray how you want to pray.

One of the most compelling reasons men enter religious life is the opportunity to pray. That is very good. But even if you enter a contemplative monastery, you will spend lots of time on things that assist the community to function and allow them to pray. Even having liturgical jobs, such as sacristan, music director, cantor, organist, where the job itself is precisely for the Church's prayer, can frustrate religious who would rather just pray like everyone else than worry about the details of liturgical beauty. There are many other tasks in a religious community besides these liturgical ones, and the community may direct you to work in the house, serve in an outside ministry, or recreate more than you would like. Some may think, "But can't I just stay in my room or the chapel and pray the way I want?" No, not all the time. Some of the ways you learned how to pray before entering religious life may end up being your bread and butter in the spiritual life, but expect to be immersed in a form of life that will expand your soul. You will want to be formed in the charism of your community and not just stick to old ways. Have some patience with your new prayer life.

Don't expect that you'll never be bored.

Boredom is a problem that afflicts many people today. Because of instant communication and instant information people get bored rather easily. Also, because people have so many options—places to visit, people to text, foods to eat, shows to watch—they can get rather tired of the familiar and wonder if there's isn't something better available. Boredom doesn't come because of a lack of things for you to do; it comes because of not caring to do what you are doing. Even if you have much to do, you can still get bored—if you don't pour yourself into the task at hand. Take this Latin saying to heart, popular in some religious communities: *Age quod agis*—"Do what you are doing."

Don't expect that the most significant trials in religious life are those that you have in initial formation.

You may realize that you won't like all the details of the novitiate. You may realize that you won't enjoy the difficulties of rigorous study. You may realize that you won't get along with every single person around you. But please don't expect that the worst trials of initial formation will pass when initial formation passes. You would delude yourself if you imagine that after final profession, you won't have trials similar to those you experienced during your formation years. In fact, expect worse trials. The man docile in his formation learns not only to accept and bear the crosses that inevitably come, but also flourishes in the midst of them. The key is flexibility and docility.

Don't expect that you will have great clarity about how your life will actually look.

You may think during religious formation that you will know what your life will look like after formation. It's far better to focus on God's providence and your obedience within the religious community than try to plan out your religious life. Distinguish between what you know will happen and what you don't know will happen. Final profession gives some certainties, but future assignments are unknown. Religious life is an adventure. Expect surprises from the Lord.

Conclusion

These categories of what to expect, and not to expect, from God, others, and yourself in religious life give only a rough sketch. If you're in some way like Noah, whose story begins this chapter, it may help you in some small way. But you don't really know religious life until you experience religious life for yourself. Experience gives you an insight that book-knowledge will never give. Many religious find that their life is extraordinarily full and varied; it's like living a dozen lives, and all are to be lived for Christ. At the same time, if you become a religious, don't fool yourself in imagining that your life is so much busier and more demanding than all others. Think about a young husband and father who has a cranky baby that wakes him up at night, a very stressful job, and a relationship with his wife that requires more work than he expected. That man, too, is called to the perfection of charity and needs God's grace to live his vocation.

Just as every religious has a unique experience, so too every community has its own particular experience of religious life. The various expressions of religious life within the many institutes in the Church today each have their own living traditions of how to form a man—what works and what does not work.

For example, when a religious institute has foundations that go back centuries, you should expect that it will take time to be initiated into that way of life—ancient as it is. If you join a community that is new, there will be different challenges in your formation. In either case, you will have to depend on your brothers to process and understand what will transpire in your life. Only then you will be formed into a consecrated man of God. Trust in God and talk honestly with your spiritual director and formators.

The Lord can and does work through them. Expect much from the Lord—and never forget to brace yourself for his surprises in your life.

Virgin Mother, you waited expectantly nine months for the birth of your Son, our Savior. Pray that I may grow in the virtue of hope for what God will do in my life.

—PART FIVE—

HEARING FROM
OTHER RELIGIOUS

CHAPTER 13

HOLY RELIGIOUS OF THE PAST ON RELIGIOUS LIFE

"We heard with our own ears, O God, our fathers have told us the story of the things you did in their days, you yourself, in days long ago" (Psalm 44).

O ur fathers have told us the story. Religious life has been lived from one generation to the next. We who enter religious life are not its inventors. We receive it—gratefully. Every religious community has a story about its beginning, when the founder received from the Spirit of God a charism, that spiritual gift for the sake of the community. If you enter a religious community, you will hear repeatedly their founding story. If you are meant to be in that community, that founding story will be a part of your own story, and your own story expresses something from that founding story.

In addition to the founding stories, you can find all sorts of reflections, customs, laws, teachings, and actions that express what the religious life is about for a community. This chapter gathers together just a few passages from holy religious in Church history about the meaning of religious life. Such words obviously pertain to the author's own form of religious life, but many times they instantiate something broader than that particular way of life. They tell us about what religious life is.

Before a passage is given, it is prefaced by a few words to put the passage in context in terms of the author, setting, and purpose. We invite you to ponder these words from men who speak across time and space to our hearts today. The Holy Spirit may inspire you to pray in a particular way as a response.

From St. Pachomius (died ca. 348)

Listen first to St. Pachomius, the one credited with beginning coenobitic (community) monasticism. Pay attention to how one who wants to enter the monastery must be tested in a number of ways before he may be admitted to serve in the community and receive the monastic habit.

No. 49: When someone comes to the door of the monastery, wishing to renounce the world and be added to the number of the brothers, he shall not be free to enter. First, the father of the monastery shall be informed [of his coming]. He shall remain outside at the door a few days and be taught the Lord's prayer and as many psalms as he can learn. Carefully shall he make himself known: has he done something wrong and, troubled by fear, suddenly run away? Or is he under someone's authority? Can he renounce his parents and spurn his own possessions? If they see that he is ready for everything, then he shall be taught the rest of the monastic discipline: what he must do and whom he must serve, whether in the *synaxis* [liturgical gathering] of all the brothers or in the house to which he is assigned, as well as in the refectory [dining room]. Perfectly instructed in every good work, let him be joined to the brothers. Then they shall strip him of his secular clothes and garb him in the monastic habit. He shall be handed over to the porter [door keeper] so that at the time of prayer he may bring him before all the brothers; and he shall sit where he is told. The clothes he brought with him shall be given to those in charge of this matter and brought to the storeroom; they will be in the keeping of the superior of the monastery.[109]

From St. John Cassian (died ca. 435)

St. John Cassian learned from the Egyptian monastic tradition and transmitted much of its wisdom to the West. His large book called the Conferences collects together various teachings of monks for the benefit of his Western readers. The first conference, from the great Abba Moses, communicates how the end or purpose of monastic profession is the kingdom of God, and the means of achieving that end is purity of heart. Consider now the importance of having a pure heart in religious life.

> All the secret places of our heart... must be constantly scrutinized and the prints of whatever enters them must be investigated in the most careful way, lest perchance some spiritual beast, a lion or a dragon, pass through and secretly leave its dangerous traces; then, once our thoughts were neglected, access to the sanctuary of our heart would be offered to still others. Thus at every moment we should cultivate the earth of our heart with the gospel plow—that is, with the continual remembering of the Lord's cross—and we shall be able to root out from ourselves the nests of harmful animals and the hiding places of venomous serpents.[110]

From St. Gregory the Great (died 604)

St. Gregory the Great lived a monastic life at St. Andrew's Abbey in Rome before becoming pope. He applies to religious life the

---

109. "Precepts of our father Pachomius," in *Pachomian Koinonia*, vol. 2: *Pachomian Chronicles and Rules,* trans. Armand Veilleux, Monk of Mistassini, Cistercian Studies Series 46 (Kalamazoo, MI: Cistercian Publications, 1981), pp. 152-53.

110. Conference 1 in *John Cassian: The Conferences,* trans. Boniface Ramsey, Ancient Christian Writers 57 (New York: Newman Press, 1997), p. 63.

image of the whole-burnt offering, what is called a holocaust, as the supreme animal sacrifice commanded by God in the Mosaic Law. Why? In the whole-burnt offering, the complete animal is given to God without any other purpose, as no one may eat of something burnt to a crisp. Consider how that completeness in the offering is considered better than giving a portion to God and keeping another portion. This is St. Thomas Aquinas's favorite image for religious life.

> Truly it must be known that there is this difference between a sacrifice and a whole-burnt offering, that every whole-burnt offering is a sacrifice but not every sacrifice is a whole-burnt offering. For in a sacrifice only part of the beast is customarily offered, but in a whole-burnt offering the whole beast is offered. Thus "holocaust" in the Latin tongue denotes a whole-burnt offering...
>
> When a man shall consecrate to Almighty God everything he has, everything he knows, his entire life, it is a whole-burnt offering. For there are those who are still held by the mind in this world, and yet from their possessions administer aid to the needy, and hasten to defend the oppressed. These make a sacrifice in the good they do because they both offer something from their action to God and reserve something for themselves. And there are those who keep nothing for themselves but offer to the Almighty Lord the sense, tongue, life and substance which they have received. What do they offer if not a holocaust, nay rather that they become a holocaust?
>
> ...Therefore, as was said, although a sacrifice may also be a whole-burnt offering, a whole-burnt offering is nevertheless greater than a sacrifice because all that is owned by a mind

which is not oppressed by love of this world is burned as a sacrifice to Almighty God.[111]

From a letter to his Carthusian sons, St. Bruno (died 1101)

St. Bruno founded the Carthusian monks and writes to them of his joy in their progress in religious life.

> From the frequent and pleasant reports of our most blessed brother, I know of your reasoned and truly praiseworthy discipline, carried out with unwavering rigor. Since I have heard of your holy love and constant pursuit of honesty and virtue, my spirit rejoices in the Lord. I rejoice and am drawn to praise and give thanks to God, and still I long to love him. I rejoice, as I should, in the growing fruits of your strength, and yet I grieve and grow ashamed that I lie idle and senseless in the mire of my sins.
>
> Therefore rejoice my dearest brothers, because you are so blessed and because of the bountiful hand of God's grace upon you. Rejoice, because you have escaped the various dangers and shipwrecks of the stormy world. Rejoice, because you have reached the quiet and safe anchorage of a secret harbor. Many wish to come into this port, and many make great efforts to do so, yet do not achieve it. Indeed many, after reaching it, have been thrust out, since it was not granted them from above.
>
> Therefore, my brothers, you should consider it certain and well-established that whoever partakes of this desirable good,

---

111. St. Gregory the Great, Homily II.8, in *Homilies on the Book of the Prophet Ezekiel*, trans. Theodosia Tomkinson, 2d edition (Etna, CA: Center for Traditionalist Orthodox Studies, 2008), pp. 409-10 [translation altered].

should he in any way lose it, will grieve to his death, if he has any regard or concern for the salvation of his soul.[112]

From St. Bonaventure (died 1274)

St. Bonaventure, one of three Franciscan Doctors of the Church, contributed many beautiful writings to assist the Church. He was a successor to St. Francis as Minister General of Franciscans. The following is not one of his most famous texts, but is written especially to remind the reader what is most important in religious life. He wants you to experience the love that the Lord has for you.

> Let us not permit our hearts to be concerned with any created good, except as long as such goods move us with feelings of love and charity. When the manifold charm of temporal goods is given too much attention, not only does it distract the spirit and disturb the mind's happy peace: as it arouses the imagination, it actually destroys this peace by sadly vexing it with violent commotions. Let us, instead, drop the load of earthly love; let us run to the One who invites us, who refreshes the soul and provides peace ... "which surpasses all understanding" (Phil 4:7).
>
> "Come to me," he said, "all you who labor and are burdened, and I will give you rest" (Matt 11:28). O Lord, what need have you? Why do you call? What do you have in common with us? Oh, true voice of kindness! "Come to me," he says, "and I will give you rest." Oh, admirable condescension of our God! Oh, love beyond words! Who else has ever done so much? Who has ever heard or seen anything like this? Behold: he invites his enemies, he exhorts the guilty. He attracts the ungrateful! "Come to me, all you," he says, "and learn from me: take my yoke upon you, ... and you will find rest for your souls." Oh,

---

112. Extracted from the Office of Readings, Second Reading, Memorial of St. Bruno, October 6.

most sweet and pleasing words! Oh, divinizing words, keener than any two-edged sword; heart-writing words filled with extreme delight, extending even to the division of soul and spirit!

Wake up now, O Christian soul, to a love so kind, to a flavor so sweet, to a fragrance so delightful! Anyone unable to perceive all this is most certainly ill, bereft of reason, at the threshold of death.

O my soul, please, be set afire, be fattened, be sweetened by the mercy of your God, by the kindness of your God, by the love of your Spouse! Be set afire by the fervor of your Beloved; be fattened with his love; be sweetened with his savor. Let none prevent you from entering, holding, and tasting![113]

From Blessed Humbert of Romans (died 1277)

Blessed Humbert of Romans was the fifth Master (head) of the Order of Preachers. He spent considerable time writing on religious life, especially on the form of life of the Friars Preachers. Notice his emphasis on the centrality of God for all action in life.

Make every effort, my Brothers, to show yourselves worthy of all praise, by being sincere in purity of mind before God, and before men noted for due discipline. Show yourselves in such service always reverent and devoted. Diligently find out what is pleasing to God, and ardently desire it and accomplish it. Endeavor to do all things in charity and out of charity, so that with God's help you may also possess the habit of charity, and by your efforts bring it into operation.... Therefore, whatsoever come your way, refer it devoutly to God, and unweariedly cling to him by love for his own sake.

---

113. St. Bonaventure, *Letter Containing Twenty-Five Points to Remember*, in *The Works of Bonaventure: III: Opuscula Second Series*, trans. José de Vinck (Paterson, NJ: St. Anthony Guild Press, 1966), pp. 250-51.

Let your way of going to God be by adversity as well as by prosperity, so that you may be humble and grateful in your successes and patient in trouble and difficulty.

Rejoice over nothing except that you fight for Christ; nor grieve over anything except in so far as it may separate you from his favor. Desire to please God alone, and him alone fear to displease. Let those things alone be sweet to you which unite you to God; those alone bitter which are opposed to him.

Regulate your whole life to God's glory, give thanks always to him for his benefits, and whatsoever does not belong to his praise look upon as something altogether lost.[114]

From St. John of the Cross (died 1591)

St. John of the Cross, together with fellow Doctor of the Church St. Teresa of Avila, began a Carmelite reform that continues to inspire many to deny themselves, pick up their crosses, and follow Jesus. He is famous for his great works *The Ascent of Mount Carmel, The Dark Night, The Spiritual Canticle,* and *The Living Flame of Love.* In response to a friar's request, the following emphasizes four points that sum up St. John's teaching on how to live a truly religious life. A list concerning degrees of perfection seems to have been meant for this same friar, and only the first is given to end this extract.

Your holy Charity, with a few words, asked me for a great deal. An answer would require much time and paper. Seeing, then, that I lack both of these, I will try to be concise and jot down only certain points and counsels that in sum will contain much, so that whoever observes them perfectly will attain a high degree of perfection.

The one who wishes to be a true religious and fulfill the prom-

---

114. Bl. Humbert of Romans, *The Religious Vows and Virtues,* ed. James Harrison, O.P. (London: Burns, Oates & Washbourne, 1922), pp. 62-63 [translation altered]. Humbert is not beatified, but is called Blessed in Dominican tradition.

ises of the profession that was made to God, advance in virtue, and enjoy the consolations and the delight of the Holy Spirit, will be unable to do so without trying to practice with the greatest diligence the four following counsels concerning resignation, mortification, the practice of virtue, and bodily and spiritual solitude....

If your Charity observes these four counsels with care, you will reach perfection in a very short time. These counsels are so interdependent that if you are lacking in one of them, you will begin to lose the profit and gain you have from practicing the others.

Do not commit a sin for all there is in the world, or any deliberate venial sin, or any known imperfection.[115]

From St. Alphonsus de Liguori (died 1787)

St. Alphonsus de Liguori founded the Congregation of the Most Holy Redeemer, commonly called the Redemptorists. He was a holy bishop who suffered greatly. He wrote many treatises on doctrinal, moral, and ascetical themes, and was renowned for his devotion to the Blessed Virgin Mary. A Doctor of the Church, he is patron saint of moral theologians and confessors. Notice his emphasis on becoming a saint in religious life.

No saint has ever attained to sanctity without a great desire. As wings are necessary to birds in order to fly, so holy desires are necessary to the soul in order to advance in the road of perfection. To become a saint, we must detach ourselves from creatures, conquer our passions, overcome ourselves, and love

---

115. St. John of the Cross, *Counsels to a Religious on How to Reach Perfection* and *Degrees of Perfection*, in *The Collected Works of Saint John of the Cross*, rev. ed. trans. Kieran Kavanaugh, O.C.D., and Otilio Rodriquez, O.C.D. (Washington, DC: Institute of Carmelite Studies, 1991), pp. 725 and 728.

crosses. But to do all this, much strength is required, and we must suffer much....

St. Bernard, being in religion, in order to excite his fervor, used to say to himself, "Bernard, for what did you come here?" I say the same to you: what have you come to do in the house of God? To become a saint? And what are you doing? Why do you lose the time? Tell me, do you desire to become a saint? If you do not, it is sure that you will never become one. If, then, you have not this desire, ask Jesus Christ for it; ask Mary for it; and if you have it, take courage, says St. Bernard, for many do not become saints, because they do not take courage. And so I repeat, let us take courage, and great courage. What do we fear? What inspires this diffidence in us? That Lord, who has given us strength to leave the world, will give us also the grace to embrace the life of a saint.[116]

From St. Eugene de Mazenod (died 1861)

St. Eugene de Mazenod founded the Missionary Oblates of Mary Immaculate, during a time of re-building of the Church following the French Revolution and its immediate aftermath. Notice in this letter his concern both for the interior life of the men of his society and for the souls of those they encounter in mission. He is writing to someone who is already in the clergy, and St. Eugene wants him to join his new community.

My dear friend, read this letter at the foot of your crucifix with a mind to heed only God and what is demanded in the interests of his glory and of the salvation of souls. ... Stifle the voice of cupidity, love of comfort and convenience; dwell deeply on the plight of our country people, their religious situation, the

116. St. Alphonsus Liguori, "The Choice of a State of Life, and the Vocation to the Religious State," in *The Complete Works. The Ascetical Works*, vol. III: *The Great Means of Salvation and of Perfection* (Brooklyn, NY: Redemptorist Fathers, 1927), pp. 440-41.

apostasy that daily spreads wider with dreadfully ravaging effects. Look at the feebleness of the means employed to date to oppose this flood of evil; ask your heart what it fain would do to counter these disasters and then reply to my letter.

Well, dear man, what I say to you, without going fully into details, is that you are necessary for the work which the Lord inspires us to undertake. Since the head of the Church is persuaded that, given the wretched state in which France finds herself, only missions can bring people back to the Faith which they have practically abandoned, good men of the Church from different dioceses are banding together in response to the views of our supreme Pastor. We likewise feel that it is utterly necessary to employ the same remedy in our regions and, full of confidence in the goodness of Providence, have laid down the foundations of an establishment which will steadily furnish our countryside with fervent missionaries. These will ceaselessly engage in destroying the empire of the demon, at the same time as providing the example of a life worthy of the Church in the community which they will form. Indeed, we will live together in one house, that which I have bought, under a Rule we shall adopt with common accord and for which we will draw the elements from the statutes of St. Ignatius, of St. Charles [Borromeo] for his Oblates, of St. Philip Neri, of St. Vincent de Paul and of the Blessed [Alphonsus] Liguori.

Happiness awaits us in this holy Society which will have but one heart and soul. One part of the year will be devoted to the conversion of souls, the other to seclusion, study and our individual sanctification. I say no more for the moment; it suffices to give some intimation of the spiritual delights we will taste together. If, as I hope, you wish to be one of us, you will not find yourself in unknown terrain; you will have four companions. If presently we are not more numerous, it means we wish to choose men who have the will and the courage to walk in the footsteps of the apostles. It is important to lay solid foundations. The greatest regularity must be planned and introduced in the house as soon as we enter it. And it is precisely for that reason that you are necessary to me because I know you to be capable of embracing an exemplary rule of life and of persevering in it.[117]

From Blessed Basil Moreau (died 1873)

Blessed Basil Moreau founded the Congregation of Holy Cross. As the founding Superior General, he gave many Circular Letters to express the charism he received and promote the work of the congregation. In this excerpt, Blessed Basil Moreau emphasizes ideas essential to religious life, and applies this in a particular way to his new congregation.

> I firmly trust ... that the same God who has begun this work under such favorable auspices will carry it through to its completion. This he will do, provided that you strive constantly after the perfect life. This perfect life is characterized by obedience, discipline, punctuality, community spirit, zeal for the interior life, edification, and devotion to work. The perfection of this life stands out, particularly in that purity of intention that seeks not self, but God alone; aims only at heaven and not at anything earthly; strives for nothing but the happiness of possessing Jesus and belonging to him and to his blessed mother; and directs all interests, goods, and rights to the sole honor of the divine master and the salvation of souls. Obedience will so completely animate the whole tenor of such a life that no one will engage in any activity except at the will of the superior. This kind of life will be marked by devotion to regularity and punctuality, by a constant and universal fidelity to the rules and constitutions of the society in a spirit of love

---

117. St. Eugene de Mazenod, Letter to l'Abbé Tempier, in *Letters to the Oblates of France: 1814-1825*, trans. John Witherspoon Mole, O.M.I. (Rome: General Postulation O.M.I, 1984), pp. 6-7.

rather than of fear, and in a spirit of faith rather than for human motives.

This life will promote community spirit by humility, meekness, and charitable forbearance with others. It will follow scrupulously the maxim of the pious author of the *Imitation [of Christ]*: "We must mutually support, console, aid, instruct, and admonish one another." Such a life will give edification by its modesty, its sacrifices of personal viewpoints, its self-forgetfulness, its religious gravity, and its careful avoidance of all criticism, unkind jesting, and even the slightest trace of frivolity. It will be a life of devotion to the work of teaching or of any other employment, to punctuality to the common exercises, and to the shunning of idleness. Lastly, it will be an interior life, elevated to God by the habitual practice of acts of faith, hope, and charity, after the example of Jesus Christ, who is to be the particular model of our conduct. Unless we wish to ruin the work of Holy Cross, it is absolutely essential for us to lead with our Lord a life hidden in God.[118]

From Blessed Columba Marmion (died 1923)

Blessed Columba Marmion was an Irishman who became abbot of the Abbey of Maredsous in Belgium. He is one of the greatest spiritual writers of modern times, with classics such as *Christ in His Mysteries, Christ, the Life of the Soul,* and *Christ, the Ideal of the Priest.* The following is taken from a work where he considers Jesus Christ as the ideal for the monastic life.

It is above all on days of weariness, sickness, impatience, temptation, spiritual dryness, and trials, during hours of sometimes

---

118. Bl. Basil Moreau, *Circular Letter* 14, Notre-Dame de Sainte-Croix, Le Mans, France, September 1, 1841 in *Basil Moreau: Essential Writings,* edited by Kevin Grove, C.S.C., and Andrew Gawrych, C.S.C. (Notre Dame, IN: Ave Maria Press, 2014), pp. 380-81.

terrible anguish which press upon a soul, that holy abandonment is pleasing to God.

More than once we have considered this truth, namely, that there is a sum total of sufferings, of humiliations and sorrows, which God has foreseen for the members of Christ's mystical body in order to "fill up those things that are lacking in the sufferings of Christ." We cannot reach perfect union with Christ Jesus unless we accept that portion of the chalice which our Lord wills to give us to drink with him and after him.

Our Lord knew all about the terrible way along which his Father had ordained that he should travel; did he refuse to accept the divine will or refuse to fulfill it? No, he embraced it. "Behold, I come, O Father; I have placed this law of suffering in my heart, and I accept it for love of thee." The Word of God, Eternal Wisdom, Christ likewise foresaw the part that we should have in his Passion. What is there better than to surrender ourselves, with him, to our Father and accept this participation in the sufferings and humiliations of his Son Jesus? "O Father, I accept all the sorrows, all the humiliations, all the sufferings that it shall please thee to send me, all the misunderstandings to which it shall please thee to subject me, all the painful obediences that it shall please thee to impose upon me; and all this for love of thee, in union with thy beloved Son."

If we could always keep ourselves in these inward dispositions, never stopping at secondary causes, never asking, murmuringly, when annoyed and contradicted: "Why has this happened? Why do they treat me in this manner?" If we could lift ourselves up to that supreme will which permits everything, and without the permission of which nothing happens; if we could always look up above creatures with hearts uplifted, *sursum corda* [the priest's liturgical call: lift up your hearts], to see only God, to abandon ourselves to him, we should constantly abide in peace.[119]

Holy Mother of my Lord, your saints in religious life can show me the holiness of a life dedicated to your Son. Help me to learn from the saints so that I too may be close to Jesus.

---

119. Bl. Columba Marmion, *Christ the Ideal of the Monk*, Part II, chap. 16, sec. 14, quoted in *Suffering with Christ: An Anthology of the Writings of Dom Columba Marmion, O.S.B.*, compiled by Dom Raymund Thibaut, O.S.B. (Westminster, MD: The Newman Press, 1952), p. 128 [translation slightly altered].

CHAPTER 14

A DAY IN THE LIFE OF DIFFERENT RELIGIOUS

"Yours is the day and yours is the night" (Psalm 74).

hat does the typical day of a religious look like? That's a difficult question to answer, as religious communities are so different from one another. Daily life and work will vary greatly for a Carthusian monk in Vermont, a Discalced Carmelite friar in Washington, DC, a Jesuit priest at Boston College, a Salesian missionary in Chile, and a Missionary of Charity brother in India.

Religious within the same community could have very different days. The same Benedictine abbey could have such varied figures as abbot, prior, subprior, procurator, novice master, junior master, librarian, sacristan, guest master, porter, oblate director, novice, junior monk, high school teacher, college professor, college chaplain, prison chaplain, liturgical director, organist/abbey cantor, infirmarian, and someone dying in the infirmary—all in the same abbey. Often monks have two or three roles to play at the same time. Moreover, some religious say that no two days are the same.

But there are certain commonalities among all forms of religious life, perhaps best expressed when religious pray Psalm 74, "Yours is the day and yours is the night." Because their whole existence is meant to be worship of God in charity, all of the time of religious belongs to the Lord. This is not a nine-to-five job. Also, as it is said, there's no vacation from your vocation.

Religious typically carry within themselves an ancient sense of the rhythms of the hours of a day, especially in sanctifying the hours of the day through what some call the horarium. *Horarium* is a Latin word meaning the schedule of a day, broken down into various hours, especially for the times of prayer. The Church's liturgy has never lost the sense of the deep symbolic significance of the setting of the sun, as a sign of death in Christ, and the rising of the sun, as a sign of the resurrection in him. You could say that religious are "liturgical creatures" who pray, minister, study, eat, recreate, and sleep within a rhythm of the hours of each day. And what is communicated by this rhythm? Let's return to the Psalms:

> The heavens proclaim the glory of God
> and the firmament shows forth the work of his hands.
> Day unto day takes up the story
> and night unto night makes known the message. (Psalm 19)

One Dominican friar who is a Doctor of the Church and patron of the natural sciences, St. Albert the Great, said, "The whole world is theology for us, because the heavens proclaim the glory of God."[120] Religious are called to have in each day a holistic sense of the unity of all things in God, and join their lives to God's purpose in creation: giving God the glory and receiving his happiness—especially in the midst of pain and sorrow. That never gets old. For as we read in the Book of Lamentations:

> The Lord's acts of mercy are not exhausted,
> his compassion is not spent;
> They are renewed each morning—
> Great is your faithfulness! (Lam 3:22-23)

---

120. St. Albert the Great, quoted in Simon Tugwell, O.P., *Albert and Thomas: Selected Writings*, Classics of Western Spirituality (Mahwah, NJ: Paulist Press, 1988), p. 29.

This chapter now considers a day in the life of four religious from four different kinds of religious communities. These accounts come from a monk, a canon, a friar, and a priest from a religious congregation founded in the nineteenth century. Many more examples could be given from other types of religious, but we hope that you'll be able to see something of how these men follow the Lord by living religious life.

A Day in the Life of a Benedictine Monk

By Brother Isidore Colm, O.S.B.
St. Mary's Monastery, Petersham, MA

4:35 a.m. Rise

I wake up every day by the sound of the rising bell at 4:35 a.m. I then have twenty-five minutes to wash my face, get dressed and make my way to the church. We're allowed a cup of coffee before Vigils, if we wish, and I usually take one. Another bell is rung at 4:55 to summon us to prayer. We keep silence at this time but I do my best to offer up some mental prayers as I head to the church.

5:00 a.m. Vigils

We begin praying the Divine Office while it's still dark outside, which is appropriate since Vigils is actually the "night office." When a signal is given we all make a small sign of the cross on our lips as one of the monks intones the psalm verse: *Domine labia mea aperies* (Lord, open my lips) and the rest of the choir responds: *Et os meum annuntiabit laudem tuam* (and my mouth will proclaim your praise). These are the first words I utter in the day.

6:00 a.m.—Silent prayer

Vigils usually lasts about one hour. From the end of the Vigils until the beginning of Lauds we have a period of silent prayer, or meditation. We do this together in church, although we are free to spread out and not sit in our usual choir stalls. I like to move closer to the tabernacle and make my meditation there.

6:30 a.m.—Lauds

Lauds is the first hour of the day office, and by now the sun has risen. We are joined at Lauds by the nuns of St. Scholastica Priory, our "twin community." We pray the Divine Office together with the sisters, and have some other activities in common, although we are two separate communities. The model for us is that of St. Benedict and his sister St. Scholastica, who supported each other in their spiritual lives. During the Divine Office we form two choirs, sitting across from each other in church, chanting the psalms and hymns antiphonally, going back from side to side.

We sing the Office using Gregorian chant in the original Latin. I prefer the Latin because the Gregorian melodies were composed in this language, and there's an intimate connection between the music and the text which gets lost in translation. Many people today appreciate Gregorian chant simply as beautiful music, but we are fortunate to be singing the chant in its original context, for the purpose for which it was intended.

7:10 a.m.—Breakfast and *lectio divina*

Breakfast is not a common meal and each monk can eat it when he likes after Lauds. The time between Lauds and Mass is our main *lectio divina* period.

9:30 a.m.—Mass with Terce

We consider the liturgy to be our main work, following St. Benedict who calls it the "Work of God" (*Opus Dei*). The high point of our liturgical life is the Eucharist, being the Church's main prayer and "the summit and source of Christian life" (Second Vatican Council, *Lumen Gentium*, no. 11; *Catechism of the Catholic* Church, no. 1324). The Mass is in English but we sing some parts in Latin every day. On Thursdays we have Mass entirely in Latin (except for the readings) according to the Novus Ordo.

At the end of Mass we sing Terce (pronounced Ters), the first of the so-called "Little Hours." Terce, Sext and None (pronounced Noan), are derived from the Latin, meaning the third, sixth, and ninth hours, since these times marked the major divisions of the day in the ancient Roman world.

10:30 a.m.—Chapter and morning work

After Mass we all process into the chapter room, and the superior reads out a portion of the *Rule of St. Benedict*. This custom is known as "Chapter" since traditionally a chapter of the Holy Rule was read out at this time. Sometimes the superior makes a few announcements or gives a brief conference or spiritual talk.

After Chapter we begin our morning work. I'm the librarian and much of my work consists in cataloging books. I'm also the guest master. Welcoming guests is a traditional monastic custom and one which St. Benedict emphasized in his *Rule*. In the summer I also manage our vegetable garden. Several of us have been taking turns giving classes to the monks and nuns in formation, and at present I teach a class on the *Rule of St. Benedict.*

Work, like prayer, can be a means of sanctifying the day. The two Benedictine mottos are *Ora et Labora* (Pray and Work) and *Ut in omnibus glorificetur Deus* (That in all things God may be glorified). The latter phrase is from 1 Peter 4:11 and is found in the *Rule of St. Benedict* 57:9. These two mottos sum up our monastic life.

1:00 p.m.—Sext

Next comes our midday prayer, Sext. At the end of the office one of the monks or nuns reads aloud from the necrology, a list of the deceased members of our congregation who have died on that date. We also remember our deceased relatives, friends and benefactors at this time.

1:15 p.m.—Lunch

This is our main meal of the day. On weekdays it's a meatless meal although we eat meat on Sundays, solemnities and on other special occasions. Guests also join us for lunch in the refectory. Monastic meals follow a certain ritual, which forms a parallel to our liturgy in the church. We sit in order of seniority as we do in choir, with the superior "presiding" at table.

2:00 p.m.—Free time

After lunch we have free time until 3:00 p.m. The brothers can relax, take a nap, go for a walk, read a book, listen to music or practice a hobby. One of my hobbies is genealogy and this is a time when I can to do some research.

3:00 p.m.—None

The office of None marks the last of the Little Hours. We normally have None on our own without the sisters. Like the other Little Hours it is short and lasts about thirteen minutes.

3:15 p.m.—Afternoon work

After drying the dishes from lunch we begin our afternoon work period which lasts until 5:45 p.m. The tasks are the same as those for the morning work period.

6:00 p.m.—Vespers

At the end of the work day we have Vespers (evening prayer). Along with Vigils this is the most solemn of the monastic hours. To emphasize its importance we process into the church together for Vespers as we do for Mass.

6:35 p.m.—*Lectio Divina*

Vespers is followed by another *lectio divina* period, which can also be used as a time of silent prayer. In either case the purpose is really the same—to unite ourselves to God in prayer.

7:10 p.m.—Supper

Our evening meal is a lighter meal than lunch so we can get to bed earlier. During supper we listen to a brief scripture passage which is followed by a reading from the "martyrology," or "Lives of the Saints," which contains brief biographies of the saints whose feasts are commemorated on the following day. After the reading the meal continues in silence until the superior rings a bell.

7:25 p.m.—Recreation

After supper we process to the chapter room where we have recreation—all except the weekly server who stays behind to do the washing up. At recreation we simply sit together and talk. For the most part it's fairly lighthearted conversation. At 7:55 p.m. the superior reads out the prayer intentions for the following day. He then reads a few excerpts from a spiritual book to help us recollect ourselves before going into the church for Compline.

8:00 p.m.—Compline

We sing Compline in the dark church, illumined by only three candles. The same three psalms (4, 90, and 133) are repeated every day so we basically know them by heart. Compline concludes with the *Salve Regina* (or the *Alma Redemptoris Mater, Ave Regina Caelorum,* or *Regina Caeli,* depending on the season of the year). After this the superior sprinkles the two communities and guests with holy water and we are free to leave the church or stay behind to pray a little longer if we wish. We then retire to our rooms and go to bed shortly after that in order to get rested for another day.

A Day in the Life of a Norbertine Canon

By *Frater Urban Hannon, O. Praem.*
St. Michael's Abbey, Canons Regular of Prémontré, Orange, CA

5:45 a.m.—Matins and Lauds, *Lectio Divina*, Missa Summa

The abbey bell is ringing for the first time today—the only sound in an otherwise quiet monastery—to rouse the confreres from sleep and to call us to prayer. In silence, one white-robed figure after another is taking his place in *statio*, lining up beside the cloister gardens to prepare for Morning Office. One priest is just finishing his candlelit Latin Mass in the chapel. Some of the seminarians already are making the rounds on their rosary beads or prayer ropes. Others are sipping some much-needed coffee. This week's lector is holding his breviary, glancing over the patristic homily that he is about to proclaim in the liturgy. Now we are processing into the church in hierarchical order, bowing to the altar and to one another, and taking our places in choir. The abbot knocks, the confreres turn east, and the presiding priest intones the first words of the Divine Office: *Domine, labia mea aperies, et os meum annuntiabit laudem tuam:*"Lord, thou shalt open my lips, and my mouth shall announce thy praise." The day has begun.

8:00 a.m.—Silent Breakfast, Terce, Morning Apostolates

Thus far this morning, we have chanted Matins and Lauds, spent half an hour reading sacred scripture (*lectio divina*), assisted at our conventual High Mass (the centerpiece of our day), eaten breakfast, and prayed Terce. Now our priests are busy with their daily pastoral work, especially in the seminary and at the boys' high school which we run out of our abbey. One of the fathers is leading his freshman literature class in a dramatic reading of *Macbeth*. Another is rehearsing St. Thomas Aquinas' famous five ways with his seniors. Still another is on the air with *Catholic Answers Live* to explain divine predestination to thousands of radio listeners. And several more priests are offering Confession or counsel in various parlors around the abbey. We seminarians are in class. This morning the novices are studying Gregorian chant, the history of our canonical life, and the *Confessions* of St. Augustine. The philosophy students have just finished Aristotle's *Metaphysics*, and now they are diving into the *Prima Pars* of the *Summa Theologiae*. In our free periods, we are getting ahead on Latin translations, or writing letters to friends and family, or meeting with our spiritual father. At 11:55, the abbey bell will ring, and we will gather in the church once more to consecrate the day to God.

12:00 p.m.—Sext, Lunch with Table Reading, Afternoon Work or Play

After chanting Sext, we process to lunch, where one of the seminarians serves as table reader. At lunch we always read from the *Rule of our Holy Father St. Augustine*, from the *hagiologion of our order*, and from some other spiritual book (recent selections have included a biography of Pope Benedict XV, a theological study on the role of angels in liturgy, and a delightful British novel about St. Helena). After lunch, our priests return to their apostolic endeavors, while we seminarians clean up the refectory. If today were a Monday or Wednesday, then the philosophy students would be heading down to their cells to study, while the novices would assemble for manual labor—and if it were a Friday, everyone would be working. But today is Tuesday, so all of us seminarians have a free afternoon. Several brothers are down on the field for a fierce game of ultimate frisbee. A few others are on a bike ride through the canyon. Two are in the kitchen making apple butter and hot sauce. A handful have gathered around a piano to practice their musical act for our next variety night. Most of the painters are hanging out working on their newest icons, while one is over in the woodshop crafting a frame for his. Our confreres enjoy their leisure time in all sorts of different activities, but the common thread running through them all is *communio*—we are united in love of God and the brethren.

4:20 p.m.—None, Rosary, Vespers, Dinner with Conversation, Evening Chores, Recreation

After cleaning ourselves up, we finish the afternoon by convening to pray None. Then the lights in the abbey church are extinguished, and the men in white spread all throughout the sanctuary and nave for our daily rosary. We sanctify the evening by gathering in *statio* once again and processing into the church for Vespers. Then at dinner, our table reader begins the meal with the *Roman Martyrology* and the constitutions of our order, and he ends with a passage from the *Life of St. Norbert*. But most of dinner is spent in conversation—a "family meal" at its finest. After dinner, some of our priests find themselves in the computer room, preparing their homilies for the parishes where they assist on Sundays. A couple of others are out for a run on the trails. Several fathers are relaxing together in the priests' common room. One or two are in the parlors meeting with lay groups or individuals. As for us seminarians, several of us are bringing dinner to the elderly fathers, while others are setting up vestments and chalices for tomorrow's conventual Mass, or shelving books in the library, or doing any of the other beautifully routine tasks that help maintain our religious life. Soon we will head down for our nightly seminarian recreation. Sometimes we play a board game or sing songs, but more often we just sit back and enjoy each other's company. After recreation we will have a free hour to read or get work done, except on Saturdays when we use this time to rehearse the chant propers for Sunday Mass, and on Fridays when we have our chapter of faults, a forum in which we confess our public failings against our rule of life and beg from our brothers their pardon and prayers. After these events, our *magnum silentium* (grand silence) will begin, which will continue until breakfast tomorrow morning. Thus we begin and end each day in the silent peace of prayer.

8:00 p.m.—Holy Hour, Compline, Bed

We are right where we belong: kneeling together in our abbey church, adoring our Lord in the monstrance ("lifting high the Holy Eucharist over the miseries and errors of this world," as St. John Paul II fittingly described the mission of our order). This is the end of our day, and also the end of our nightly holy hour, which begins with chanted Compline and concludes with benediction. In a few minutes, the Blessed Sacrament will be reposed, and all of our confreres will make their way towards bed. Then we rest, we rise, and we do it all again. "Day unto day takes up the story, and night unto night makes known the message." "Seven times a day I praise you." "How good and how pleasant it is, when brothers live in unity!" As canons regular, we are blessed not only to chant these psalms each day, but to live them. Indeed, it is precisely these two aspects of the vocation which first attracted me to St. Michael's Abbey: our chant and our common life, the holy liturgy and holy friendship.

A Day in the Life of a Franciscan Friar of the Renewal

By *Br. Joseph Michael Fino, C.F.R.*
St. Leopold Friary, Yonkers, NY

5:16 a.m.—Wake

I awake into daylight sticky with heat. The noise of Nepperhan Avenue, a constant *whoosh* of traffic, colludes with the box fan's push of July humidity. On the far wall is an icon, a gold-leafed square of beloved faces. I cross myself and sigh a prayer to the God I love. Bare feet find even the linoleum floor warm as I rise up off the mattress laid out upon it. Of the usual thirteen friars inhabiting St. Leopold, our house of studies, for the summer we are only three. While other seminarians spend the break abroad assisting the brothers in Europe and Central America, we work a summer camp with our brothers in the Bronx.

Downstairs a mug of cold brew sweats on the back patio where I sip it from a plank-backed chair. For me days begin thus: prayer and coffee; ideas held in tension with the heart's experience. Days and sentiments merge in the imagination as prayer happens within God's omnipresence. Black ink scratches onto a yellow pad.

6:00 a.m.—Angelus

A bell sounds mid-scribble. It's time for office. In the chapel, another brother enters, kneels down to kiss the pine floorboards, finds his chair and raps twice at the armrest. We kneel for the Angelus. It ascends from our hearts much like we from our beds: with a little work. Six comes quickly after a long day of Summer Life. We recite the psalms together and take turns with the readings.

6:20 a.m.—Personal Prayer

This begins an hour of personal prayer which the brothers make where they wish. Often in our cells or the Chapel. Lately I've chosen the patio where the breeze is merciful. Today I pray over the material I will teach this afternoon to sixth and seventh graders—scribble a line, jot a note, practice, listen. Nothing suits one's prayer life more than sitting and listening.

7:30 a.m.—Morning Prayer and Mass

Another bell has assembled us to the chapel for Morning Prayer—all three of us—after which we walk next door, our priest being absent, to the parish for Mass.

8:23 a.m.—Travel and Basic Ministry

Having packed books and materials, I leave immediately after Mass for Harlem in a deep blue Town and Country (donated to us a few years ago). Rosary beads pass through my fingers as the Henry Hudson careens beneath the tires. Then comes the George Washington bridge, the swerve into Harlem and, in the distance, a New York skyline like watercolors through the haze.

Two young adults, two teens, and two children funnel out of their apartment on 141st street. Marie-Lou sits shotgun and, after a traveling prayer, clicks on the stereo. She snaps a selfie with digital flowers in her hair and turns up the volume. Pop music is our soundtrack into the Bronx. The kids are singing. The kids are brimming. At 155th street, they file out into the red doors of the St. Francis Youth Center, a renovated school building adjacent to the friary. I manage to park the minivan a few blocks away.

Walking the Bronx is quintessential joy. Imagine muggy mornings hanging in a low haze, a street sweeper rounding the corner at Key Food, neighbors from the projects sludging through the heat, people slow cross the street. July sticks to all of us. Faces hang. Each one passes me, amid the shrug and sag of life, so bright with being (unknowingly, I think).

Two men see my gray habit from across Melrose. It says to

them: FRIENDSHIP or PRAYERS or FREE FOOD, so they cross. They are guys in rehab, men without resources. They need food, they tell me. They want to know if God hears their prayers, and why he's not answering them. At the deli-grocery, I buy them coffee, prepackaged blueberry muffins, and orange juice. We circle up, and there on the sidewalk in the shade of a locust tree, we pray.

They walk north. I go a block south, hang a right past the fire department toward the St. Francis Youth Center where children line the sidewalk at hip-height waiting for the doors to open.

In the gym, Fr. Luke corrals the teens into a morning meeting. This apostolate belongs to the devoted brothers at Our Lady of the Angels. It is their ministry to the children, teens, young adults, and families in our neighborhood. This Summer Life has nearly ten brothers with an invaluable staff of lay volunteers and employees working together for the three-week summer camp.

10:00a.m.—Class Preparation

I'm upstairs putting my room together: a horseshoe of chairs, a podium for a weathered leather bible and notes, a knapsack of props. Downstairs the friars and staff welcome the kids into the gym. Day five of Summer Life begins. I hear them singing. I hear them laughing. I hear them silent as Fr. Xavier introduces the day's virtue and theme.

10:25 a.m.—Class

Kids clamor up the stairwell. In the classroom, they tease out similarities and differences in the created order. Comparing rocks to plants, plants to animals, and animals to people helps the kids to see the order to God's creation and intuit their unique place in the created world.

12:00 p.m.—Mid-Day Prayer and Lunch

Once class finishes, I sit down for mid-day prayer. When brothers are home, it too is prayed in common in the chapel, but during apostolic periods we pray it as we can on our own. Lunch follows, and the day continues to drive itself with its rotating wheel of activity.

3:00 p.m.—Rest

As their parents arrive, kids are free to leave. Fr. Luke closes the day with the staff and allows them time to rehearse the skit for tomorrow.

A few of us find a quiet space in the (importantly) air conditioned Padre Pio Activity Center—where we will have dinner since the friary refectory is too small to accommodate both brothers and volunteers—and we rest. On a couch, a young woman—one of the family from Harlem—unloads her day in the space between us. She's excited. It fills her eyes and all her words come skipping out. It's a new role for her managing a portion of our youth staff, and today, she successfully extinguished a few fires of teenage drama.

4:30 p.m.—Holy Hour

The brothers and volunteers make our daily Holy Hour. It begins with Evening Prayer and continues in silence. For the brothers it is the second hour of silent personal prayer in a day—a sturdy hinge to our horarium. The chapel stills around us. On days like this, tiredness often hangs our heads. What moves me about our fraternity is that these men *pray*. Time spent adoring the Blessed Sacrament anticipates that awesome event of consuming it. And, like the Lord, we too are men consumed: ground between the teeth of prayer and apostolate.

6:00 p.m.—Dinner and Recreation

Dinner and a night of games and fellowship with the brothers and volunteers.

9:00 p.m.—Night Prayer

After Night Prayer, a brother intones the *Salve*. As usual brothers remain in the chapel for the rosary, however, Br. Ignatius Pio and I drive home. This night the city decides to repaint the Deegan, which sends us winding through the Bronx. We arrive late into Yonkers. A brief goodnight at the tabernacle and I ascend the stairs to my cell.

11:00ish—Sleep

I take in a poem or a little scripture before shutting the light. So many faces propose themselves to my prayer. A friar falls asleep each night with faces and names surfacing in his memory and affections. I lay them all upon my heart which I set against the Father's. I fall asleep hard.

A Day in the Life of a Holy Cross Priest

By *Father Charles McCoy, C.S.C.*
U.S. Province of the Congregation of Holy Cross,
University of Portland, Portland, OR

6:45 a.m.—Rise

Wake up by my alarm. Immediately say a brief "morning offering" consisting of a dedication of the day to the Sacred Heart, the Guardian Angel Prayer, a Hail Mary, and the Invitatory Prayer from the Office.

My residence hall, Villa Maria, had our weekly Tuesday night Mass at 10:15 p.m. last night, so I usually get to bed late and wake up late on Wednesdays. Plus, I have something special to do this morning. So I won't pray Morning Prayer until after my 8:00 a.m. class; I don't want to rush through it.

7:00 a.m.—Prepare for the Day

Get ready and dressed in my clerics for class. Look over class notes, pack up supplies needed, and head out for the day.

I must take a detour from my normal, quick walk from my dorm to my office in the math department. Today is Fr. Dick Rutherford's 80th birthday. He is a retired theology professor who still works on archaeological digs as part of his research. He has been something of a role model for me since I joined this community shortly after my ordination in July 2009.

As the local superior of the community, I had gathered signatures on a card from the other Holy Cross priests and brothers and from Amy, our lay office administrator. I drop off the card, together with a small gift, in the mailbox for his apartment. (The priests who do not live in the dorms live in a private complex of apartments on the side of campus opposite from my office.)

8:00 a.m.—Teach Calculus Class

Get to my office in the math department in time to dash off a quick email to Fr. Dick, to wish him a happy birthday and to make sure he checks his mailbox.

Teach Calculus I. Making the transition from the conceptual and formal definition of the derivative to the more mechanical techniques.

9:15 a.m.—Morning Prayer

I say morning prayer in private in the Chapel of Christ the Teacher on campus.

9:45 a.m.—Work

Final preparation of lecture for my afternoon Linear Algebra class. Various communications (emails and/or phone calls) as local superior of Holy Cross community at UP. Final homily preparation for the noon Mass.

12:05 p.m.—Mass

I am one of about ten priests in a rotation of presiders for our main daily Mass on campus. One of the concelebrants is Fr. Dick; he's very happy and appreciative. Although it's not really our normal custom at UP to invite con-celebrants to interject at the appropriate parts of the Eucharistic Prayer, I invite Fr. Dick to do so. It is special to celebrate this Mass with him.

12:35 p.m.—Lunch on campus

At lunch, we share our Holy Cross dining room with any administrators, faculty and staff who wish to join us. (It costs them only $6 for an all-you-can eat buffet, so many folks are there each lunch hour.) This set-up allows us to build great relationships between Holy Cross and our lay collaborators and across academic disciplines.

1:35 p.m.—Teach Linear Algebra

This is one of the "bridge" courses to higher mathematics, so it's a subject I particularly enjoy teaching. The students struggle with the newness of math being about something deeper than hard computations, but so far this semester, the students are at least willing to take that "leap of faith."

2:45 p.m.—Office hours

One student comes by almost every day. He is very bright. Not many other students have been visiting office hours so far this semester, which is a bit concerning. Always wondering how to draw them in without resorting to bribery.

4:00 p.m.—Mathematics department meeting

Department meetings are often a chore, but our department has a good *esprit d'corps*, which makes them more tolerable.

5:40 p.m.—Evening Prayer

Evening prayer with the local Holy Cross community and whoever joins us. This year we have had a handful of students who often pray with us. They are an inspiring group.

6:00 p.m.—Meeting with Pro-Life Group

Normally, I'd join my Holy Cross brothers for dinner. But on Wednesdays, the UP pro-life group Voice for Life meets, and I am their chaplain. Today we are continuing to talk about apologetics and to plan events for October, which is Respect Life month. It is counter-cultural to be pro-life, even on a Catholic campus, and they interact with all of their peers, especially those who disagree with them, with remarkable grace, compassion and understanding. Although I'm their chaplain, they are a good role models for me!

7:00 p.m.—Rosary

Rosary at Chapel of Christ the Teacher. A group of about six UP students, with no prompting from Campus Ministry, started meeting once a week to pray the Rosary. I like to join them whenever I am able.

8:00 p.m.—Exercise

Workout at the gym on campus. If I don't get some exercise in most days, I begin to feel lousy.

9:30 p.m.—Movie at the Student Lounge

Watch the movie Crouching Tiger, Hidden Dragon in the Villa Maria lounge. I have been trying to find ways to bond with guys in the hall. I found out a few of them, like me, enjoy kung fu movies. We watch a different one each Wednesday, and sometimes there's a snack. The student who is my main partner said he was cooking pot stickers. About three other men show up. As an event, it's pretty much a failure. But the movie is great.

11:45 p.m.—Retire

Pray the Office of Readings, Night Prayer, and then bed.

Conclusion

Each morning God gives us the gift of another day. The question is how we spend that day. Do we strive to return that gift back to God, or do we squander the preciousness of time? Days come and go, and our eternity will come. One of these days will be our last here on earth, and then there will be a day that does not end. Religious are called to live an intense form of the Christian life every day right here and now as eschatological signs of the glory of the everlasting day.

In our final chapter we will turn to several men from many different forms of religious life to hear their advice for your thinking about the possibility of religious life. Know that Christ is inviting men to follow him in poverty, chastity, and obedience. The invitation is real. Men have followed Christ in this radical path for about two thousand years. They are following him this very day—and night.

> *Mary, your soul proclaimed the greatness of the Lord, and so many religious echo your song of praise in the evening canticle of your Magnificat. Pray that my soul may proclaim God's grace at every hour of my life.*

CHAPTER 15

ADVICE FROM RELIGIOUS PRIESTS AND BROTHERS

"If you wish to be perfect, go, sell what you have and give to the poor, and you will have treasure in heaven. Then, come, follow me" (Matt 19:21).

Recall that evangelical counsels are fundamentally forms of good advice. Counsels are not commandments, but invitations. Jesus invited the rich young man in Matthew 19, and that young man heard the invitation and went away sad. What do you want to do? Because Jesus is the wisest and best of friends, we can trust his words and find great joy in the midst of offering our bodies as a living sacrifice.

Just as Christ offers good advice, so too do his followers. We reached out to over a dozen religious men in the Unites States to collect their advice for you about your future. We asked each of them a simple question:

What is the most important piece of advice you want to give to men discerning religious life today?

As you will see, their answers offer distilled wisdom from many years of experience. These men come from a broad range of communities, and so reflect something of God's intended diversity in religious life. Read each entry prayerfully, taking to heart the advice of those who go before you.

Fr. Donald Calloway, M.I.C.
Marians of the Immaculate Conception, The BVM, Mother of Mercy Province, U.S.

Give everything to Our Lady! When you read the lives of the saints you discover that every one of them entrusted everything to Mary as they prayed about knowing and doing God's holy will. You will never go wrong by asking Mary to guide you. She is the model of consecration to God and will greatly help you.

Concretely, I encourage you to spend time with her in heart-to-heart prayer, especially by praying a daily rosary. Read good books about Mary from authors like St. Louis de Montfort, St. Alphonsus Liguori, and Fulton J. Sheen. If possible, it wouldn't hurt to try and make a Marian pilgrimage as well. It doesn't necessarily have to be to a famous Shrine in Europe. Making a mini-pilgrimage to a Marian shrine in your diocese will bring about tremendous graces as you seek to discern the religious life.

Br. Tim Jones, O.F.M. Cap.
Capuchin Franciscan Province of St. Mary

Thank you for your generosity of spirit in seeking God's will in your life. You are an inspiration to so many. I hope the following brief thoughts may prove helpful to you on your vocation journey.

- Pray: especially to the Holy Spirit, our Blessed Mother, and your favorite saint.

- Patience: you probably won't get your answer as definitively and as quickly as you'd like.

- Possibilities: there are many in following the Lord, so be open-minded.

- Presence: make yourself available to the communities you are considering (but not too many!) through visits and weekend retreats.

- Preference: go with it based on how you find the spiritual, ministerial, and fraternal combination of the groups you've visited.

- Procrastinate: don't, once you've made your mind up.

- Peace: delight in it and the joy you feel in knowing you are doing God's will in your life.

I promise my prayers for you.

Abbot Austin G. Murphy, O.S.B.
St. Procopius Abbey, Lisle, IL

How do you know where God is calling you? Among other helps in discerning this, the monastic tradition has emphasized the use of a spiritual director or mentor.

Such a person has experience faithfully living the Christian life. His experience means that he knows how to listen to God's voice. The person knows the ways in which we are often deceived when discerning God's will and, in turn, the person knows how to "test the spirits" in order to know whether they are truly from God.

The person needs to be someone you trust enough to share honestly your thoughts about your vocation. The person will then be able to offer a helpful point now and again, but also, just by sharing your thoughts you will come to see them more clearly.

This help from a spiritual guide can go a far way in gaining clarity about God's call for you.

Fr. Bill Murphy, S.J.
Society of Jesus U.S.A. Midwest Province

Aspects of discernment can seem frustratingly intangible: God's will, the future, spirituality, and endless ideas about your life's path. What solidifies things for many men is the experience of religious life embodied in community.

Fight the temptation to think about discernment—go ahead and actually discern. That means getting to know orders by visiting their communities. Understanding the texture of fraternity within a group is impossible through the written word, over the internet, or by phone. You need to personally witness the men's interactions, their laughter, and how they pray. You need to feel how you fit in as you walk among them.

As you visit, look for both friends (prospective companions over many decades) and heroes (men who embody your hopes for your best self). When you meet the right group of men you will know. The resonance you find will be God's voice in your heart, "You are home."

Fr. Thomas Esposito, O. Cist.
Our Lady of Dallas Cistercian Abbey, Dallas, TX

Fear is not a valid excuse to remain in abstract "discerning" mode for months and years on end. You must recognize that fear of the sacrifices involved in a priestly or religious vocation is a paralyzing force that does not come from God. In this regard, prudence is an essential virtue you should pray for constantly, as is courage. You might not have connected courage with the discernment process itself, but you need a strong will capable of identifying anxieties for what they are—distractions trying to distance you from God. You need courage to overcome anxiety with the calm assurance that God speaks through love, not fear! Prudence and courage, asked for calmly and consistently in prayer, will help you accept the adventurous nature of discernment and provide you with the graced eagerness to explore a particular community that naturally appeals to you.

Fr. Ambrose Criste, O. Praem.
St. Michael's Abbey, Orange, CA

Don't make the decision to enter religious life a bigger deal than it is! Deciding to give religious life a try is nothing more (and nothing less) than the decision to step out of your life in the world so that you can really discern how Jesus wants you to follow Him. Entering religious life is really the beginning of your discernment, not the end of it, so don't be afraid to take that first step into a program of postulancy or the novitiate. Then, from the inside, you'll be able to unpack Jesus' call and your response much more thoroughly.

Once you take that first step and enter a religious community, you'll discover that it really wasn't a terrifying leap across an abyss, but rather a step across the threshold of the door—where Jesus is waiting to help you come to know His will.

Br. Christopher Patiño, F.S.C.
De La Salle Christian Brothers, District of San Francisco New Orleans

The most important piece of advice I would like to share is something Pope Francis has often emphasized: Be not afraid. Do not be afraid of how God is calling you to love and to be your authentic self. As you discern, consider the life-giving relationships in your life. What do these reveal about how you best love? Consider the Christian call to service. In what ways do you feel you can best live a life with and for others? Finally, consider your relationship with Jesus Christ. In what ways do you most clearly encounter Jesus in your life? Know that if God is calling you to religious life, you will be blessed with the graces to sustain the call. Pray for the strength to respond and know that God will not abandon you. Often pray the words of our Blessed Mother, "May it be done to me according to your word" (Lk 1:38).

Fr. Neil Wack, C.S.C.
Congregation of Holy Cross, U.S. Province

To know God's will, get to know the God who knows and loves you completely. Invite Him into your heart through daily prayer, the sacraments, ministry opportunities, and your every thought, word, and deed. Listen to the Lord in your prayer. How can we answer a call if we don't hear it? Spend some of your prayer each day praying "Come, Holy Spirit" or "Speak Lord, your servant is listening" and let God fill the silence. We should pray, "Lord, what do you want me to do?" for the next conversation we are going to have, for the day's activities, or even for our vocation. Don't look too far down the road though... It is enough for now to ask for God's help in discerning the next step, and ask for the courage to take it.

Fr. Benjamin Maria Wilkinson, S.E.M.V.
Servants of the Holy Eucharist and of the Blessed Virgin Mary, St. Paul, MN

Make your life Eucharistic! Your vocation is rooted in Jesus Christ; he is the one who calls. And Jesus is alive and present in the Blessed Sacrament, waiting for you to discuss your vocation with him. The Eucharist is a participation in the Sacrifice of Christ and communion with the Risen Lord, where you can learn the virtues necessary to hear and respond to your calling: virtues like humble adoration, unconditional love, joyful acceptance of the Father's will, and being broken and shared for the life of the world.

The greatest teacher of Eucharistic spirituality is the Blessed Mother. Her entire life was a "Magnificat" of Eucharistic praise and thanksgiving to God. It was this Eucharistic outlook that enabled her to say yes to her mission as Mother of God. Entrust your vocation to her and she will lead you to the Eucharistic Savior.

Fr. Emmanuel Mary Mansford, C.F.R.
Franciscan Friars of the Renewal, St. Joseph Friary, New York, NY

The foundation of all good discernment is believing and trusting that the Father loves you and has a unique plan for your life. Only then can you begin to truly discern, that is be open, to what God wants. Trust that He desires your happiness. Every time you experience fear, it is because you doubt His love and His plan, so it is important to return to this reality of His loving plan often. Once you begin to trust Him, you can start to take concrete steps. The journey of discernment is all about taking steps, one at a time. In

His wisdom, God only gives us enough light for the next step and no more. The heart of discernment is trusting Him who you know loves you and allowing yourself to be led. The reason Jesus says "Come follow Me" is because he wants us to trust that where He will lead is for our good.

Fr. Benedict Jurchak, T.O.R.
Franciscan Friars, Third Order Regular, Province of the Most Sacred Heart

When it comes to hearing God's voice, prayer is of the utmost importance, but do not underestimate what your personal experiences are telling you. Sometimes God speaks to us through the people who know and love us, or perhaps even a stranger. Has anyone ever suggested that consecrated life would be a good fit for you? Do you find meaning and fulfillment in putting others first? Have you ever been engaged with a service project or a mission trip and found great joy? While spiritual confirmations are a great privilege and certainly welcome, God also speaks through our everyday experiences. If you are thinking about religious life, make sure you take time to visit a religious community. This will ensure that you will have an experience to take to prayer. God is—and always has been—at work in your life. Perhaps it is in looking back that you will be able to find some direction about what lies ahead.

Fr. Michael Berry of the Heart of Jesus, O.C.D.
Discalced Carmelite Friars, Province of the Immaculate Heart of Mary

Pay close attention to that keen, unyielding fascination with Christ Jesus that arises within you as you consider His invitation to follow Him. Fix the eyes of your heart upon Him in response to His call. Seek vocational guidance from a very few select persons who best know you, including your spiritual director; in your eagerness to resolve your uncertainties do not rashly disclose your heart to strangers, looking for understanding by canvassing their opinions. The touchstone for good discernment is not to resolve all uncertainty, but to respond affirmatively to that generous love that swells your heart to follow the Lord and serve His Church. Trust not in yourself but in the Lord who calls you.

Br. Stephen Balletta, S.M.
Marianists, Province of Meribah

Listen to your life. Be confident that the Lord is speaking to you through the events you experience and the people you meet. I've talked to so many young men who are looking for absolute clarity, for an unmistakable divine sign. For the most part, God's not going to issue the call that way. But He will call you in dozens of subtler ways. This principle is illustrated in one of my favorite stories from the Old Testament (1 Kings 19: 11-13). The prophet Elijah finds the Lord not in a great and powerful wind, nor in a mighty earthquake, nor in a raging fire. Instead, he hears the voice of the Lord in "a gentle whisper." If you can listen for that "gentle whisper" in your own life, you will know that God is indeed calling you to something holy for Him and for His people.

Br. M. Anthony Weber, O.C.S.O.
Abbey of the Genesee, Piffard, NY

As you continue discerning your vocation I suggest you pray earnestly to come to know God's will for you. For example, when you pray the Our Father pause for a moment at the words "Thy will be done" and ask yourself if you really mean it. Pray that you will come to know His will for your vocation. For it is in His will that is our peace.

One of the ways God indicates His will for us is through the attraction to a particular way of life. Pay attention to your attraction and ask yourself just what it is that attracts you. It is good to follow through on the attraction and seek to become acquainted with that particular way of life.

During your discernment the help of an advisor or spiritual director will be most helpful. Such a person will help you clarify and purify your motives.

Br. Leven Harton, O.S.B.
St. Benedict's Abbey, Atchison, KS

Learning how to pray is a non-negotiable. For me, that required three months of solitude and silence, working as a research assistant in small-town Kansas over the summer. No friends, nothing to distract me. I got on my knees every day and prayed the rosary with sincerity, begging. And you know what I found? Something that shocked me: I like to pray. And my interior is vast, a world unto itself! I never knew that, never knew the depth of my person, never knew my identity. I do now. And you know what allowed me the space to discover this world, to find my identity? I was unplugged. You probably don't need to spend your summer alone in a small town to discern, but you absolutely, positively need to turn off your cell phone. You need to shut off the TV. You need to get off the video games. If you want space in your heart to encounter Christ, unplug.

Fr. Richard Goodin, O.F.M.
Order of Friars Minor, Province of St. John the Baptist

Religious life today is full of challenge, trials and rewards. If God is inviting you to the challenge of religious life, then God will also protect you during any trials and eventually bestow on you any fitting rewards! The world needs men who are willing to give up everything to follow Jesus Christ. And men inherently know how to step up to a challenge. So my advice is to step forward in faith to the challenge of a lifetime: follow the Gospel of Jesus Christ as a religious! Join the company of Dominic, Francis, Ignatius and Padre Pio—men who certainly had their trials but who now know the rewards!

Mother of Good Counsel, help me to take good advice when it is offered to me, and so I may follow your Son wherever he goes.

CONCLUSION

GIVE EVERYTHING OVER TO OUR LADY

"Standing by the cross of Jesus were his mother and his mother's sister, Mary the wife of Clopas, and Magdala. When Jesus saw his mother, and the disciple there whom he loved, he said to his mother, 'Woman, behold, your son.' Then he said to the disciple, 'Behold, your mother.' And from that hour the disciple took her into his home" (John 19:25-27).

Think of yourself standing at the foot of the cross with the mother of Jesus. You are the beloved disciple. The Son gives you over to his mother and gives his mother over to you. She is now your mother. What does it mean for you to be her son?

Religious typically have a profound sense of the care of Mary as mother, especially in times of anxiety and trial. In the thirteenth century, a young Dominican friar found that in religious life "everything jarred with his tastes and feelings." He always found himself in hunger and distress, and he couldn't sleep properly. This young man came from a comfortable background. He wasn't used to walking the distances expected of friars who were forbidden to use horses. (That was considered too luxurious in the thirteenth century.) What saved this young friar was his devotion to Our Lady. "O most blessed Virgin," he cried, "it was to serve you and your Son that I entered this Order, and see me now fainting from weariness at the very outset. Get me the strength needed." The friar reported that he found himself sprinkled with a fragrant dew. The account records: "From that hour he continued strong and healthy, so that what up to that point he could not endure, became a pleasure. Helped in this way by Our Lady's merits, he happily endured to the end his earthly course."[121]

Are you experiencing some anxiety and trial about your vocation? Young men who are apprehensive about their vocation often find relief from Our Lady once they, by her help, put an end to discernment and make a decision. They accept her as their mother and welcome her in a powerfully new way in the decision they make. Religious can testify that once they entered religious formation, professed first vows, or professed final vows (three critical points)—the fears during the time of their discernment were cast far from their minds. It's true!

The first chapter of this book considers truths to free you from discernment traps. We want to end the book with the image of untying a knot. When you were a little boy, did you ever get frustrated with a knot in your shoe laces? Do you presently see your vocation as similarly knotted? Does it seem twisted in complications; so tight that you can't see where things are going, and still insolvable after you've tried with all your might to pull your way through?

One of Pope Francis's favorite Marian devotions is Our Lady Undoer of Knots. The original Baroque painting for this devotion is in Augsburg, Germany. It beautifully shows the Blessed Mother, surrounded by angels, untying the knots of a ribbon. The image makes visible a teaching of St. Irenaeus of Lyons from the second century about the connection between the Garden of Eden and the Annunciation. St. Irenaeus contrasts Eve with Mary, the New Eve. Eve tied a knot of disobedience, of saying no to God. St. Irenaeus writes, "The knot of Eve's disobedience was loosed by the obedience

121. Gerard de Frachet, O.P., *The Lives of the Brethren*, Part 1, Chapter 5.

of Mary. For what the virgin Eve had bound fast through unbelief, this did the Virgin Mary set free through faith."[122]

Our Lady will not fail you. She will help you turn to her Son through faith. Satan will be crushed. Do not settle for little pleasures, when God wants you to have great happiness. Commit your vocation to Our Lady's Immaculate Heart. Give everything over to her. Pray the rosary each day for her help so that you may respond well to the Lord's invitation in your life. Pray other Marian prayers so that you see how Our Lady is truly your mother, standing to receive you and to be received by you, at the foot of the Cross.

Yes, it is at the Cross where you will discover your vocation. But do not be afraid. Ask Our Lady, whose heart was pierced by a sword of sorrow and whose joy never faded, to give you the strength to make a sacrifice of love. She will help you untie the knots of your life so that you can become a living sacrifice.

Prayer to Our Lady, Undoer of Knots

Virgin Mary, Mother of fair love, Mother who never refuses to come to the aid of a child in need, Mother whose hands never cease to serve your beloved children because they are moved by the divine love and immense mercy that exists in your heart, cast your compassionate eyes upon me and see the snarl of knots that exist in my life. You know very well how desperate I am, my pain, and how I am bound by these knots. Mary, Mother to whom God entrusted the undoing of the knots in the lives of His children, I entrust into your hands the ribbon of my life. No one, not even the Evil One himself, can take it away from your precious care. In your hands, there is no knot that cannot be undone. Powerful Mother, by your grace and intercessory power with your Son and my liberator, Jesus, take into your hands today this knot. (Mention your petition here.)

---

122. St. Irenaeus, *Against Heresies*, III.22.4.

I beg you to undo it for the glory of God, once for all. You are my hope. O my Lady, you are the only consolation God gives me, the fortification of my feeble strength, the enrichment of my destitution, and, with Christ, the freedom from my chains. Hear my plea. Keep me, guide me, protect me, O safe refuge. Amen.

STATES OF LIFE FOR CATHOLIC MEN

Clerical life[A]	Consecrated life[B] *(whether from clerical or lay)*	Lay life[C]
Bishops Priests Deacons *(transitional and permanent)*	Religious institutes *(monks, canons, friars, clerics regular, other religious in congregations)* Secular institutes Societies of apostolic life New communities[D]	The baptized *(who are not clerical nor consecrated):* Single men Married men Widowers

A. Second Vatican Council, *Lumen Gentium*, no 28: "Christ, whom the Father has sanctified and sent into the world, has through His apostles, made their successors, the bishops, partakers of His consecration and His mission. They have legitimately handed on to different individuals in the Church various degrees of participation in this ministry. Thus, the divinely established ecclesiastical ministry is exercised on different levels by those who from antiquity have been called bishops, priests and deacons." From apostolic times there has been an emphasis on clerical celibacy. In Eastern Christian practices, it is common for married men to be ordained to the diaconate and the priesthood. In the Roman discipline, it is presently common for married men to be ordained to the permanent diaconate. Also, in Rome's Pastoral Provision, one may find some married men ordained to the priesthood, such as an Anglican priest come into full communion with the Catholic Church and then ordained.

B. *Code of Canon Law*, can. 588 §1: "By its very nature, the state of consecrated life is neither clerical nor lay." Second Vatican Council, *Lumen Gentium*, no. 43: "From the point of view of the divine and hierarchical structure of the Church, the religious state of life is not an intermediate state between the clerical and lay states. But, rather, the faithful of Christ are called by God from both these states of life so that they might enjoy this particular gift in the life of the Church and thus each in one's own way, may be of some advantage to the salvific mission of the Church."

C. Second Vatican Council, *Lumen Gentium*, no. 31: "The term laity is here understood to mean all the faithful except those in holy orders and those in the state of religious life specially approved by the Church. These faithful are by baptism made one body with Christ and are constituted among the People of God; they are in their own way made sharers in the priestly, prophetical, and kingly functions of Christ; and they carry out for their own part the mission of the whole Christian people in the Church and in the world."

D. St. John Paul II, *Vita Consecrata*, no. 12: "The perennial youth of the Church continues to be evident even today. In recent years, following the Second Vatican Council, new or renewed forms of the consecrated life have arisen. In many cases, these are Institutes similar to those already existing but inspired by new spiritual and apostolic impulses. Their vitality must be judged by the authority of the Church, which has the responsibility of examining them in order to discern the authenticity of the purpose for their foundation and to prevent the proliferation of institutions. similar to one another, with the consequent risk of a harmful fragmentation into excessively small groups. In other cases, it is a question of new experiments which are seeking an identity of their own in the Church and awaiting official recognition from the Apostolic See, which alone has final judgment in these matters."

GLOSSARY OF RELIGIOUS LIFE TERMS

Abbey: An independent monastery headed by an abbot.

Abbot: Meaning "father," this is an ancient term designating the superior of a monastery with a sufficient community for a full monastic life.

Active: A community dedicated in its charism especially to works of ministry external to the community.

Apostolate: Either the general work of ministry in a community's charism or a specific work of time and place for that community or individual.

Application: Process for entrance into a community.

Aspirant: One who hopes to enter a community.

Assignment: Duty given to a religious, usually meaning a life's work for a time, but could also be for something of less significance.

Brother: New Testament term of family for a member of the Christian community applied within a religious community. In some religious communities, those who are not priests are called this. In some religious communities, all may be called this.

Canon: Similar to monk or friar as a broad term, this term identifies a man living in a form of life dedicated to communal celebration of the sacred liturgy of a particular church, such as the Praemonstratensians (Norbertines).

Canon law: Law of the Church. The fundamental legal text is the code. In 1983, the post-conciliar *Code of Canon Law (Codex Iuris Canonici)* was issued for the Latin Church (Roman Catholics). In 1990, the *Code of Canons of the Eastern Churches (Codex Canonum Ecclesiarum Orientalium)* was issued for the Eastern Catholic Church (Eastern Catholics).

Canonical hours: Times of prayer for the Liturgy of the Hours/ Divine Office, such as: Office of Readings/Matins; Morning Prayer/Lauds; Midmorning Prayer/Terce; Midday Prayer/Sext; Midafternoon Prayer/None; Evening Prayer/Vespers; Night Prayer/Compline. A religious community may have variations.

Chapter: A gathering of religious for some sort of spiritual or practical business (such as a superior's talk, reports, discussions, votes), taking its name from reading from the chapters of a rule. Depending on the community, a chapter may be on the local, provincial, or global levels.

Charism: Extraordinary gift of the Holy Spirit given to a founder that expresses the particular call to holiness and mission of a religious community.

Cleric regular: A religious from the 16th-century communities (e.g., Jesuits and Theatines) that stress the apostolic mission of their clergy, not monastic practices.

Congregation: A term for a religious institute or apostolic society usually founded in modern times.

Congregation for Institutes of Consecrated Life and Societies of Apostolic Life (CICLSAL): For much of the twentieth century known as the Congregation for Religious, this department of the Roman Curia performs its duties in the Pope's name and with his authority in its charge of overseeing the consecrated and apostolic communities of the Church.

Contemplative: A community that is entirely devoted to prayer, study, and spiritual works without an active apostolate, or an aspect of religious life which is devoted to prayer, study, and spiritual works.

Continuing formation: See Permanent formation.

Convent: From the Latin word for a community gathered together, this name can be an official name for houses of men (such as Franciscans or Dominicans) or, more commonly, for women. In some houses of men, the "conventual Mass" or "conventual chapter" expresses the Mass or the chapter of that community.

Departure: When someone formally leaves a community.

Diocesan priest: A priest "incardinated," or placed under the immediate authority of a bishop to serve the local church, and not a priest in religious life. Also known as a secular priest.

Exclaustration: Exceptional, serious process of living outside of a community for a limited time, such as three years, for a member in perpetual vows to think and pray about the future.

External forum: A public setting or discussion of matters that may be shared with others.

First Order: A medieval categorization popularized by Franciscans to denote friars, in contradistinction to the cloistered nuns of the Second Order and those in the Third Order who embody the charism in their proper states of life.

Formation: Initial process whereby one is changed by the charism of a community and is incorporated more and more into that community. Today it can also mean, as permanent or ongoing formation, the renewal of living out religious life until death.

Formator: One tasked to oversee those in initial formation, and especially indicating one in charge of that process, such as the director of formation (novice master, junior master, et al.)

Friar: Coming from the word that means "brother," a friar is a member (whether ordained or not ordained) of many communities emphasizing a humble, fraternal life present in the thirteenth century (and today)—such as Franciscans, Dominicans, Carmelites, Augustinians, and Carmelites.

Friary: A local house of Franciscans or others friars who might use that term. More properly, it may be a convent of men. See also: Convent.

Habit: Common religious clothing. It comes from the Latin word meaning "to have," and is used to denote clothing for certain male and female religious.

Holy Orders: Sacrament instituted by Christ expressed in the three grades of bishop, priest, and deacon.

Horarium: Schedule of the community's day, especially noting common times for prayer as well as meals and other activities.

House: A local community of religious, at times differentiated from a large community of religious, which might have a different, technical name.

Initial formation: The beginning stages of incorporating someone into full membership of a community.

Internal forum: A private setting or discussion of matters that may not be shared with others, such as spiritual direction.

Junior master: Monastic formator for monks in temporary vows.

Junior monk: A monk in temporary vows.

Local superior: One who leads a particular house within a larger religious network, such as a province.

Ministry: A church work done for the glory of God and the good of others.

Mixed life: A term used to express a form of life that is both active and contemplative.

Monastery: A house where monks or other religious (such as Carmelite friars, Passionist men, cloistered nuns, Benedictine sisters) live. The monastery may have another name, such as abbey or priory—depending on size, governance, and particular religious tradition.

Monk: From the Greek word for "one" denoting his seeking to be alone with God or in a community seeking to be one in God, a monk is a male religious (either ordained or not ordained) in one of the traditional forms of religious life, such as the Benedictine, Cistercian, or Carthusian communities, and different from canons, friars, clerics regular, and members of modern congregations.

Novice: From the Latin word that means "new," a novice is someone beginning religious life in a time period called "novitiate," and not yet made first profession of vows.

Novice master: The head formator of novices within a community's novitiate.

Novitiate: A time that begins one's religious formation, certainly before first profession of vows, and may be preceded by a pre-novitiate or postulancy. It may also refer to the place where the novitiate occurs.

Nun: A female religious, usually belonging to a cloistered/contemplative community (as a female equivalent of monk), but commonly also said of active sisters.

Order: A term for a religious institute usually founded before modern times.

Ordinary: One who holds an office that involves executive governing authority, such as a diocesan bishop, an abbot, and a religious provincial, as well as their vicars (i.e., those who govern in the name of the Ordinary).

Permanent formation: After initial formation, this process occurs to emphasize the ongoing change of a religious in following Christ until death. Also known as continuing formation.

Postulant: One in a period of time (postulancy) who is asking, or considering to ask, to enter the novitiate.

Postulant director: A community official who oversees the program that prepares for the novitiate.

Priest: A sacred minister ordained between the levels of bishop and deacon in Holy Orders.

Prior: Coming from the Latin word for first, this community official may mean the first one after the abbot (in monastic communities) or the first one who leads the brethren in certain religious communities.

Priory: A community headed by a prior. For Benedictines, this means that the monastery is not an independent abbey. For Dominicans, this is the name of its standard-sized house.

Procurator: One who takes care of the monies and temporal needs of a community, assisting the superior, and may also be known as a bursar or treasurer.

Province: A geographical area of several religious houses that forms one part of an institute and is under the authority of a major superior.

Profession: A recitation of vows (first, renewal, or final) that binds one to God and the religious community according to the community's proper law.

Religious: One who is consecrated by a public profession of the evangelical counsels to worship God.

Religious brother: A man, not ordained or seeking ordination, consecrated by public profession of the evangelical counsels to worship God.

Religious priest: A priest consecrated by public profession of the evangelical counsels to worship God.

Rule: A written, set way of life, as found in such examples as the *Rule of St. Augustine* or the *Rule of St. Benedict.*

Secular Institute: Formally approved by Pope Pius XII, this way of life has a form of consecration, but unlike a religious institute, exists in the world and does not have the common life as an essential aspect.

Secular priest: See diocesan priest

Simple vows: These vows may be temporary for orders with solemn vows and either temporary or lifelong, permanent vows in religious institutes that do not have solemn vows.

Sister: New Testament term of family for a member of the Christian community applied within a religious community. In some religious communities, one calls the superior "Mother" rather than "Sister."

Solemn vows: Lifelong vows that traditionally hold differences regarding poverty and commitment to celibate chastity within religious orders in comparison to simple vows.

Superior: One who is elected or assigned to be in charge of a community on whatever scale. Institutes have different customs of particular terminology, such as Abbot, Prior, Guardian, and Servant.

Superior General: See Supreme Moderator

Supreme Moderator: The superior of a worldwide institute.

Vocation: A call from God. Often it means to a particular state of life of holiness.

Vocation Director: Someone tasked to oversee a vocation process. In a diocese, the vocation director has oversight of the entire diocesan program, usually focused on diocesan seminarians. In a religious community, usually the vocation director has oversight of the process until a man's entrance into that community.

Appendix C

Lectio Divina Meditations for a Religious Vocation

Introduction to Lectio Divina *by Abbot Austin G. Murphy, O.S.B., Abbot of St. Procopius Abbey, Lisle, Illinois.*

So, you never heard of *lectio divina*? Well, if you can read and you have faith, then you can do it.

Lectio divina (or *lectio* for short—sounds like LEX-ee-oh) is an ancient, yet straightforward way of praying. It literally means "sacred reading" in Latin, but it simply refers to prayerfully reflecting on Scripture. Spending time with God in prayer is important, but we might wonder how to do this. Well, it normally requires having something to think about and turn over in your mind once you have put yourself in God's presence. *Lectio* uses the great gift of Scripture to provide what to think about while spending time with God.

The 4 steps will help you better understand this prayer method. But don't get too caught up in method! Ask the Spirit for guidance. I'd recommend 15 min. for *lectio* (if you want to do more, great!).

READING: of course, you start by reading Scripture. Take only a few lines to a paragraph (yet if the Spirit prompts you, read more). Read so as to listen. What is God saying to us, or *to me*? Read slowly, and repeatedly.

MEDITATION: having read the passage, start thinking about

it. Perhaps a word or phrase will jump out as especially meaningful. Stay with it, repeat it, ponder it. Sometimes, it helps to use your imagination: imagine yourself as a character in the story, picture details in the scene, etc. However you meditate, recall that you are listening for what God is saying.

PRAYER: here you respond to God's words with your own words. Speak what's in your heart. If you have no words to say, just keep looking to God.

CONTEMPLATION: sometimes a sense of the Lord's loving presence will come upon you. Active thinking and praying will stop, and you'll simply rest in the Lord's presence.

Note: you will not always reach all 4 steps; you might remain at the first two. That's okay. And remember, any practice of prayer will be dry at times, and thus takes perseverance.

Abbot Austin makes something that sounds so difficult to be so easy—as long as you can read and have faith. Are you willing to try? Another way of thinking about *lectio* is through the image of a feast, which can be consumed only one bite at a time. **Reading** is like taking a bite, one verse at a time. **Meditating** is the process of chewing. Don't forget to chew your food many times before swallowing, and don't forget to let the Word of God stay with you as you think on it. Food needs to be chewed, and the Word of God can be like tough meat (cf. Heb 5:14). You may have reactions to the food in your chewing process, such as "Oh my, this is so good!" or "What is this?" or "Um, I think this has a strange taste." Similarly, **praying** may come in your meditating on the Word: "Thank you, Lord" "Yes, this is great!" "What do you mean, Lord?" "Oh my God, I don't understand why this hurts me." Finally, just as you have a process of digestion that is beyond your control when the food changes your life through its nourishment, so there could be **contemplating** that is beyond your control when the Word changes your life. In fact, we are the ones who are changed when we feast on the Word. St. Augustine heard God say: "I am the food of strong men. Grow, and you shall feed upon me. You shall not convert me, like the food of your flesh, into you, but you shall be converted into me" (*Confessions* 7.10.16).

Pick up a Bible and choose one of the following passages. Five are from the Old Testament, and five from the New Testament. As you read, you could use *lectio divina* questions given under the biblical citation to assist your pondering, if you wanted.

Gen 12:1-3

What do you think Abraham was thinking when the Lord first called him, when Abraham was still known as Abram? Why do you think Abraham is called "our father in faith"? What kind of faith do you need to answer the Lord's call?

1 Sam 3:1-10

What is the significance for young Samuel to realize that it was not Eli calling him, but the Lord calling him? What is the significance for you to realize that the Lord is calling you? How did Samuel listen to the Lord? How can you listen to the Lord?

Psalm 40 (Psalm 39 in some bibles based on the Greek and Latin numeration)

What is the importance of waiting for the Lord in your life? How does the Lord put a "new song" into your mouth? How can doing the will of the Lord be your delight? How can you let the assembly, that is the Church, know of your obedience to the Lord?

Psalm 73 (Psalm 72 in some bibles based on the Greek and Latin numeration)

How do you know the goodness of God in your life? How important is it to have purity of heart to see God's goodness? In what ways have you been stupid and not understood the ways of God in your life? What does it mean for you to be able to have God as your "possession" forever, and not be concerned about any other possession?

Isa 6:1-8

What does the holiness of the Lord mean for you? How do we need purification when we encounter the Lord's holiness; what was Isaiah's purification and what is yours? How can you respond with a generous heart to the Lord's question of who will go?

Matt 19:16-30

Why do people turn away from Jesus sad? What is the usefulness of riches during this life on earth? How can you prioritize in your life to keep the Lord more important than anything else? What does God's ability to do all things mean for your vocation?

Luke 1:26-34

What does it mean for the sinless Virgin Mary to be deeply troubled at the greeting of the angel? What does the angel promise her? What are you promised? How can you rely upon the Mother of God to be made worthy of the promises of Christ? How can you echo the Virgin Mary's fiat (Let it be)?

John 1:35-42

What does Jesus' title of Lamb of God mean for you? How does the sacrifice of the Lamb help you think about the possibility of making a living sacrifice? What are you looking for, what are you seeking, what do you want when you follow the Lamb? How does Jesus invite you to come and see about a religious vocation? How can you be like St. Andrew in not only following after Jesus, but also telling another about him?

Rom 12:1-2

What does it mean to offer your body as a living sacrifice? In what ways does that hurt? In what ways is it joyful? How can you use your mind now in giving rational, spiritual worship to God?

What are some specific temptations to conform yourself to this age? How can you be transformed by the renewal of your mind?

Phil 3:7-16

Is knowing Christ Jesus your Lord more important than anything else for you? For his sake, what do you hope to do? How can you forget what lies behind but strain forward to what is ahead in life?

ROSARY MEDIATIONS FOR A RELIGIOUS VOCATION

The holy rosary of the Blessed Virgin Mary has been recommended by Popes for many centuries in a unique way. Many people want to have the rosary in their hand in their life and even in their death when they are buried. The *Code of Canon Law*, can. 246 §3 promotes the rosary for priestly formation. Many religious find the rosary to be an important part of their daily prayer. If you would like to read more about the rosary, consider St. John Paul II's *Apostolic Letter on the Most Holy Rosary, Rosarium Virginis Mariae*, October 16, 2002, available online.

Also, three of many recommended books on the rosary are: St. Louis de Montfort, *The Secret of the Rosary* (Bay Shore, NY: Montfort Publications, 1972), Richard Gribble, C.S.C., *The History and Devotion of the Rosary* (Huntington, IN: Our Sunday Visitor, 1992), and Donald H. Calloway, M.I.C., *Champions of the Rosary: The History and Heroes of a Spiritual Weapon* (Stockbridge, MA: Marian Press, 2016).

The following gives a brief suggested prayer to make in connection with each mystery of the rosary. Notice that in each one we pray in Christ to the Father, asking for the Gift of the Holy Spirit.

The Joyful Mysteries

1. *The Annunciation.* O my God, you chose the Blessed Virgin Mary, and she said yes to your will to bear your Son as our

Savior. Send forth your Holy Spirit to overshadow me so that I may say yes to your will for my vocation.

2. *The Visitation.* Most merciful Father, your lowly servant rushed to help her kinswoman Elizabeth in her need. May your Holy Spirit rush into my heart so that I may be generous in Christ to serve those around me.

3. *The Birth of Our Lord.* Almighty God, your Son took flesh from the Virgin Mary, was born in poverty, and was placed in a manger. Send the Spirit of holiness into my life so that I may find your Son in poverty.

4. *The Presentation of the Lord.* Most Holy God, the Blessed Virgin Mary and St. Joseph did not hold Jesus back, but gave him over to you. Let your Spirit fill me so that I may not hold anything back from you.

5. *The Finding of the Lord in the Temple.* Righteous Father, your Son was found where he was meant to be: in your Temple. Give his Spirit to me so that I may be found where I am meant to be.

The Luminous Mysteries

1. *The Baptism of the Lord.* Almighty Father, you announced that Jesus was your beloved Son in the river Jordan. Let your Spirit fall on me so that I may always be pleasing to you.

2. *The Miracle at the Wedding Feast of Cana.* Lord God Almighty, the Blessed Virgin told the servants of your Son: "Do whatever he tells you." May I drink of your Holy Spirit, and do what I am told when pondering the mystery of my vocation.

3. *The Proclamation of the Kingdom and Call to Conversion.* All-holy God, your Son preached repentance and the coming of the Kingdom. Let his Spirit rule my life to shun what keeps me from following your Son wherever he goes.

4. *The Transfiguration.* Most loving and wondrous God, you allowed a few apostles to witness the transfiguration of your Son on Mount Tabor. Let your Holy Spirit open my eyes to see the beauty of being with Christ in the consecrated life.

5. *The Institution of the Most Holy Eucharist.* Lord God, heavenly King, to you do I lift up my eyes. Send down your Spirit on my life so that I may adore your Son present most mysteriously in the Sacrament of the altar and may join my life to his sacrifice.

The Sorrowful Mysteries

1. *The Agony in the Garden.* Abba, Father, I give thanks and praise that your Son in his humanity obeyed your holy will. Strengthen me with his Spirit so that I may be willing to suffer with him.

2. *The Scourging at the Pillar.* My God and my all, your Son allowed himself to be beaten for my salvation. Let your Holy Spirit come down on my body so that in chastity I may be a living sacrifice for you.

3. *The Crowning of Thorns.* King of all the nations, your most beloved Son was most cruelly mocked by the soldiers. Give me the Spirit so that I may have the strength to behold the King of the Jews in a life of truth and love.

4. *The Carrying of the Cross.* Lord of heaven and earth, your Son invited me to pick up my cross and follow him. Fortify me with the Spirit of power so that I may do what Jesus invites me to do.

5. *The Crucifixion and Death of Our Lord.* My God, my God, you wanted us to see boundless mercy in the Cross of your Son. Put into my heart your Spirit so that I may find that mercy to worship in an obedience until death.

The Glorious Mysteries

1. *The Resurrection of Our Lord.* God who makes all things new, the resurrection of your Son changes everything in life. Give me the Spirit, who is the Giver of life, to live only for you.

2. *The Ascension of Our Lord.* O God beyond my sight, your Son brought human nature to the glory of heaven. Help me by giving the Spirit of hope to my soul so that I may be faithful and loving during this life of pilgrimage.

3. *The Descent of the Holy Spirit.* Father most holy, your Son asked the first disciples to wait for "the promise of the Father." Give me what you have promised, your Holy Spirit.

4. *The Assumption of Our Lady.* Most good and loving Father, you willed that the Blessed Virgin Mary should share in a pre-eminent way the bodily resurrection of your Son. Let your Spirit stir my heart to trust in your loving goodness for my own body.

5. *The Coronation of Our Lady.* All-powerful King of the universe, I give you thanks and praise that the Blessed Virgin Mary is crowned Queen and Mother of mercy. In Jesus' Name, put the Holy Spirit in my life so that I may live heaven's thanks and praise here on earth and so one day may join the Mother of God and all the saints crowned in happiness forever.

HOLY HOUR PRAYERS FOR A RELIGIOUS VOCATION

Eucharistic adoration quiets our life and allows us to be with Jesus, who came to be with us. We offer our thanks and praise, and ask God to make our lives worthy of the sacrifice of the altar. The following are ten very brief prayers addressed to Christ present in the Most Blessed Sacrament so as to assist you in meditating during a Holy Hour on a religious vocation.

Lord Jesus Christ, Son of God, have mercy on me, a sinner.

Jesus, my Savior, what are you inviting me to do in my life? I want to live for you alone.

My Lord and my God, thank you for being with me. May I be with you.

Be my food, my nourishment, my life this day.

I believe you, Lord. Help my unbelief. Give me an increase of faith to do whatever you ask me to do.

I hope in your promises in my life, Lord Jesus.

I love you. I love you so much, Lord. Thank you for your love for me, and loving me more than I can understand.

My wisest and best of friends, let me praise you now for your goodness to me.

Lord, open the eyes of my heart to see who you are, and to see who I am meant to be.

Thank you, Jesus, for everything.

RECOMMENDED READINGS

The most important recommended reading is the Holy Bible. This is why we have an appendix to help you practice *lectio divina* over some select passages. We highly recommend that you pray over the readings of the daily Mass. If you don't have a monthly *MAGNIFICAT*, missal, missalette, or other print version of the readings, you may go to the United States Catholic Conference of Bishops (USCCB) website for the readings:

Also, as we mention earlier in the book, read about the lives of great religious saints, about the founder of a religious community that interests you, writings from that institute, and anything else your spiritual director and a community's vocation director recommends.

This brief lists gives a very few additional suggested readings, first from the Church and organized by pontificate, then from theologians and spiritual writers.

St. Paul VI (1963-78)

Second Vatican Council, *Lumen Gentium, Dogmatic Constitution on the Church*, November 21, 1964. Available online.

Second Vatican Council, *Perfectae Caritatis, Decree on the Adaptation and Renewal of Religious Life*, October 28, 1965. Available online.

St. John Paul II (1978-2005)

St. John Paul II, *Vita Consecrata, Post-Synodal Apostolic Constitution on the Consecrated Life and its Mission in the Church and in the World*, March 25, 1996. Available online.

Congregation for Institutes of Consecrated Life and Societies of Apostolic Life, *Directives on Formation in Religious Institutes*, February 2, 1990. Available online.

Pope Benedict XVI (2005-2013)

Pope Benedict XVI, *Called to Holiness: On Love, Vocation, and Formation*. Edited by Pietro Rossotti. Washington, DC: Catholic University of America Press, 2015.

Pope Francis (2013-)

Pope Francis, *Apostolic Letter to All Consecrated People on the Occasion of the Year of Consecrated Life*, November 21, 2014. Available online.

Congregation for Institutes of Consecrated Life and Societies of Apostolic Life, *Identity and Mission of the Religious Brother in the Church*, October 4, 2015. Available online.

Final Document of the Synod of Bishops on Young People, Faith and Vocational Discernment (2018). Available online.

From theologians and spiritual writers

Francis Cardinal Arinze, *Radical Discipleship: Consecrated Life and the Call to Holiness*. San Francisco: Ignatius Press, 2015.

Raniero Cantalamessa, O.F.M. Cap., *Obedience: The Authority of the Word*. Trans. Frances Lonergan Villa. Staten Island, NY: Society of Saint Paul, 2018.

Raniero Cantalamessa, O.F.M. Cap., *Poverty.* Trans. Charles Serignat. Staten Island, NY: Society of Saint Paul, 1997.

Raniero Cantalamessa, O.F.M. Cap., *Virginity: A Positive Approach to Celibacy for the Sake of the Kingdom of Heaven.* Trans. Charles Serignat. Staten Island, NY: Society of Saint Paul, 1995.

Basil Cole, O.P. and Paul Conner, O.P., *Christian Totality: Theology of the Consecrated Life.* Revised and updated edition. New York: Alba House, 1997.

Dominic Hoffman, O.P, with Basil Cole, O.P., *Consecrated Life: Contribution of Vatican II.* Mumbai: The Bombay Saint Paul Society, 2011.